DIGITAL SIGNAGE BROADCASTING

Digital Signage Broadcasting
Content Management and Distribution Techniques

Lars-Ingemar Lundström

ELSEVIER

AMSTERDAM • BOSTON • HEIDELBERG • LONDON
NEW YORK • OXFORD • PARIS • SAN DIEGO
SAN FRANCISCO • SINGAPORE • SYDNEY • TOKYO

Focal Press is an imprint of Elsevier

Publisher: Elinor Actipis
Senior Acquisitions Editor: Angelina Ward
Series Editor: S. Merrill Weiss
Publishing Services Manager: George Morrison
Project Manager: Marilyn E. Rash
Marketing Manager: Christine Degon Veroulis
Developmental Editor: Beth Millet
Copyeditor: Joan Flaherty
Proofreader: Jodie Allen
Indexer: Ted Laux
Typesetting: Charon Tec (A Macmillan Company)
Photos and Text Illustrations: Lars-Ingemar Lundström
Text and Cover Printing: 1010 International Ltd.

Focal Press is an imprint of Elsevier
30 Corporate Drive, Suite 400, Burlington, MA 01803, USA
Linacre House, Jordan Hill, Oxford OX2 8DP, UK

Recognizing the importance of preserving what has been written, Elsevier prints
its books on acid-free paper whenever possible.

Library of Congress Cataloging-in-Publication Data
Lundström, Lars-Ingemar.
  Digital signage broadcasting : content management and distribution techniques /
  Lars-Ingemar Lundström.
    p. cm.
  Includes index.
  ISBN 978-0-240-80976-2 (alk. paper)
  1. Digital signage. 2. Advertising—Audio-visual equipment. 3. Communication—
Methodology. 4. Multimedia communications. I. Title.
  TK4399.S6L86 2008
  659.13'42—dc22   2007041469

British Library Cataloguing-in-Publication Data
A catalogue record for this book is available from the British Library.

For information on all Focal Press publications
visit our website at *www.books.elsevier.com*

08 09 10 11 12   5 4 3 2 1

Printed in China

CONTENTS

ACKNOWLEDGMENTS

Authors need to earn the right to write their books, and this would never be possible without the support and encouragement of other people sharing their interests.

I would like to thank my friends in the United States as well as in Sweden who have all participated in digital signage broadcasting projects where I found the inspiration to write this book.

Especially, I would like to give my gratitude to the U.S. staffs at Wegener Communications in Atlanta, GA , KenCast in Stamford, CT, and the Swedish companies MultiQ in Malmö and Parabolic in Kungsbacka. All the people, along with my dedicated colleagues at Teracom, also in Sweden, have been my great sources of inspiration.

But most of all I would like to thank my wife, Marianne, and my two sons, Niklas and Filip, who have been incredibly patient and understanding while I worked on this all-consuming project.

This book is dedicated to people all over
the world who struggle at the bleeding edge
of technology to make new products become
reality instead of staying just as ideas.

PREFACE

After writing about television broadcasting systems for more than two decades in a world of conventional radio and television and then the Internet, I did not think it was very likely that a completely new medium would show up. It seemed that most things were already invented and that most innovation would be in the realm of improvements. However, one day it happened. I understood that something new was on the move.

When I started to work with satellite IP distribution a few years ago, I saw digital signage as a very specialized business media–related application. Retail chains and gaming companies used VHS recorders and DVD players in their stores to improve business. Some closed-circuit television networks also were used for gaming and betting. All seemed to be spin-off effects of the TV and video media that used conventional home electronics.

As time passed, however, flat-panel display devices and computers and Internet and satellite distribution were introduced. Suddenly I realized that digital signage really is a new medium that encompasses most other kinds of digital media. It also became clear to me that people in this business, including me, did not see the full picture. This is not unusual because digital signage involves both broadcasting and telecommunications technologies in a way that may seem to be a complete mess. Broadcasting people do not know telecom very well and vice versa. Still, everyone has been talking about the convergence of the two for a decade or more.

Exploring this new medium has meant new "A-ha!" experiences almost every day, so obviously there is much more to learn. I soon found that there was not much written about the whole digital signage phenomenon, and that probably a lot of people want to know what digital signage is all about. Clearly, there was a need to put the pieces together to try to find the structure of this new medium.

Digital signage is very different from most other kinds of media because it is really a combination of existing technologies. Internet technologies merge with digital broadcasting, and computers develop toward set-top boxes. On the media production side, television, radio, web site development, and conventional printed media join to form one new medium.

When you start to study digital signage, you soon realize that you have to find out most things by yourself piece by piece. My intention in writing this book is to give readers a comprehensive view of the key elements in digital signage systems and of ways to manage the content and distribution in different applications. Especially important is the need to put the spotlight on broadcasting IP data for digital signage applications.

ABOUT THIS BOOK

I have arranged the content of this book in a way that I believe most people would approach digital signage technologies.

When starting to think about establishing digital signage services in stores, most people probably begin by thinking about the screens, such as, where to install them (which is much easier with flat-panel displays than the old cathode-ray-tube TV sets)? Second, what content should be put on the screens? Third, what content should be exposed in different departments of the store at different times? Finally, what about customizing information depending on the stores' geographic locations?

Most people still seem quite unaware of the unique possibilities for tailoring the displayed content for each application, geographic location of screens, and time of day. Even fewer people have a deeper insight into the problems involved in distributing content and controlling what kind of content appears on each screen.

For this reason, and to give you new ideas and stimulate your imagination, we begin in Chapter 1 with some of the numerous applications for digital signage. In Chapter 2, we take a more in-depth look at display devices and address how to choose the right technology for the application and location of the screens.

Digital signage has completely new ways of combining information from different sources. Getting to an understanding of how the visual message in digital signage systems is put together is described in Chapter 3.

To get all this to work, we need a different kind of device from conventional broadcast receivers. Media players are computers somewhere between broadcast receivers and personal computers. They exist in many shapes, and Chapter 4 describes these key devices in detail.

One consideration that is often neglected when planning digital signage applications is the means of distribution. This behind-the-scenes issue is critical to the types of applications that can be implemented. Chapters 5, 6, and 7 shed some light on questions that are rarely fully analyzed.

A store or public area with many screens may benefit from a local site server that stores all the information that is to be provided to the screens. The site server, described in Chapter 6, leads us to another important element in the retail environment—the customer terminal.

In the long run, the choice of distribution method affects the economy of the system in a significant way. Chapter 7 describes and explains the most powerful means of distribution—digital signage broadcasting.

Digital signage systems would never work without someone controlling which content is shown on which screens. The content management server, described in Chapter 8, is not only the heart of a digital signage system but also the spider in the web when it comes to collecting information from the Internet that is to be distributed to the screens.

Perhaps you have heard the expression, "There is no success without the right content." Chapter 9 discusses in more detail the ways to use web site information and TV commercials on the screens of the digital signage system. The possibilities prove to be even greater than most people think. Much of the content production needed for a digital signage application may already exist on your web site or in your video archives.

Digital signage must be regarded as a new kind of medium. Completely new approaches may have to be used. Such new systems also require new ways of operation with completely new operational problems. Chapter 10 investigates the known facts about the new challenges.

Digital signage systems are a part of the environment in retail stores and affect the atmosphere in them. Therefore, it may be a part of or significantly affect the culture of a brand. Chapter 11 raises some questions related to this very complicated question concerning this new medium. To stimulate your imagination, the chapter contains examples of screens in various environments, outdoors as well as indoors.

Today's digital signage systems are mostly seen in stores and public areas. But other kinds of applications may be a part of the media of tomorrow. Chapter 12 speculates on how digital signage may develop in the decades to come. Already, many people have media players in their homes to view digital photos and play their MP3 music using their TV set or home theater systems. Much of the digital signage you find in stores already exists in many homes, even though you may not realize it! And I am sure you already have one or more media players on your laptop or desktop computer. Whether you know it or not, your computer screen works more or less the same as a digital signage screen.

Digital Signage Broadcasting does not delve deeply into topics such as the Internet Protocol, digital television, satellite distribution technologies, and design of outstanding advertising signs. Other books describe such topics in detail. Instead, my aim has been to fill the gap between these topics and to link them closely. I hope you will find a new world of possibilities here (see also *www.digitalsignagebroadcasting.com*).

Welcome to the world of a new medium—digital signage.

1

AN OVERVIEW OF DIGITAL SIGNAGE

IMAGINE THE WORLD IN 20 YEARS

The bulky cathode-ray tubes of the twentieth century have all long been replaced by ultrathin, inexpensive, high-resolution, and high-quality display panels. These panels can be located indoors or outdoors and can have any format or shape. The panels are fitted to suit the walls in any public area or your home.

The screens are filled with live television as well as *near-real-time* information that is mixed with *non-real-time* video spots or still images that are suited to the screen's location or to the person who is watching it at that moment.

This scenario may seem like science fiction, but really, why should this be an impossible forecast of the media of tomorrow?

We can already see an obvious trend where flat-panel display systems become larger, cheaper, and thinner, with improved resolution. Therefore, it is not impossible to imagine that in the not-too-distant future we will find one or more of these thin flat-panel displays in each room of a home. Nevertheless, the world where wallpaper is replaced by electronic display systems is probably still far away.

But in stores and other public areas, things are already on the move. The introduction of flat-panel TV sets and computer screens has meant that dynamic digital media can be found everywhere. The need for content suited for the specific location and the specific moment has made this a reality in these kinds of environments.

However, to get the scenario of the future to work, we need the right content on the screens. In a society of hundreds of thousands or even

Figure 1.1 Future digital signage applications will make use of thin, inexpensive, high-resolution electronic display devices that may be easily located everywhere. Imagine all the new opportunities!

Figure 1.2 Digital signage is becoming a more common sight, both indoors and outdoors. The same messages might appear on plasma or LCD screens in stores as well as on large LED screens outdoors. Actually, they are all the same medium.

millions of display panels, all this content must be managed and distributed. And that is what this book is all about.

This can be done using computers, some people might say. This is certainly true, but still, there is so much more to it.

THE DAWN OF A NEW MEDIUM?

Modern society is a world of satellite, cable, and terrestrial television, now accompanied by *Internet Protocol Television (IPTV)* and broadband Internet access in an increasing number of homes. Could there really be another medium to discover and to exploit?

It is quite obvious that conventional television is not suited to provide content that is specific to the individual screen, especially not if the content on the screen depends on where the screen is located or who is watching it. In an ideal digital signage system, the screen location, the time of day, or the actual viewer would decide that content. The TV set has one simple way of handling all this: The viewer simply switches the channel using a remote control device.

Digital signage means moving one step further in other respects as well. The content on the screen does not necessarily originate from one single source or channel, as in television broadcasting. Instead, the different picture components can originate from several separate data files in a manner similar to the content on your computer screen. Also, some content may be live broadcast in *real time* and other information may be stored on its way to the screen. The content may have been stored for a fraction of a second, a couple of minutes, hours, days, months, or perhaps even years.

DIGITAL SIGNAGE: A BRIEF DESCRIPTION

Digital signage is based on various methods of using computer and television screens (as well as other kinds of display devices) in ways that are as efficient as possible to provide advertising and information to people in public areas.

In modern digital signage systems, the screens are divided into regions and layers, and the content on the screens is made up of several files. Inside all this, there may be real-time streaming media as IPTV.

However, the content files and data streams are not enough. Information and instructions are needed to control how, where, and when the content files and streams are displayed on the screens. This control information is stored in *scheduling* and *playlist* files. Content files, data streams, scheduling, and playlist files are discussed further in Chapters 4 and 8.

Figure 1.3   The screen is divided into regions and all content does not necessarily originate from the same source.

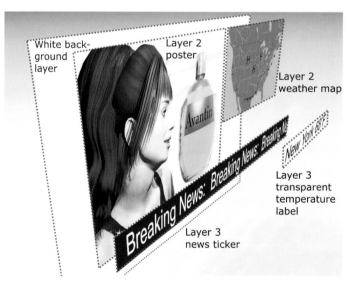

Figure 1.4   Regions, layers, and tickers originating from separate files and IP streams are the basic digital signage screen content components.

How Is Digital Signage Different from Television?

When you watch television or listen to the radio, you are seeing a picture on the screen or hearing the sound from the speakers that originate from a single stream of analog or digital information. When you use your computer, the things you see on your screen do not originate from one single source of information but rather from a large number of files from a large number of providers. In most cases, this also applies to *digital signage*: modern electronic commercials and information in stores and public environments.

In radio and television, there are ready-made, live-transmitted signals that are processed by the receiving equipment and then presented to the listeners and viewers. The content on a digital signage screen may originate from several different data files. Each file represents the content in a specific region of the screen or in a specific layer or the text content of a ticker. However, this is not the only difference. Conventional broadcasting is based on real-time distribution. This is not necessarily the case in a digital signage system.

Of course, television today is often combined with *non-real-time* elements such as hard drive storage of programs. In conventional television, however, storing information in the distribution chain is not an automated process, even though a timing feature may be used for automatic recording when you are not able to make the recordings manually. Digital signage systems allow automatic content storage at several locations en route to the viewer. The stored content may also be updated at any time. (See Table 1.1.)

There is another significant difference between conventional radio and television broadcasting and digital signage. In both analog and digital broadcasting, the transmission formats and protocols are specifically designed to carry audio and video signals. In digital signage systems, the *Internet Protocol (IP)* is used to carry the files and the streams to their destinations. IP is not designed to carry any specific type of information, but it can be a carrier for any existing or future media. As a result, investments in the distribution infrastructure are more or less insensitive to changes in audio and video compressions standards and other transmission formats. And if someone should come up with something completely new, such as some kind of 3D display device, it is likely that an existing IP-based distribution system would be able to carry this content as well. The bitrate of an IP distribution channel can be easily increased to fit any future need.

Table 1.1   Conventional television versus digital signage systems

Conventional television	Digital signage systems
One region originating from one source	Several regions originating from several files and/or streams
One single layer originating from one source (an exception is subtitling in digital television systems)	Several layers originating from several files and/or streams
Content transferred in real time	Content may be transferred in real time or near-real time or stored in the distribution chain
Specific recording formats for audio and video. Storage of other kinds of information only has limited support	Any kind of file format may be used to store audio, video, and other kinds of information
Specific transmission formats for audio and video (DVB, ATSC)	General transmission formats for all kinds of information (IP)

Figure 1.5   The differences between conventional television (*left*) and digital signage systems (*right*).

Finally, there is another advantage to IP-based distribution: Local area networks exist almost everywhere. Even if there is no network available, it may be possible to quickly establish a wireless local area network (WLAN) for digital signage use. However, as we will explore later, WLANs are not suitable for all kinds of digital signage applications and must be used with some care.

In traditional broadcasting systems, IEC and F connectors are used for the coaxial cables carrying analog and digital TV signals. These TV broadcasting systems usually carry only audio and video, along with some metadata as teletext and program-related "event information." In an IP-based distribution system, twisted-pair cables

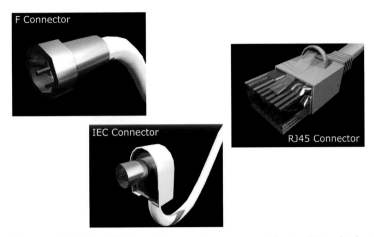

Figure 1.6   Both IEC and F connectors are used for traditional television; RJ-45 connectors are used for IP communication and IP broadcasting.

with RJ-45 connectors are used to carry IP Ethernet traffic (Figure 1.6). Using IP, which can carry any kind of information, the distribution part of the system becomes quite future-proof.

How Is Digital Signage Different from a Web Site?

So, digital signage is created from several kinds of files or IP media streams rather than just one ready-made, continuous live signal. Why, then, is digital signage not the same as the presentations of content that are bought to us when visiting a web site using a personal computer? web site content is most certainly based on separate files and IP streams.

In digital signage systems, the content is presented to us in a more or less automatic way, just as it is with radio and television once we have selected the desired channel. We do not have to constantly request specific information. In digital signage systems, an automated process handles most things. The key elements of this handling are the schedules and the playlists.

The content is based on one or more files being combined into a complete message on a screen just as they are on the screen of a personal computer. However, just as with television, we do not have to work actively to get the message on the screen. That is done automatically. When surfing the Web, you actively fetch content from web sites by selecting the pages you want to view. In digital signage systems, the content is automatically fetched from somewhere or, as we will see later in the book, it may be broadcast directly to a large number of users. In that respect, digital signage is much more like broadcast media than a web site.

But digital signage can also be configured to allow interaction between the user and the system. In some applications, the user can control the screen content by selecting or editing playlists. This could be compared to a TV viewer using a remote control device to change channels or select subtitling or alternative languages. Consequently, digital signage, like the museum information display in Figure 1.7, may be regarded as something between traditional TV broadcasting and Web browsing on the Internet.

Television and radio are old media that have been in stores for decades. Living in the shadow of home entertainment media, VCRs and CRT TV monitors have been used in the stores to provide commercials and product demonstrations closer to where the purchasing decisions really take place. Presenting products at the *point of purchase (POP)* is the core idea of digital signage.

Can digital signage be regarded as a new medium coexisting with radio, television, and the Internet? Or perhaps radio and television should be regarded as a part of the much larger medium of digital signage.

When television was first introduced, it was immediately regarded as a new medium, in addition to traditional radio broadcasting. But in reality, radio broadcasting is a part of the television medium because an audio signal (radio channel) is needed to carry the TV sound channel(s).

The same is true for digital signage systems that comprise audio, video, and all other kinds of information in real time, near-real time, and non-real time. These systems may make use of broadcast distribution and may then be regarded as a new kind of medium beyond television. Radio and television broadcasting may be regarded as a part of the new medium because one or more regions on a digital signage screen may be live IPTV broadcasts. Alternatively, the audio may be a real-time IP radio channel. This means we now have a new medium that encompasses live radio and television as well as real-time and non-real-time presentations of media files. An interesting point is that newspapers and other printed media are non-real-time

Finding content is a
manual task on the Web.

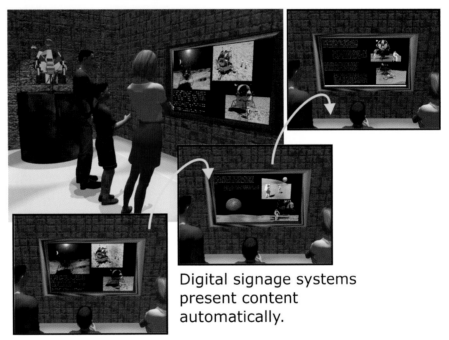

Digital signage systems
present content
automatically.

Figure 1.7 Although there are similarities between web sites and digital signage, a digital signage system provides information in a much more automated way.

media and that digital signage methods may be used to integrate these with traditional broadcast media.

Digital signage is perhaps not the best name of this media because it encompasses much more than just digital signs. Digital signs are actually only one application of this kind of file- and IP-stream-based media. Today there is no appropriate name for this medium. A better name of this new medium would have been Digital Media

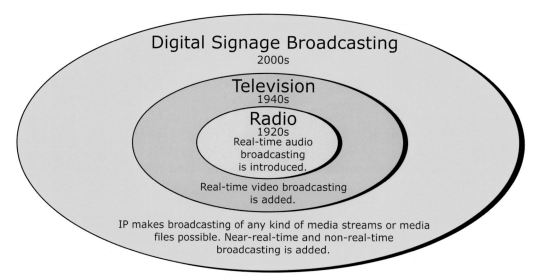

Figure 1.8 If digital signage uses a broadcast transmission chain, it can be regarded as a new medium that encompasses traditional radio and television as well as the non-real-time possibilities available on the Web.

Broadcasting. However, DMB is already taken as an acronym for Digital Multimedia Broadcasting, used for terrestrial data broadcasting associated with digital radio.

In this book, we use digital signage as the name of the new medium. If a broadcast medium is used for distribution, it could be called digital signage broadcasting. In the future, this might be shortened to just signage broadcasting (since today's technologies are all digital anyway). But *digital signage* and *digital signage broadcasting* will have to do for now.

RETAIL APPLICATIONS FOR DIGITAL SIGNAGE

Digital signage could be used for any electronic signage or visualization application. However, it is evident that the most popular application today is for commercial and advertising purposes in stores and public areas such as railway stations and airports. There are both indoor and outdoor applications.

Today people are exposed to electronic advertising media primarily in their homes—watching commercials on TV or surfing the Internet. However, except for e-commerce and some TV shopping accomplished by ordering the merchandise using the phone, both done at home, customers have not been exposed to much electronic advertising at the point of purchase, that is, in the stores.

With digital signage systems, it becomes possible to get electronic advertising—just like on the Internet—into the stores where the customers are making their purchasing decisions. This is important because it may be more efficient to reach consumers at the point of purchase. In the shops people are more focused on looking for products than when watching TV at home. And it is well known that a large portion of the purchase decisions are made right in the shops.

Accessibility of Internet Content

The Internet is very much a marketplace for commercial purposes and is filled with advertising. However, Internet information reaches the consumers only in their homes, at their workplaces, and possibly on their cell phones.

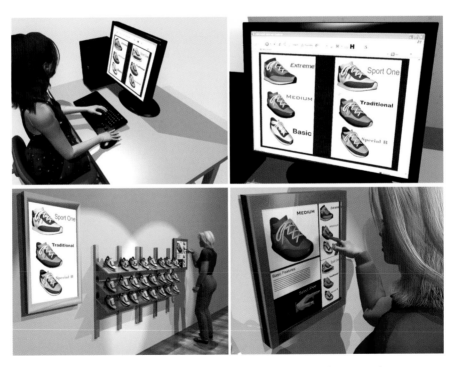

Figure 1.9 Digital signage in stores is a way to get the marketing and advertising information from the Internet out into the real world.

It seems quite strange that electronic media have been present in the homes for such a long time while printed media have completely dominated retail environments. Radio has been present in homes since the 1920s, and television has been the largest commercial medium in many countries since the late 1940s or early 1950s. Still, printed material is essential to reach people in their homes but the gap between the retail environment and the home environment when it comes to the use of electronic media is astounding.

Digital signage systems can move commercial content from the Internet into the stores. This is quite important because customers now often get more and better updated information from sources on the Internet than in the stores. But increased e-commerce comes at the expense of the retail industry. Therefore, getting Internet information to the brick-and-mortar stores as well is essential.

Greater Control and Flexibility of Content

Digital signage provides the possibility of changing the message all the time. The dynamics allow the content to be adapted to different hours of the day and other circumstances. Using suitable means of

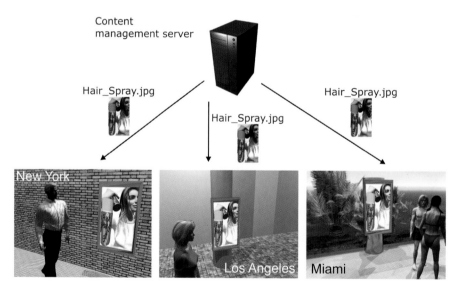

Figure 1.10   The image file Hair_Spray.jpg is simultaneously sent to all locations and shown on the screens according to playlists that are also downloaded to the screens.

distribution (see Chapters 5, 6, and 7) also allows near-real-time or live update of the content.

Finally, digital signage provides very accurate control of what appears on the screens. Printed signage has to be changed manually in the stores, making the advertiser dependent on the manual work of the staff to display the most current message. An even greater benefit to digital signage is that content on point-of-purchase screens can be changed simultaneously and automatically across a whole continent. This has never been possible before.

CURRENT HOME APPLICATIONS OF DIGITAL SIGNAGE–LIKE DEVICES

A technology similar to that used for digital signage is already in use in many homes without people really noticing its connection to digital signage systems in public environments. Many people collect their digital photos and video recordings in their computers rather than use more traditional ways of doing so (such as photo albums, videocassettes, and CDs). Separate media players are used to watch the photos and video stored in the computer.

The media players are used to bring video clips, digital photographs, and music to the TV set and the home cinema system. Of course, media players also exist in computers to play video files and music. These media players are based on the ability to play files and streams of many formats. They also include playlist features so the user can create slide shows and other presentations. The media players fetch files from a PC somewhere in the home via the local area network IP switch. Many of these media players are rather thin; they do not have a hard drive and depend on specific server software installed in the PC. Some media players also enable Internet access from the TV set.

The in-store applications for digital signage discussed in this book resemble these home media networks that consist of computers or other centralized storage, a home Ethernet IP network, and a variety of media players suited for different kinds of applications. As shown in Figure 1.11, the user can retrieve files from a PC in another room using the media player's remote control. Then the files are combined

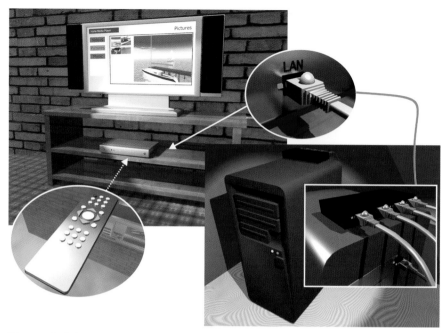

Figure 1.11   Several types of hardware media players now in many homes use the home's local area network.

by the player to generate the final screen content. (In Chapter 12, we will dig deeper into how these present-day hardware and software media players might evolve into the home digital signage systems of tomorrow.)

The closest thing you can get to a home digital signage system today is a Home Theater PC (HTPC), which is a PC designed and equipped to provide easy access to television as well as digital files and the Internet. The only thing missing from such a system is the availability of content streams and files that are controlled by schedules and playlists that do not have to be created by the consumer. Today you simply have to be your own digital signage content provider. But that is about to change as completely new kinds of media providers begin to show up and capitalize on this new medium.

In the following chapters, I discuss the elements of digital signage as well as content management and distribution methods that are available today and how they seem to be evolving.

2

DISPLAY SYSTEMS

Every technology occupies a certain window in time. Most people have learned that it is essential to use the right technology in the right era.

The reason digital signage systems have become popular is very much due to the increasing availability of very thin, inexpensive, high-resolution screens that can display large pictures. These new display devices can be installed on any wall, anywhere. The future development of these display devices will also undoubtedly decide the success or failure of the digital signage medium.

How do you choose the right kind of digital signage display device? Today there are many kinds of display devices to choose from (see Figure 2.1). Before the plasmas and liquid crystal displays (LCDs), the only option was equipment that used a cathode-ray tube. There were some LCD projectors, but these only reached the required performance levels for digital signage applications quite recently.

One of the basic ideas of the digital signage medium is to divide the display area into regions, layers, and tickers, and this requires a large screen in order to offer content that is reasonably easy to read or view. And to fit a large screen into a store or home, it has to be quite thin.

This chapter focuses on the display options and applications that are most suitable for each alternative.

Figure 2.1 There are many kinds of digital device. This 360-degree LED video display system is designed to create an exotic digital signage experience.

CATHODE-RAY TUBES

In stores, conventional TV sets have been used for a long time to make product presentations, but cathode-ray tube (CRT) TV sets (Figure 2.2) are heavy and bulky. Therefore, they have only been used when absolutely necessary and with suitable stands or shelves to get these ugly devices into the retail environment. These ordinary TV sets that are used to display demonstration videos on a VCR are regarded as the first electronic (though not digital) signage display appliance. To use VHS-based systems for in-store signage purposes, it was necessary to rewind the tape again and again. The idea of using multiple recordings on a tape combined with an autoreverse capability to repeat the commercial message was the predecessor of the playlists that can be considered as the fundamental core of any digital signage application.

CRTs and TV sets have also been used for live coverage of horse racing and other sports in gaming parlors around the world (Figure 2.3).

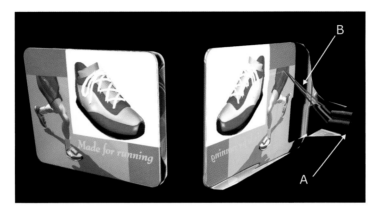

Figure 2.2 Cathode-ray tubes are based on electron guns **(A)** that generate beams of electrons **(B)** propagating in a vacuum toward a surface of zinc sulfide where light is radiated as a result of the collision between the electrons and the sulfide.

Figure 2.3 The conventional CRT-based TV set and VCR were combined to present the first electronic display appliances for product demonstrations in stores and presentations of live events such as horse races in gaming parlors.

CRTs do not have an easy life these days. The competition with LCDs, plasma screens, and projection systems will probably be impossible to beat in the long run. However, new slim CRTs have been developed that might make it possible for this technology to survive. Until now (2008), however, these new display devices are not yet competitive in the market.

One thing is clear: The market wants thin display systems that are easy to put on any wall and that do not occupy much space. The display device has to be able to provide a large picture with a sufficient contrast ratio during daylight conditions.

FLAT-PANEL DISPLAYS

Flat-panel display systems have opened up many new ways to use digital media in stores. In contrast to the bulky CRT-based displays, flat-panel displays give an awesome impression and improve the atmosphere in the store.

Liquid Crystal Display Panels

For screen diagonals smaller than 40 inches (102 cm), the liquid crystal displays are the most cost-efficient flat-panel displays. As shown in Figure 2.4, LCDs are based on a large fluorescent white light source in front of which there is a filter that provides polarized light. In front of this filter is a grid of tiny pixel-sized liquid crystals that can be electrically prodded to twist the polarized light to the same polarization angle as the second polarization filter. In this way, the light is either allowed to pass through or not. Additional filters give the pixels their red, green, and blue colors.

The LCD screens are popular because they are very insensitive to burn-in effects, which can be caused by the sometimes static content used for digital signage. (In the long run, still pictures and graphics may cause burn-in effects in virtually any type of display; smart digital signage managers will design their content to change occasionally to avoid this.)

In comparison to the competing technology of plasma flat-panel displays, it is easier to make tiny pixels and achieve high resolution on an LCD. On the other hand, the contrast ratios are usually better for plasma display systems.

Thin Film Transistor LCDs

Unlike television, digital signage does not rely completely on display devices that are specifically made for television. Computer monitors can also be used. As discussed in Chapter 4, media players have

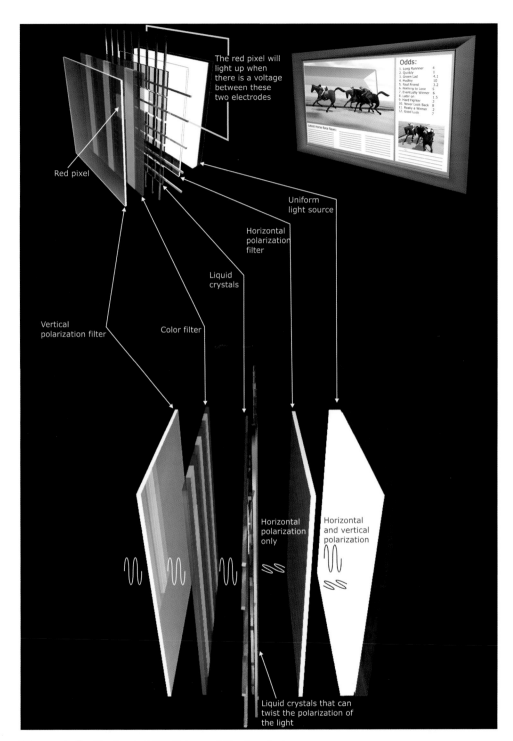

The red pixel will light up when there is a voltage between these two electrodes

Red pixel

Uniform light source

Horizontal polarization filter

Liquid crystals

Vertical polarization filter

Color filter

Horizontal polarization only

Horizontal and vertical polarization

Liquid crystals that can twist the polarization of the light

Figure 2.4 The basic LCD flat-panel display design.

video interfaces other than television set-top boxes; they are actually computers. Therefore, conventional flat-panel computer screens are used for applications where smaller screens are needed.

The most common type of computer screen is the thin film transistor (TFT), which works in a similar way to TV LCD displays. Today's TV LCD displays, however, are of the same class as computer monitor LCDs.

One thing to remember is that computer TFT screens do not always have the 16:9 aspect ratios that are normal in TV-type displays. The screen may be narrower than a standard aspect ratio television display. This will affect the kind of applications that the screens can support. In digital signage applications, the computer TFT LCDs are often installed in portrait rather than landscape position (Figure 2.5).

Interactivity can be added with touch-sensitive screens (Figure 2.6). They can be added quite easily to the smaller TFT screens. There are four basic kinds of touch-sensitive screen: resistive, capacitive, acoustic surface wave–based, and infrared light–based touch screens. All these touch-screen-sensing technologies determine the coordinates on the screen where the user places a finger. These X and Y coordinates are connected to various actions within the

Figure 2.5 For applications that require screen sizes smaller than 26 inches (66 cm), general computer TFT screens are often used.

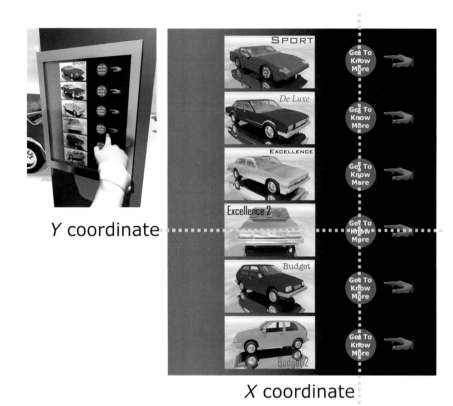

Figure 2.6 Touch-screen displays make it possible for customers to interact with media players without a keyboard or mouse.

software of the interactive application, such as zooming in on a product image or selecting different content to view.

Plasma Screens

For 42-inch (107 cm) and larger screens, plasma display systems are the most popular for digital signage just as they are for television.

Plasma flat-panel displays consist of small pixel-sized cells containing ionized gas that glows when an electrical field is built up around it by a grid of electrodes. Each pixel actually consists of three fluorescent lamps: one red, one green, and one blue (Figure 2.7).

Plasma screens have a high contrast ratio and are therefore suitable for store environments. The improved contrast ratio is possible because each pixel can be completely shut off and appear completely

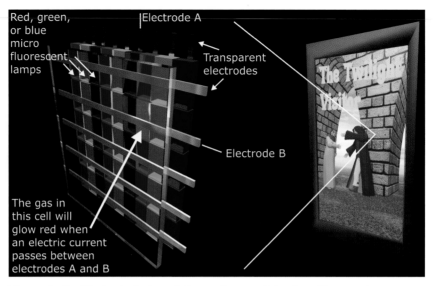

Figure 2.7 The basic design of plasma flat-panel display. When an electric current passes between the transparent electrodes (*top*) the gas in the addressed cell will glow (*left center*).

black. (This is not true in an LCD pixel element, where it is not possible to completely block the light.)

On the other hand, the same technology that allows a plasma pixel to be completely shut off requires that its only option for "on" is to be completely on. In other words, the only way to create gray levels is to make each pixel flash very quickly. As a result, there are significant demands on the electronics controlling the plasma display. In an LCD display, it is easy to create any grayscale level by letting the liquid crystal twist the light into the appropriate polarization angle. In a plasma screen, the grayscale is harder to achieve.

Another problem often discussed about plasma displays is the risk of burn-in effects. One way to avoid them is to avoid content that is too static.

Organic Light-Emitting Diodes Displays

Organic light-emitting diodes (OLEDs) are used only in very small display devices. But OLEDs are definitely one of the more exciting technologies for future display systems. OLED technology can be used for larger screens as well. They have low power consumption and are based on an emissive layer of organic compounds. In contrast to LCDs, OLEDs do not require a backlight.

OLED displays can be manufactured using a process that resembles conventional printing techniques. It is also possible to apply OLED technology to flexible materials; this might be the ultimate solution to creating self-illuminating digital paper. A competing technology for digital paper is described in the "Electronic Paper" section of this chapter.

Figure 2.8 shows a three-layer color OLED. The three polymer layers contain organic compounds. OLEDs are based on the principle that light is emitted in certain organic compounds when electrons and electron holes (lack of electrons) are joined. To the right is a cathode grid, and in front of this grid is an electron transport layer. The negatively

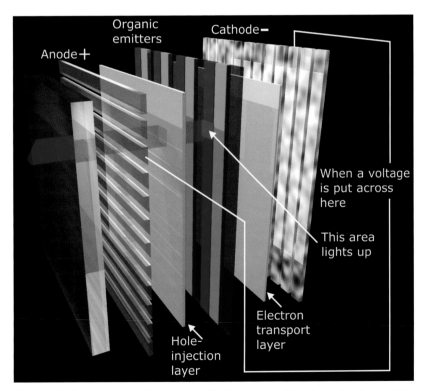

Figure 2.8 Organic light-emitting diodes may well be the technology of the future even for larger screens. When a voltage is put between the electrodes addressing a certain pixel, the electrons and electron holes (lack of electrons) will join in the organic emission layer and cause the pixel to light up.

charged electrons in the electron transport layer try to move left toward the organic emitter layer and the positively charged anode. At the same time, electron holes (a lack of electrons) are created in the hole-injection layer since the electrons of this layer also move toward the anode. These holes move to the right into the layer containing the organic emitters where they meet and join the electrons originating from the electron transport layer. When the holes and the electrons join in the organic emitters layer, light is emitted. The color of the light is determined by the kind of organic material in the emitting layer.

There are also simpler two-layer OLEDs that may be put on top of flexible substrates. This is probably one of the most important and exciting characteristics of the OLEDs.

Today OLEDs are used primarily in very small displays like mobile phones, MP3 players, and digital cameras. However, there are prototypes for up to 40-inch TV displays. LCDs and plasmas will likely face tough competition from OLEDs in the next few years.

Shelf-Oriented Digital Signage Systems

Of course, LED outdoor display systems provide the largest pictures, but there are also applications that call for very small screens. For example, small screens located next to specific products to promote that product's benefits (Figure 2.9) may create a stronger impression

Figure 2.9 Small media players with integrated LCD screens that are only a few inches wide can be mounted next to merchandise. Often the content of such media players is stored in flash memory.

on the customer since he or she is probably more focused when searching for a certain product among the shelves. This is one example where OLEDs may be effective.

PROJECTORS

Projection systems are most suited to cinema-like applications. There are modern high-intensity projectors, however, that may be used in retail environments and public areas even where there is quite a lot of background light. Using a projector is no doubt the most inexpensive way to provide a very large picture. The only thing required is somewhere to put the projector and a wall to project on to.

There are two main competing technologies when it comes to projection: LCD and digital light processing.

LCD Projectors

The LCD projector technology is based on blocking the light using polarization filters and liquid crystals that twist the polarization plane of the light. Using dichroic mirrors (see Figure 2.10), the light of a common white light source is separated into three rays of light (red, green, and blue). These rays pass through three LCD elements. Since blocking light means heating the LCD elements, it is an advantage to use a separate LCD for each color so the LCDs share the heat load from the lamp.

There are also projectors based on one common LCD handling all three colors, but this means that a weaker light source has to be used (in order to maintain lower heat). This solution leads to worse brightness than in the three-element LCD projectors.

The principle of blocking the light and the associated heat problems is a limitation to the brightness that can be achieved using LCD technology in projectors. Just as with LCD flat-panel displays, another problem is achieving a high contrast ratio, though this has improved over the years.

Digital Light-Processing Projectors

Digital light processing (DLP) is based on a mosaic of hundreds of thousands of small, electrically controlled mirrors. By controlling

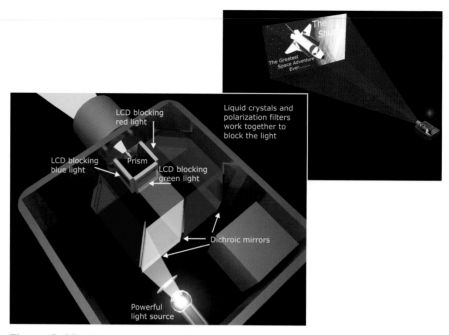

Figure 2.10   The basic design of an LCD projector. Dichroic mirrors reflect and filter the light from the common white source of light into red, green, and blue light, which is directed into the LCD responsible for each of the basic color components. Liquid crystals and polarization filters work together to block the light of the pixels that should appear dark or black.

electrical signals to each micro-mirror, its orientation can be altered. This reflects the incoming light from a strong source of white light. However, before hitting the mirror, the light is filtered through a wheel with red, green, and blue (Figure 2.11). So the three basic colors are shown in sequence.

Because the control of light is achieved by reflecting—rather than obscuring—the light, as is the case for the LCD projector, very bright light sources may be used. For this reason, DLP systems may be the best choice in well-lit environments such as stores. In home applications where it is possible to use the projector in a completely dark room, this is of less significance.

One digital micro-mirror device (DMD) is enough to provide a color picture if a rotating wheel with three color filters is put in front of the device. Then the red, green, and blue components of the picture are

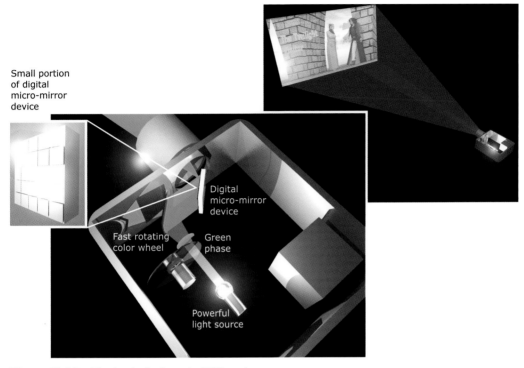

Small portion
of digital
micro-mirror
device

Digital
micro-mirror
device

Fast rotating
color wheel

Green
phase

Powerful
light source

Figure 2.11   The basic design of a DLP projector.

shown in fast sequence, making the eye believe that it is actually seeing a full-color picture.

Short-Range Projection Systems

Conventional projectors must be several yards or meters away
from the flat surfaces onto which they are projecting. In many situations, as in store windows, a shorter projection range is necessary.
Short-range projection systems have been developed to meet these
needs. These projectors use special lenses combined with a special
mirror to reduce the projection range, as shown in Figure 2.12.

Remember that a projected picture created by this kind of projection
system, just as with any kind of projector, is a two-dimensional flat
picture. A projected image does not have the same effect or appearance as a real store window with mannequins.

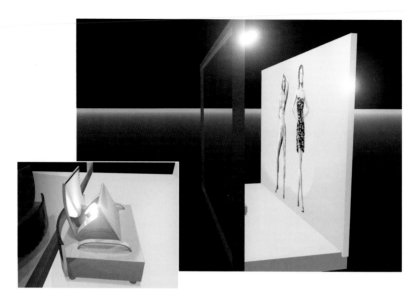

Figure 2.12   A short-range projector (such as this one from NEC) works well for store windows and other small spaces.

OUTDOOR DISPLAY SYSTEMS

Outdoor display systems are very expensive because they are not made in large volumes and they have very expensive components. Screens of this kind include a lot of electronics to control the pixel elements. Naturally, these electronics are quite customized, which is a partial explanation for their high cost.

It is interesting to study these giants among electronic screens because—just as with any computer TFT screen or flat-panel screen— we find ordinary graphics interfaces (e.g., DVI, HDMI, and others that are described in the High-Definition Television section later in this chapter). This means an ordinary computer or some other kind of video device can be connected to these large outdoor screens. Going one step further, there is nothing stopping us from connecting a digital signage media player to the screens as well.

LED Outdoor Display Systems

LED-based outdoor display systems, as shown in Figures 2.13 and 2.14, have been used for a long time at sports arenas because although projectors provide large pictures, they still have insufficient brightness for daytime outdoor use.

Figure 2.13 Large-scale LED screens are built in sections, like this one from Hibino, which means that you can get any size you want (and can afford). If you stand in front of the screen, it appears as just one large surface of LEDs (*left*). If you look at the LED display from behind, it becomes obvious that the screen consists of sections that can be combined into any size and shape of screen (*right*).

Figure 2.14 Outdoor LED display systems, like this one from Barco, are the picture-producing giants of our time. If looking closely at the screen you will see the red, green, and blue LEDs. The color nuance in a particular area of the screen depends on the combination of light intensities of the red, green, and blue LEDs, respectively, as shown in the circles.

In recent years, these very large screens have also entered the digital signage arena in large public areas. LED displays are very bright and work well in daylight. There are several tricks, such as using small curtains above each row of LEDs, to prevent sunlight from striking the LEDs directly (Figure 2.15). This improves the brightness considerably.

A major problem with LED outdoor display systems is the very high power consumption, which may be several kilowatts due to the large number of LEDs. But undoubtedly, the LED display systems are still the most popular option for outdoor use. They are insensitive to high and low temperatures and there are no real alternatives during tough outdoor conditions.

LED techniques are also used for smaller digital signs—for example, text messages on busses, in railway stations, and sometimes even in airports. The most modern LED outdoor screens are based on high-intensity multicolor LEDs (Figure 2.16). Because each LED can produce any color, each LED can be located farther from the others, unlike traditional screens, which have an LED for each basic color.

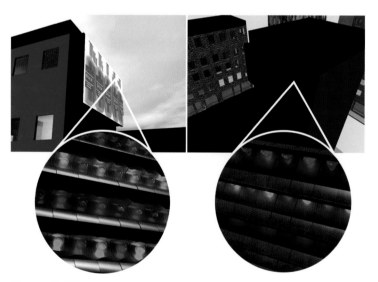

Figure 2.15 In some large outdoor LEDs, incoming light is stopped by clever "light traps," a kind of curtain that stops light from above without obscuring the visibility from below (*left*). Viewed from above (*right*), the image is almost completely blocked by the light traps.

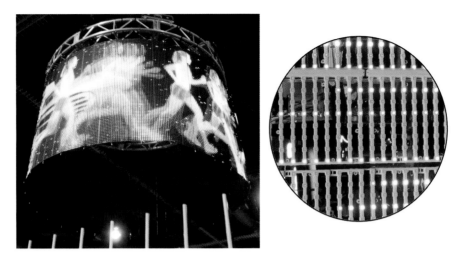

Figure 2.16 New kinds of LED screens use multicolor LEDs (*right*) such as this cylindrical display, using the "Stealth Technology" from Element Labs.

These modern LED outdoor screens are very thin and easy to handle. Screens of many sizes and shapes can be constructed using this technology. The only disadvantage is that the picture will not get as dense as when using conventional LED technology.

Daylight-Use LCD Display Systems

For outdoor and especially nighttime use, LEDs are undoubtedly the most common display systems, although there are LCD alternatives that can be used in broad daylight. LCDs consume much less power than LEDs but they cannot be made very large (at least not compared to large-scale LED displays). They also require temperature-controlled, indoor environments. But they can be used in store windows, where they work quite well even though exposed to daylight.

Figure 2.17 shows an LCD that is designed to be put in very bright environments such as store windows. The screen has a back light consisting of a set of fluorescent lamps in front of which there is an array of closely tiled optical fibers that get wider as they get closer to the display surface. This magnifies the picture provided by the LCD and rejects incoming light from outside. As a result, a very bright picture with a very tiny distance between the pixels is achieved.

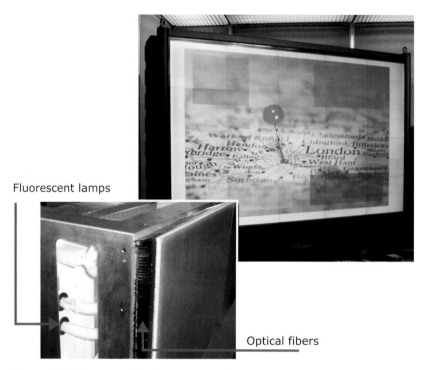

Fluorescent lamps

Optical fibers

Figure 2.17   Large LCD displays use fiber optic techniques to make the screen less sensitive to incoming light. In this display system from Screen Technology, fluorescent lamps serve as the back light to optical fibers that are placed very close together and act as light guides to magnify the image from the LCD.

Transreflective and Reflective LCDs

Another way to avoid the problem of sunlight hitting the display is to turn the worst enemy into the best friend. In transreflective and reflective LCDs, the incoming light can be used to increase the contrast (Figure 2.18). In the back of the LCD, a retroreflector transmits light from external light sources back through the LCD. In this kind of display, the built-in light source may be switched off when the display is exposed to daylight (Figure 2.19). This preserves power and makes LCD technology a strong alternative to LEDs for outdoor applications in the long run.

However, the problems in making large LCD screens remain. LCDs are usually made for indoor use but an alternative to introduce the screens to people might be to place them in store windows. This may be one of the most suitable places to put a transreflective LCD flat-panel display.

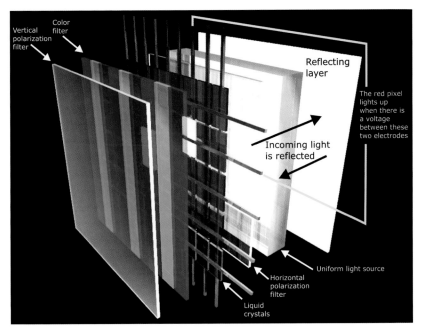

Figure 2.18 The basic design of a transreflective LCD flat-panel display turns a difficulty into an asset. Incoming light is converted so that it improves contrast. The uniform light source is lit in darkness but shuts off automatically in bright light.

Figure 2.19 Transreflective and reflective LCDs may be one way to get low-energy outdoor display systems. At night, the built-in light source is used (*left*). In daylight, no light source is required (*right*).

Most of today's transreflective LCDs are quite small and used in customer terminals that need to be in daylight conditions.

SCREEN ORIENTATION AND ASPECT RATIOS

Television and movie theater screens are always in landscape orientation. Only video artists have experimented with video recordings in portrait orientation.

In digital signage, there is much more flexibility in screen orientation. The portrait orientation is quite common to simulate printed posters. Using portrait orientation is also a way to make digital signage look different from television.

When installing a display system, it is essential to be sure that it really can be installed in portrait orientation. Not all display devices are designed for this. There might be issues related to cooling and fans when installing plasmas vertically.

Projection systems cannot be easily used to provide pictures in portrait orientation, but it has been attempted for special purposes like electronic and digital art (Figure 2.20). The portrait orientation is very powerful when displaying people in standing or walking positions, such as a video from a fashion show.

Another important consideration is the aspect ratio of the display device. The most common aspect ratios are:

- TFT computer monitors, 1.25:1
- Standard TV set, 1.33:1 (4:3)
- Widescreen TV set, 1.78:1 (16:9)
- Cinema, 2.35:1

In television display systems, it is common practice to add black bars at the top and the bottom of the picture to "convert" the old standard television ratio of 1.33:1 to display movies with an aspect ratio of 2.35:1. This conversion is called *letter boxing*. Black bars are added to the sides to display regular 4:3 (1.33:1) aspect ratio programs on widescreen 16:9 (1.78:1) TV screens. Letter boxing is not an option in digital signage systems, where it is essential to use the complete screen area. The aspect ratio of the content to be displayed will affect

Figure 2.20   In digital signage, portrait orientation of screens is quite common.

the choice of display system. Remember that conventional TFT screens are quite narrow (aspect ratio 1.25:1).

It is especially important to think about the aspect ratios of the display devices when using a variety of screen sizes to display the same content in the same environment. It may be hard to mix aspect ratios if the same content is to be displayed on screens of different sizes. TFTs with aspect ratios of 1.25:1 are often 17 inches or 19 inches; larger screens, TV-type LCDs, and plasmas are 16:9 (1.78:1). Cinema applications have several wider aspect ratios. Many movies are shot in 2.35:1 format, which is also often used in movies on DVDs unless the format is converted into 16:9 (Figure 2.21).

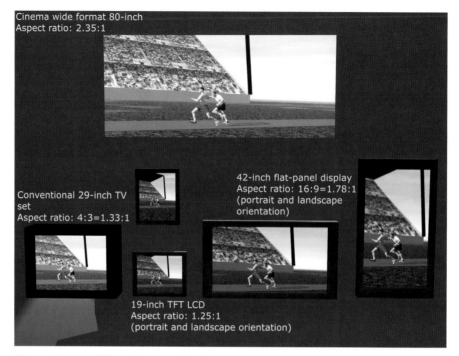

Cinema wide format 80-inch
Aspect ratio: 2.35:1

Conventional 29-inch TV set
Aspect ratio: 4:3=1.33:1

42-inch flat-panel display
Aspect ratio: 16:9=1.78:1
(portrait and landscape orientation)

19-inch TFT LCD
Aspect ratio: 1.25:1
(portrait and landscape orientation)

Figure 2.21 When choosing display systems, it is necessary to consider the picture aspect ratio.

Projectors often adapt the computer screen or conventional 4:3 aspect ratios but there are also projectors with a 16:9 (1.78:1) aspect ratio.

To get relatively inexpensive display systems, we are more or less forced to use the standard 16:9 widescreen format. Doing so means we are limited (with today's technology) in aspect ratio options; this is not the case with printed signs and posters, which can be virtually any size and proportion the designer can dream up. This has caused a special debate in the cinema business where traditional cinema posters have a specific, standard aspect ratio. However, it is much too expensive to make custom flat-panel displays and the entire digital signage business is rather dependent on the mass production of flat-panel displays for consumer use.

DISPLAY DEVICE RESOLUTION

The digital signage of tomorrow definitely will be high definition. Computers already operate with high-resolution graphics to display

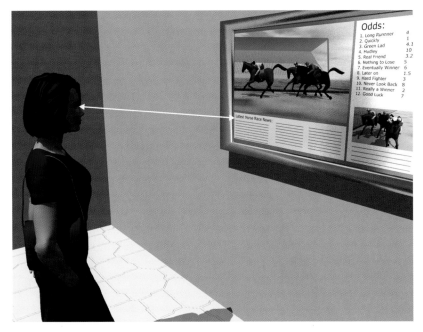

Figure 2.22   The demands for high image resolution vary in digital signage systems. The highest demands are probably in indoor applications, where the viewer is close to the screen when reading text, such as on customer terminals.

text. People tend to compare the quality of text on computer screens with printed text on paper. As a result, high-resolution displays for computers were required long before high-resolution television, HDTV was requested by the viewers or the TV stations.

Computer Display Devices

A common resolution in computer screens of today is SXGA 1280 × 1024 pixels. This is certainly much better than the standard resolution of TV sets and it provides excellent display of text and graphics. Remember that the expectations for the quality of text on an electronic display are the same as expectations for the quality of text on a poster or sign that is produced using high-quality printing at close range, as in Figure 2.22.

High-Definition Television

Traditional standard TV sets have a very low resolution. Even though conventional TV sets have meant a lot for the development of in-store television, screen resolution is too low for the reproduction of high-quality text messages. For this reason, much of the digital signage business has been based on computer displays. However, computer screens are not wide enough, and often not big enough, to display commercials at a distance.

High-definition television screens are much improved and better for digital signage than conventional television sets used to be. They are large and have sufficient resolution. The introduction of HDTV makes TV display devices much more interesting and practical for digital signage applications. Also, the HDTV development means a convergence of computer screens and display systems for television. In that respect, HDTV screens are ideal for digital signage.

Since production of TV commercials in high definition will increase, this will call for the installation of HDTV digital signage systems. Chapter 8 discusses the use of HDTV content for digital signage in greater detail, but here is an overview as it relates to the display device.

What really drives HDTV forward is the same thing that drives digital signage forward: the development of new display devices. Early plasma displays had a resolution of 852×480 pixels and were well suited for the standard-definition (SDTV) resolution signals with 720×576 (Europe) and 720×486 (U.S.) pixels.

Today LCD and plasma flat-panel systems are the major display devices for HDTV. Until recently, the screen resolution has been limited to 1366×768 pixels for the low- and medium-priced panels. Most of the more advanced consumer projectors are still limited to 1024×768 or 1024×720 pixels. However, LCDs and plasmas with 1920×1080 pixels are already on the market. The resolutions of 1366×768 and 1920×1080 pixels are in accordance with the 16:9 aspect ratios (Figure 2.23). Figure 2.24 compares the pixel densities in display systems with different resolutions but the same screen size. This gives you a sense of the clarity of details at different resolutions.

A primary difference between CRT TV sets and modern flat-panel and projection systems is that the resolution of the displayed signal is not necessarily the same as the resolution of the transmitted signal. The signal is scaled from the transmission format to the display format. Scaling the picture is also necessary when receiving standard-definition signals. This scaling requires processing in the display devices.

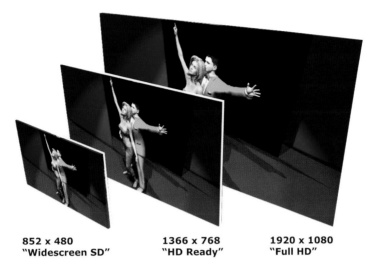

852 x 480   **1366 x 768**   **1920 x 1080**
"Widescreen SD"   **"HD Ready"**   **"Full HD"**

Figure 2.23 The more pixels on a screen, the larger the picture. This figure shows one image on screens of three sizes, even though all pixels are the same size.

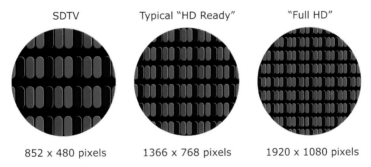

SDTV   Typical "HD Ready"   "Full HD"

852 x 480 pixels   1366 x 768 pixels   1920 x 1080 pixels

Figure 2.24 Assuming the same screen size, we will get a higher density of pixels with an increasing number of pixels. This figure shows the pixel densities for SDTV, HD-ready, and full-HD screens that are all the same size.

The most common transmission formats for HDTV broadcasting is 720p (progressive) or 1080i (interlaced). They exist in 720p/50 as well as 720p/59(59.94) and 1080i/25 as well as 1080i/30 versions depending on were they are used.

The European Information & Communications Technology Industry Association (EICTA) has issued the "HD Ready" logo for products that support a minimum vertical resolution of 720 pixels. These HD-ready devices must also be capable of handling 720p and 1080i input signals as well as the High-Bandwidth Digital Content Protection (HDCP). HDCP is the system used to prevent unauthorized copying of HDTV content.

What will be the standard format of the future? Until recently, the resolution of most HD display devices has been limited to 1366 × 768 pixels. This means that 720p may be an alternative to 1080i since the increased resolution may not be fully used anyway.

But things are beginning to change. For 40-inch and larger screens, there are now 1920 × 1080 pixel flat-panel displays and projectors that handle progressive scanning at this resolution. These devices are still quite expensive but no doubt they will eventually reach the mid-price consumer market quite soon. These 1920 × 1080 pixel display devices are referred to as "full HD" or "real HD." This makes it interesting to reconsider the choice of 720p instead of 1080i or even 1080p, which seems to be the ultimate HDTV standard of today. Certainly 1080p would require a lot more capacity than 720p.

The 1920 × 1080 pixel systems are the only systems where the distribution and display formats are the same. This might simplify the image processing in the display devices and could perhaps affect the final quality of the picture to some extent.

Video files based on HD are much larger than standard-resolution video files. Therefore, HDTV signals will require more bitrate capacity for distribution and more time will be required for file transfer if the distribution channel's bitrate is not increased accordingly. Of course, the same goes for live streaming. In addition, the larger files will require more storage space. (Capacity issues are discussed in greater detail in Chapter 9 and in Appendix A.)

OTHER DISPLAY ASPECTS

The quality of the HDTV signals is affected by several things, including the quality of compression and the bitrate. In addition, the electrical interface used on the screen will affect the result. Digital interfaces or component interfaces are much better than the conventional analog CVBS composite video baseband signals (NTSC or PAL) interfaces. Finally, the screen resolution is of great importance.

In digital signage applications, where people must be able to look at screens in bright environments and from different angles, things are a bit trickier than when watching TV at home or in home theater systems. Suddenly, the brightness of the screens, the contrast ratio, and the viewing angle of displays become very important (Figures 2.25 and 2.26).

At home, viewers tend to sit directly in front of the TV and do not move about while watching. With digital signage systems, the audience is likely standing and moving about. When more than one person is watching, the audience may be clustered around the display in a semicircle—meaning some are viewing the screen from the side rather than directly in front. How well the display device works in these situations greatly depends on the viewing angle.

The contrast ratio often decreases as the viewing angle increases. In general, plasma screens offer better quality at greater viewing angles than LCDs, which tend to lose contrast ratio more quickly. Also, plasmas are better at producing almost black regions on the screens. On the other hand, LCDs are better than plasmas at producing brighter

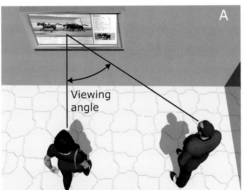

Figure 2.25   **(A)** Digital signage viewers may move around in front of the screen and watch it from many positions. **(B)** At larger viewing angles, the contrast ratio decreases. **(C)** The viewer experiences the best contrast ratio when directly in front of the screen.

Figure 2.26 Even large outdoor LED screens lose quality when observed from a greater viewing angle. The contrast ratio decreases and other strange effects may occur.

areas. This is of less importance in home applications because most people do not watch TV in very bright rooms. However, digital signage display systems may be installed in bright environments and therefore brightness is a very important characteristic of the screens.

Note that the viewing angle might be reduced when a screen is turned into portrait orientation because many manufacturers optimize their design for landscape orientation.

Display System Interfaces

The question about resolution leads to another very important discussion about which graphical interfaces should be used on the screens.

The screens have to be connected to devices that provide the graphical signals that are fed to the screens. However, there are several options when it comes to graphical interfaces, including analog and digital interfaces. There are also interfaces that allow high-definition signals and others that provide only standard TV resolution. On top of this, there is the question of scanning type. (Chapter 4 describes the video and audio interfaces in detail.)

Computer Graphical Interfaces Digital signage has developed from two directions. One line is from the TV business, using TV sets and VHS VCRs (which has evolved into DVD players). The other development line originates in the computer- and Internet-oriented world, where the VGA (Video Graphics Array) 15-pin D-Sub connector is the primary interface.

HDTV Interfaces Television viewers are familiar with the SDTV composite video connections between the set-top box and the TV set. A large improvement can be made by using S-VHS or SCART (widely used in Europe) RGB connections. Using these interfaces, the color component is separated from the luminance signal, which avoids classic problems such as cross-color interference.

But HDTV calls for even more interfaces on the display device (Figure 2.27). The analog HDTV alternative is the Y-Pb-Pr component connection that allows higher resolution as well as progressive scanning. In the SDTV world, the component connections have been used for progressive scanning playback from conventional DVD recorders.

There are also two digital alternatives: the Digital Video Interface (DVI) and High-Definition Multimedia Interface (HDMI). DVI originates from computer graphics cards and is not well suited for consumer audio-visual electronics. The cable is thick and only carries the video. To use DVI, the audio must be connected separately either by the analog RCA connectors or the separate Sony/Philips Digital Interface Format (S/PDIF) electrical or optical connections. S/PDIF is the standard way to connect digital audio sources to external multichannel amplifiers. A common problem is that flat-panel displays contain a lot of processing, which can delay the video relative to the audio, resulting in synchronization problems. External or internal audio delay devices may be used to compensate for this.

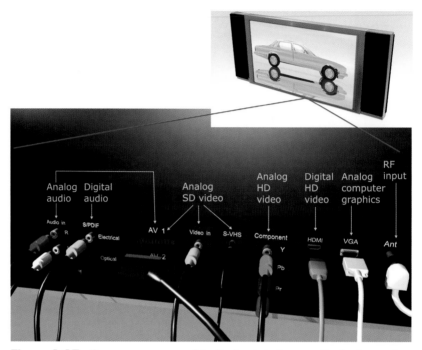

Figure 2.27   Some common graphic display interfaces on the back panel of LCD and plasma TV sets.

HDMI includes both digital audio and digital video. This facilitates pure digital connection to display systems that include the audio system, such as LCD and plasma flat-panel TV sets.

OTHER KINDS OF DISPLAY DEVICES

There are other kinds of display devices that can be controlled by a digital signage system. The 360-degree cylindrical video display (Figure 2.28) is one of the most spectacular display devices that exists today. These 3D-inspired display devices are fast rotating cylinders with a number of vertical rows of LEDs. This gives an impression of the cylinder being completely coated by LEDs. However, if studied carefully, you will see the horizontal lines that are created by the LEDs on the spinning cylinder. The LEDs can be fed with video clips and other kinds of images, just like flat displays. Of course, advanced software is required to feed the LEDs correctly to provide an impression of a picture.

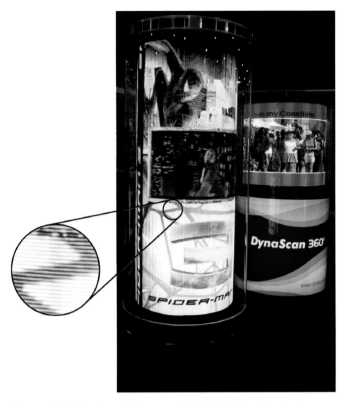

Figure 2.28 The 360-degree cylindrical video display is amazing. In the detail, you can see the horizontal lines indicating that the cylinder is spinning very rapidly. Here are two versions from Dynascan.

Although the most common 360-degree LED displays are used indoors, there are outdoor installations. These work well in broad daylight, just as large flat-panel LED displays do. It is very impressive when the moving picture rotates around the cylinder.

But there is more to it. Since modern digital signage distribution systems are based on data files and IP streaming, there is no real limitation to what devices can be supported by such a system. One example might be laser projection systems. And who knows, we might even see holographic 3D displays in the future (discussed in Chapter 12). At some locations in the world, very artistic digital signage systems have been constructed. Indoors digital signage may be used more or less as furnishing and outdoors it might be used as architecture (Figure 2.29).

Figure 2.29 Example of a display device other than projectors or flat-panel displays, such as laser projection systems. These digital signage devices may be a part of a digital signage network.

Figure 2.30 Example of 3M self-adhesive film used as a projection screen on a window.

The 3M company has invented a special kind of self-adhesive film that can be applied to shop windows or other transparent surfaces and used as a projection screen (Figure 2.30). From a projector inside the shop, a message can be displayed directly on the window. The most fascinating thing is that the film may be cut into any shape, adding a new dimension to digital signage in a quite inexpensive way.

ELECTRONIC PAPER

This chapter describes display devices that are self-luminous systems that work in the dark. They have some problems in operating in broad daylight, but this may be counteracted by using the transreflective LCD display systems, as described earlier in this chapter. Common to all these technologies is that they are based on the idea of creating a flat TV screen. But there is a completely different approach to digital signage displays: electronic paper.

The electronic ink (E-ink) technology is based on the idea of a creating a screen display that looks like printed paper but that uses incoming light. This concept is a way to preserve power and may be considered a modern type of dynamic printing technology. The display consists of many tiny capsules filled with a transparent liquid, a number of black, negatively charged particles, and a number of white, positively charged particles. By controlling a matrix of electrodes, each location of the surface behind the display capsules can be positively or negatively charged. This way, the surface facing the user becomes dark or light, since the white and black particles will be attracted or repulsed from the electrodes depending on the charge (Figure 2.31). The device consumes almost no power except when the displayed message is to be changed.

Today's applications for E-ink are small reading devices intended for digital books or newspapers. But in principle, any kind of dynamic sign that does not have to be self-illuminating could use this technology. In the long run, this technology might be applied on any material to create unique display devices, such as fabric, making T-shirts with dynamic digital signage a possibility.

The main difference between the E-ink technology and the competing OLED technology for applications on flexible materials is that

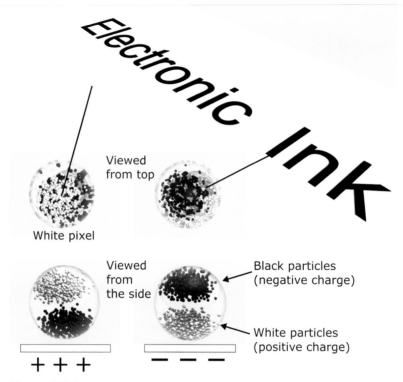

Figure 2.31   The capsules of the E-ink display form a grayscale
presentation that can be used for reading books or newspapers.

E-ink depends on external light to be seen, just like a printed sign
or poster. The advantage is the almost insignificant consumption of
power. OLEDs are self-illuminating. They can be used in the dark but
at a cost of increased consumption of power.

Color E-ink display devices can be produced by dividing each pixel
into subpixels representing the basic colors, just as in other kinds of
display devices.

A great feature with E-ink displays is that they provide extreme
viewing angles, very similar to printed material.

3

MAKING THE BEST USE OF DISPLAYS

The new flat-panel display systems offer possibilities never seen before. No matter what kind of content you'd like to display, digital signage probably has a solution. And the displays are probably the first thing you think about when starting to plan for a digital signage system. However, the display units are only a very small part of an entire system.

Before installing a digital signage system, it is necessary to decide the system's purpose and the way it is going to be used. Just finding a system that replaces the old paper posters is, in most cases, not a good alternative. Instead, you should try to explore all the new possibilities that are provided by digital signage.

The content displayed on a digital sign may originate from several files or live IP streams. Each source of content provides a content element on the screen. As described in Chapter 1, there are at least three kinds of content element: the region, the layer, and the ticker. We will certainly see even more content elements invented as the technology matures.

A conventional TV screen consists of only one layer of video all contained in one region. In Europe, sometimes teletext is used to add a layer of subtitling on top of the live video layer. In digital television, this is done locally by the digital receiver (set-top box). Also, the set-top box itself adds menus and program information screens (program metadata) on top of the received TV content. This is quite similar to the way a digital signage media player works, but the concept of layers and regions is not generally used to describe the makeup of a conventional TV screen. The difference in the digital signage world is that the screen may be divided into a multitude of regions, tickers, and layers (Figure 3.1).

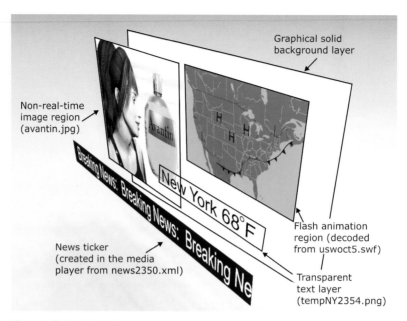

Figure 3.1 Digital signage can combine many types of information divided into regions, layers, and tickers. Each piece of information originates from a separate file.

Understanding the possibilities of layers and regions is the key to using digital signage systems in the most efficient ways. It is essential to remember that each content element—layer, region, and ticker—originates from a separate file or stream. In addition, we might have audio originating from a separate audio file or a video clip file. Of course, most live video IPTV streams also contain audio.

Media players are the devices that locally create the video and audio content on the screens. A media player works in a completely different way from a TV set-top box even though there are some similarities. A set-top box just decodes a ready-made television signal; the media player goes through a complex process of reading playlists and decoding media files accordingly. The final result is then put together into one single video signal that is fed to the screen. The regions, layers, and tickers are just virtual elements that come from the media player as a combined video signal.

The advantage to combining the content elements on the final screen is that the different elements can originate from completely different

One way to summarize the basic difference between digital signage and ordinary television is that in a digital signage system the combined video signal is created locally in the media player instead of at the TV station.

sources and the user decides what the final screen should contain. In addition, the appearance of each screen can be different even though the files are picked from a common library. This is all decided by the play-list read by the particular player. The screen being divided into picture elements means that in an interactive customer terminal, the customer can affect only selected regions or layers of the picture on the screen.

SCREENS WITH REGIONS

Successful digital signage is not just about using screens to show single digital still pictures. There is so much more to it.

As we have already discussed, a basic TV screen has only one region. The TV station can split the screen in separate areas, but that is done at the station playout, and the received signal really consists of one picture.

In digital signage systems, the new possibilities of using computers to feed the screens are utilized to their full extent. Instead of just one pic-ture area, as in television, the screen is split into regions (Figure 3.2).

An interesting possibility is showing commercials at the same time as information and entertainment. In conventional TV, the commer-cials are concentrated in breaks; in digital signage, the commercials can reside in one or more of the regions of the picture at all times. In a future home digital signage application, the viewer may get con-tent for free by allowing a region (or regions) to present commercial messages. Of course, this leads to completely new and challenging business ideas.

Another feature is that the content of the commercial regions can be selected individually for each screen depending on where the screen is located. This means that using the same basic content, the final appearance of the screens can be customized to each department of a store or to specific product advertising campaigns. Another possibility

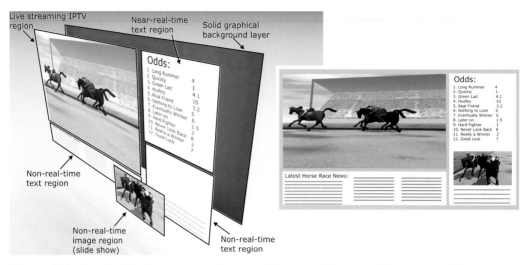

Figure 3.2   In a digital signage screen there might be a combination of live, near-real-time, and non-real-time information all displayed at the same time.

Figure 3.3   Digital signage offers the possibility of simultaneous exposure to commercials, information, and entertainment.

is to adapt the content according to geography, allowing local content in some of the areas on the screen (Figure 3.4). Local maps and advertising are good examples of combining national coverage material and local content.

Figure 3.4 The content of digital signage can be tailored to a screen's location.

Dynamic Regions

In advanced digital signage systems, the regions also can be dynamic in size. The screen may change to provide just one region and then may switch back to a number of smaller regions. By changing the size of regions, it becomes possible to focus the attention on important content. Changing a screen region's size to focus the customer on something specific is also used in common television commercials.

Finally, it could be possible to have moving, dynamic regions to achieve certain effects. This kind of dynamic effect may be used to catch customers' attention. In Figure 3.5, a larger text shrinks as the dynamic video clip region grows. This makes the text easy to read from a distance, while the video clip becomes more dominant and much more interesting. Using dynamic regions is a way to provide transitions between messages or between parts of a message.

Figure 3.5 The regions can be fixed or dynamic. In this case, the video clip region grows as the font size of a text layer decreases.

In many ways, you can say that digital signage works very much like web pages, where regions of the page are created from several kinds of file. So, this part of the digital signage medium is picked up from the world of the Internet and computers. However, other parts of the medium have roots in television and broadcasting.

Still Regions

The regions on the screens can be used for several purposes. One way to use a region is to project a still picture that can be changed easily for another picture. This is a very dynamic way of providing a visual message compared to a static printed poster. The picture can change during the day or the week to fulfill different information needs; for example, a fast-food restaurant could automatically change its signage to reflect whether it is serving breakfast or lunch.

People often expect more from digital signage systems than just an exchangeable electronic poster. The early digital signage applications failed because they were not ambitious enough. The dynamics in successful digital signs have to be extremely eye-catching. The retail environment is quite "noisy," with lots of impressions and attempts to grab customers' attention everywhere. Digital signage must offer more than just still pictures—adding animation or video clip regions is necessary.

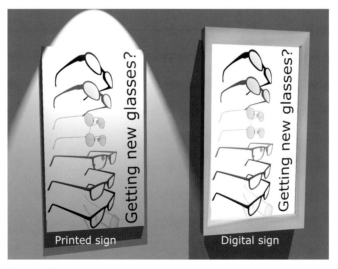

Figure 3.6   A screen with still pictures is the simplest kind of digital sign, but it's not enough in today's environment.

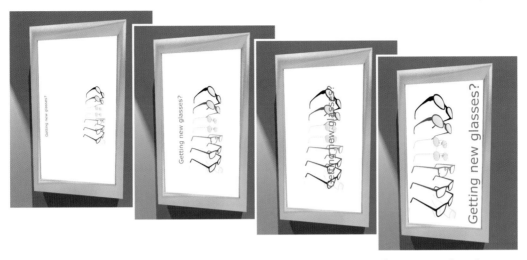

Figure 3.7   Animated regions containing a moving message are something new and tend to catch people's eyes. Here the Flash animation sequence glasses.swf creates a dynamic poster.

Animated Regions

The environment in stores and public areas is full of visual impressions. It is not easy to get the messages on the screens to the customers because their attention is being drawn to so many visual (and audio) presentations. For this reason, animated regions or full-screen animations have become very popular (Figure 3.7) and Macromedia Flash animations have found their way into the retail business. Flash animations easily can handle moving logos and other movement to show, for example, how products work. Macromedia Flash has been widely adopted on web sites around the world, and this popularity is translating to use on digital signage systems.

Video Regions

An alternative to animations is to use video clip regions. A problem might be that video clips tend to resemble the commercials that you watch at home on your TV set. But in some cases, even conventional TV commercials are used in digital signage applications. Commercials of this kind are often shown as full-screen regions.

Video clips require that the customer stop to watch the entire clip. People often have to wait in line to check out and, depending on the video's content, the time customers wait may be more pleasant with commercials to watch. At the same time, the store gets a chance to promote a product or service. The problem with show-ing commercials at the checkout is that people are about to leave and have already done most of their shopping.

Until now, most video clips used for digital signage have used the standard-definition television formats. However, the flat-panel dis-plays of modern digital signage also allow high-definition signals. Most certainly, TV commercials will evolve toward the various HD for-mats. This will affect the development of digital signage significantly when it comes to the capacity required for distribution of the signals.

Most content in current digital signage systems comes from material originally presented on web sites. But video clips often originate from the world of television commercials. For this reason, it is suitable to have the commercials delivered in television formats as well as vari-ous video clip formats if both television and digital signage are used in the same advertising campaign. Also, it is very important to be sure that all contracts cover the copyright aspects of distributing material via various media including digital signage. (See Figure 3.8.) Although

Figure 3.8 Video clips are used to get customers' attention. TV-style commercials are often shown in a full-screen region.

Figure 3.9 Video clip regions may be used to put life into otherwise stiff digital signage graphics. This figure shows a theme park promotional video clip that has been requested by a customer in a tourist information center.

content may be broadcast far and wide in various places and by various means, it is not necessarily free to be used; someone probably has a copyright on material even though it is displayed for public consumption.

Sometimes it is interesting to introduce a live video region or video clip into a graphics screen. This gives it more life. (See Figure 3.9.) At interactive customer terminals, it is quite impressive to let the customers choose to watch video clips related to the kind of products they are actually looking for.

Aspect Ratios

In digital signage, it is undesirable to have black borders on the top and bottom of the screen to handle different aspect ratios, as is often done in television. Most display systems have the 16:9 aspect ratio. It is quite easy to fit an image or a video clip of a different aspect ratio by adapting the aspect ratio of the region to the aspect ratio of the content. By using several regions, content with a different aspect ratio

Figure 3.10 Most display systems have the 16:9 aspect ratio. (**A**) In television, black borders on the top and bottom of the picture compensate for wider ratios. (**B**) In digital signage, a video clip with a wider aspect ratio can be used as a design element on the screen. It is quite easy to fit an image or a video clip of a different aspect ratio by adapting the aspect ratio of the region to the aspect ratio of the content.

from the screen can be adapted in an aesthetically acceptable way. Figure 3.10 shows the traditional letter-boxing solution for television and an alternative way to handle this for digital signage displays. Problems arise only if you go for full-screen video clip regions.

SCREENS WITH LAYERS

Another way to split up the content on the screen is to use layers. This makes it possible to put a text message on top of a still picture,

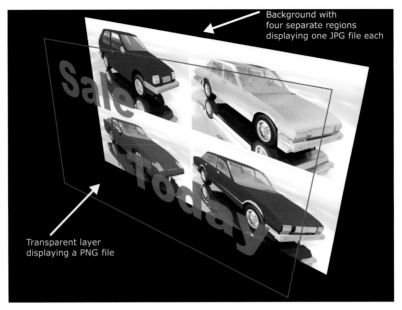

Figure 3.11 Using layers and files with transparency makes it possible to superimpose text or graphics on top of other screen content.

an animated region, or a video clip. Localized content can be used in one layer while the background content can be the same everywhere.

In some digital signage systems, the layers can be used completely independently from the regions, meaning that a text layer can be put on top of several other layers simultaneously.

Transparent Layers

Some picture file formats, such as PNG, can have transparent areas. This means that such a file can be easily put on top of any screen content (Figure 3.11). The PNG format is very handy in digital signage because it is suitable for creating transparent layers. Transparent layers can be used to add different logos or temporary messages on top of any other graphics without disturbing the background content too much.

Screens with Tickers

Tickers are often used by conventional TV stations such as CNN to present news or stock market information. The main purpose of tickers is to include continuously updated information in a TV broadcast.

Figure 3.12 Tickers can run horizontally or vertically. They may have various colors, not just black and white, and they may be transparent.

In television broadcasts, the ticker is put on the TV picture by the TV station. In digital signage systems, the tickers are added locally on each screen by the media player, which means the tickers can be tailor-made for each site and screen.

Tickers contain only text (Figure 3.12), making the capacity required to continuously update the tickers very small. In systems based on broadband distribution, tickers are the easiest way to create something that seems to behave like live, near-real-time information. The content files for tickers may be text or XML files. These file formats contain only the characters to be presented and for this reason are quite small.

AUDIO

Retail shopping environments, such as malls, grocery stores, and other public areas, are usually quite noisy, and the digital signage system's soundtrack must be handled with care. It could be used to achieve a certain atmosphere and, of course, may be necessary to present a demonstration video.

One way to create useable audio in shopping environments is to use directional speaker systems. This provides acceptable audio in limited areas instead of trying to create the traditional background sound channel that covers the entire store. Selective audio makes it

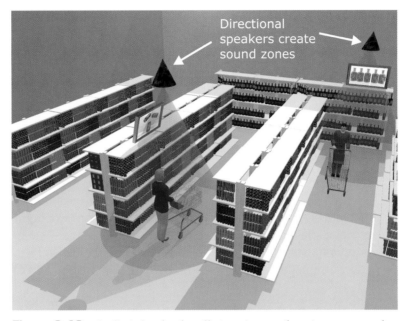

Figure 3.13 Audio is hard to handle in noisy retail environments and public areas. Directional speaker systems considerably improve the use of audio in stores.

easier to create a certain atmosphere related to specific products and also makes it easier to get specific information to the customers.

To be effective, it is necessary to divide the store into sound zones in a way that keeps the digital signage sound sources from disturbing each other. Otherwise, there will be a competition among different signs. This is a new problem that did not exist in the world of printed signs. In smaller shops, there might only be room for one digital sign with audio.

COMBINATION OF PICTURE ELEMENTS USING PLAYLISTS

So far, we have discussed the different elements of content that are the building blocks of a digital sign. To combine the different content elements of the digital sign, *playlists* must be built. Playlists tell the media player in what order and at what time certain files should be shown on the screens. Playlists can be looped so they start over when they reach their end and are constantly running.

Each region could have separate playlists or common playlists that control all content elements on the screen at any one time. Both alternatives have advantages and disadvantages. There might also be different levels of playlists with a separate playlist for each region or layer, combined with higher-level "macro" playlists deciding which lower-level playlists are going to be used in different regions or layers at different times of the day, week, or month. These higher-level playlists are used for scheduling and are sometimes called *scheduling files*.

The playlists and scheduling files are not standardized across all manufacturers of media players. Every kind of media player has its own playlist and scheduling file formats. The most common playlist file formats are the playlist formats of software media players such as Windows Media Player. (This is discussed further in Chapter 4.) However, in most digital signage systems, the playlists are proprietary and unique.

Figure 3.14 shows a display that has five regions, two of which are designated for video clips. These video clip regions have separate playlists to call a series of video clips so that the content is constantly rotating. The regions operate independently since they have independent playlists.

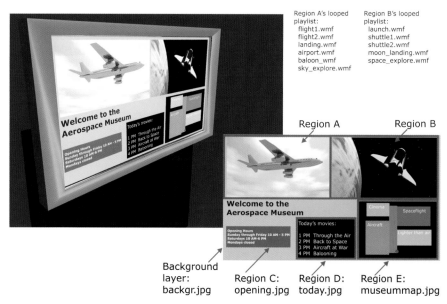

Figure 3.14 Playlists and scheduling files control what is exposed on the screens. Each digital signage system has a proprietary playlist and scheduling file format.

OPTIMIZATION OF DYNAMIC DIGITAL SIGNS

When first implementing digital signage, the first kind of application is probably a dynamic replacement for the printed posters and signs. Suddenly it becomes possible to change the content on a screen many times a week or perhaps even more often. To do this, a playlist may decide for how long each still picture animation or video clip is to be shown. Completely different kinds of file formats can be combined into one playlist (Figure 3.15). It is possible to combine video clips with animations and still pictures any way you like. However, the compatible file formats are limited by the capabilities of the media players.

Digital Dynamic Signs and Posters

Wherever there is a paper poster, there is an application for digital signage. This requires only one region and one layer on the screen. However, people expect much more from digital signage than from printed signs. Content cannot be too static. Therefore, still images

Figure 3.15 One playlist can contain different kinds of files, such as still pictures, video clips, and animations.

Figure 3.16   A number of images presented in a sequence form a kind of slide show.

have to be changed often. In Figure 3.16 the images are arranged in a sequence to form a slide show.

Using only still pictures results in very dull digital signage presentations, and consumers expect more interesting presentations. One simple way to compensate for dullness when using still pictures is to put clever transitions between the pictures. The transitions could be one picture pushing out the other one or more complex transitions including different patterns, and so on. Dynamic transitions can make the signage more interesting and is an inexpensive way to avoid a boring sequence of still pictures. Therefore, a large library of transitions can be useful.

A digital sign also has the advantage of ambience, making it clearly visible even at night without external illumination. Therefore, it works very well even after dusk. In Figure 3.17, the kind of message is also decided by the time of the day; a scheduling file controls which playlist to be used.

Virtual TV Channels

Something slightly more sophisticated than a slide show on a dynamic poster is the virtual TV channel. A virtual TV channel is created by replacing still images with video clips and playing them all in sequence (Figure 3.18). This version, while more engaging, would still require just one region and one layer.

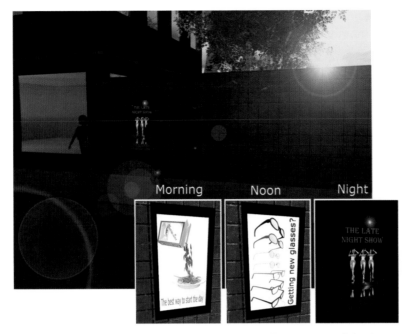

Figure 3.17 The digital poster can adapt to different hours of the day and various occasions by using a number of playlists selected by a scheduling file.

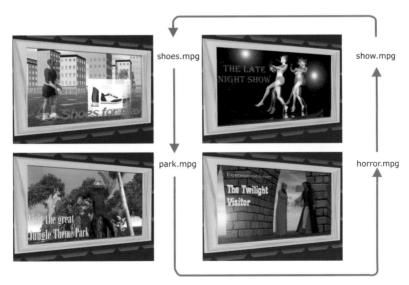

Figure 3.18 A sequence of video clips played according to a playlist forms a virtual TV channel.

Of course, it is also possible to have still images between the video clips, maintaining the impression of a virtual TV channel. A playlist is used to mix the video clip files with the still image files. Just as for still image slide shows, most virtual channels are looped because viewers tend not to stay for more than 10 or 15 minutes in each department of a store.

Virtual TV channels are often used to replace the old VCR-based demonstration videos that were shown on regular TV sets in stores. In those days, one problem was that the tape had to be rewound and restarted regularly. Looping a playlist in a computer is much easier and then the display requires no attention to restart.

It is especially important to get smooth transitions between the video clips in virtual TV channels. The general way to achieve this is to ensure that all video clips use the same settings for frame rate, resolution, and so on. When evaluating the performance of a digital signage system, you should observe the quality of the transitions carefully. In all digital signage applications, smooth transitions among images and video clips improve the presentation.

In most cases, the aim of a virtual TV channel is to resemble a conventional TV channel, so only one region of the screen is used. A large library of video clips could be combined in different sequences. Changing the content of a virtual TV channel is as simple as replacing the playlist. The same files can be reused as elements of different playlists.

Digital Cinema Virtual TV Applications   While in-store playlists are looped for repetition, in other applications, the playlist is only played once but the content of the list may vary from one show to the next. One example is the cinema preshow commercials application in Figure 3.19. The ability to put several commercials together by using different playlists—rather than gluing strips of conventional film together—is a compelling reason to move to this new technology. Each video clip can be reused as many times as needed and in any order just by replacing or editing the playlists.

When trying to get video projection to work in the cinema, it is essential to use the proper television standards. HD is a necessity. But in addition, progressive scanning should be used. Choosing 25 progressively scanned pictures per second provides the most cinema-like impression on the audience; interlaced scanning gives a less expensive result that is more like TV. It should be mentioned that conventional film scans 24 pictures per second.

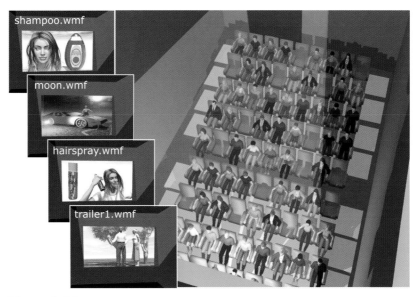

Figure 3.19 Preshow advertising can be made in a very flexible way using separate video clip files and playlists that are specific to each show.

Standard television using MPEG-2 requires about 4 Mbps and simple electronic cinema format runs from 4 to 20 Mbps. The highest quality expected to be used in cinemas for the main movies is D-cinema, which requires a bitrate faster than 30 Mbps. For preshow advertising, DVD-quality signals might suffice.

The cinema audience is quite particular when it comes to quality. An electronic picture must resemble a "real" analog movie. Progressive scanning is more similar than interlaced scanning to conventional film. It has always been the goal of the cinema business to stay "ahead" of television when it comes to quality. This goal becomes more challenging as more people install increasingly advanced home theaters.

Real-Time Video and Live IPTV

For some applications, such as sports and gaming, which take place in real time, live coverage is required. Live broadcasting to stores has long been used for event television and gaming purposes. However, broadcasting live requires a different kind of distribution system. (This is discussed further in Chapters 5 through 7.)

Quite fascinating digital signage applications can be created by combining live IPTV feeds and near-real-time graphics, such as data for betting

HDTV Used in D- and E-Cinema

This virtual TV channel E-cinema application makes it easy to customize a set of commercials to appear before each show in a way never possible before. To be able to deliver cinema commercials this way, it is necessary to use HDTV techniques.

Because of copyright issues and other problems, the purely digital cinema—D-cinema—is still not very common. Thanks to greatly improved HDTV projection techniques, D-cinema will eventually become more pervasive.

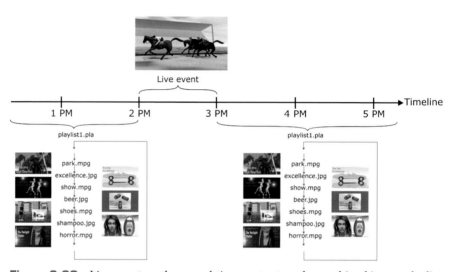

Figure 3.20   Live events and non-real-time content can be combined in one playlist.

odds. Using real-time coverage adds a dramatic touch to a digital signage system. This is essentially a closed-circuit television system.

Real-time video in a digital signage system means live TV that is streamed via IP packets—exactly the same thing as IPTV. Real-time video requires a real-time distribution medium. When it comes to playlists and scheduling files, it is possible to include even live coverage events in schedules at certain times of the day. Figure 3.20 includes an all-embracing scheduling file (top-level playlist) that controls when to use the lower-level playlist (playlist1.pla) and when to switch to live event and when to return to the playlist.

Near-Real-Time Applications

Near-real-time applications are based on immediate distribution of updated files to media players. There is a significant difference between real-time and near-real-time applications. A near-real-time application is based on files that are transferred almost instantaneously to the receiving media player. The files may have been stored briefly during transfer to the user. In real-time applications, the transfer is a continuous stream of information that is not stored en route to the user. Live IPTV is perhaps the best example of a real-time application. Examples of near-real-time applications are transfer of the changing odds in a horse race and news ticker updates.

In most cases, only some of the content elements on the screens are updated (Figure 3.21). This means that non-real-time background

Figure 3.21 With digital signage using the suitable means for distribution, live streaming IPTV regions can be combined with regions containing real-time (live) and near-real-time as well as non-real-time information.

content is combined with near-real-time and real-time information. This might include odds data or stock market information or any other information that needs to be updated instantly. Near-real-time applications also put restrictions on the kind of distribution media that can be used.

Real-time and near-real-time applications require special means for distribution. This is discussed further in Chapter 7.

Store Windows

We have already discussed the possibility of using store windows to display digital signage and to reach people outside the store or venue. This can be achieved by putting flat-panel display systems in the store windows instead of mannequins.

Conventional shop windows are expensive to decorate. Modern short-range projectors may provide a more flexible and cost-efficient solution. Because of the two-dimensional nature of a projected picture, the results will not be exactly the same. But the ability to make "moving mannequins" may compensate for this. Also being able to instantaneously change the complete content of the window is of great value. Of course, audio might also make an addition to the final impression.

Conventional store window

Dynamic digital store window

Figure 3.22   The conventional store window contains three-dimensional mannequins that stand still; the dynamic digital store window can project two-dimensional mannequins that move.

INTERACTIVE DIGITAL SIGNAGE

Some applications allow the customer to decide what to view. Adding an element of interactivity, enabling the customer to affect what is shown on the screens, makes digital signage much more useful and engaging.

Customer Terminals

A significant problem in today's retail business is that customers often find a larger selection of products and more product information on the Internet than in a store. Some people are no longer prepared to wait for assistance and instead want to have immediate answers to product-related questions. These new issues for the retail industry are all consequences of e-commerce.

One way to solve these problems is by introducing customer terminals in the stores. Based on digital signage techniques, touch-screen displays can provide the customers with possibilities to search for the desired information. This is not the same as surfing the Internet for information, but the customer terminals have access to information related to the products that can be purchased or ordered from the store.

One example is a bookstore, which can house only a few thousand titles. Online book stores include databases with hundreds of thousands or even millions of titles. Using customer terminals might provide a similar selection to the people visiting the bookstore.

Other possible applications are travel agencies or online gaming parlors, where constantly updated information, such as available tickets and game odds data, is of importance.

Finally, there is a need for knowledge in any shop that sells complex products, ranging from sports shoes to electronic devices. In such stores, the customers always have plenty of questions. In many cases, information may be a stronger weapon in selling complex products than advertising. The digital signage system can also educate the staff in the shops; a more knowledgeable sales force always improves sales.

With a user interface device, such as a mouse, keyboard, or a touch-sensitive screen, it becomes possible for the customer to control the media player to show the content that is of interest to him or her.

One of the most exciting features of interactivity is that the customer terminals provide much more than advertising. The interactive terminal offers the possibility for the customer to actually search for information. As a result, the customer is much more focused than when exposed to the passive screens with commercials. Also, the terminals simplify the work for the shop personnel and increase the service level in the shop. In the most advanced customer terminal applications, the user can navigate through a large tree structure to find very specific information about products.

Many people also find information more appealing and more valuable than pure advertising. The success of e-commerce is very much a result of people themselves actively pursuing and finding information. A bit of this less pressured self-direction may be moved to the shop environment by introducing media players that offer interactivity.

In customer terminals, there might also be regions for commercial messages that are adapted according to the choices made by the user of the terminal. The basic principle of such a customer terminal is that the customer can move to any location within the playlist. Another alternative is to navigate through a tree structure to select the right playlist and then to navigate within the selected playlist (Figure 3.23).

If not touched for a while, the touch screen can be configured to return to a default slide show or virtual TV channel, like any digital sign used for advertising does.

An interesting way to spread even more information to the customers is to make it possible for them to download pamphlets, recipes, or even parts of a song (in a music store) to their cell phones using Bluetooth technology (Figure 3.24). (Of course, contacts related to the content must address copyrights on material to be distributed in this way.) Then the customer can select how to use the information, either by using the phone directly or by downloading the collected files to the computer when he or she gets home. Bluetooth communication is free and introduces a completely new way of handling your mobile. This just might be one of the killer applications for customer terminals.

Motion Detectors

Another way to create some kind of customer interactivity is to use motion detectors that trigger the playlist in the media player when a customer passes close to the terminal. They might be used to restart a commercial video clip or an instructional movie clip related to a

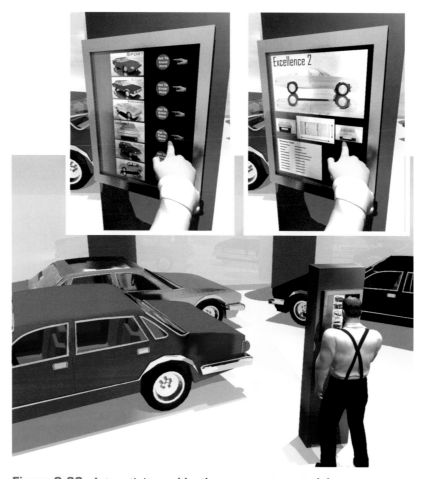

Figure 3.23 Interactivity enables the customer to control the content on the screen. Customer terminals are improving the service level in the shops.

certain product (Figure 3.25). When nobody is near the screen, the playlist just loops over and over again. In this case, the motion detector solves the classic problem of how to let the customer watch a promotional video without having to wait for it to start all over again. When somebody moves in front of the detector, the media player immediately moves to the start of the playlist and the problem is solved.

The possibilities of digital signage systems include dynamic digital posters and signs, virtual TV channels, live IP radio and TV, and near-real-time digital posters and signs. The services that can be implemented depend on the distribution techniques and the features of the digital signage system chosen for a project.

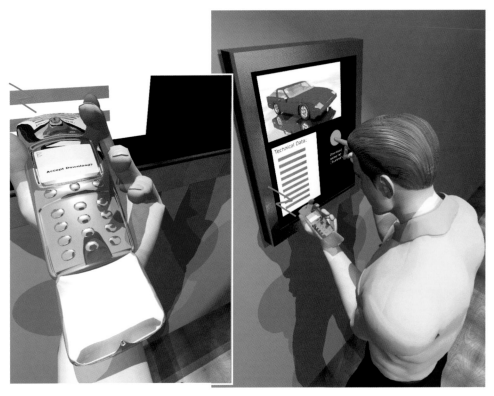

Figure 3.24   Bluetooth technology provides the ability to download myriad types of content, such as pamphlets (e.g., for tourism, retail items, health information), instructions (e.g., recipes, do-it-yourself projects, online classes), and MP3 music samples.

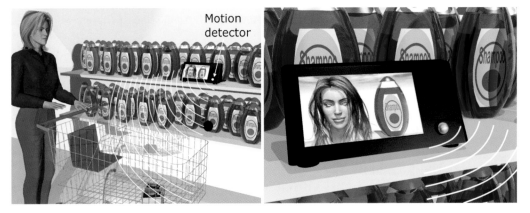

Figure 3.25   Movement detectors can be used to trigger a video clip or other kind of message on a screen as a customer approaches.

Digital Signage Standardization

There are hundreds of digital signage systems on the market. They all use standardized media file formats but they are still not compatible. Most systems have been developed from very specific digital signage applications and started out on a small scale and expanded into larger systems.

However, the lack of standardization is in the various ways to create and read the playlists, and scheduling files are different for each digital signage system. The ways the media players interpret the playlists into screen content are also different.

In the long run, standardization will be needed just as it was during the development of television and the Internet. Some steps toward standardization have already been made. One such initiative is being taken by Point of Purchase Advertising International (POPAI), which has been around since the 1930s. POPAI has started a giant work within the digital signage field to establish the standard terminology that I try to use in this book. The organization has also proposed a standard for playlog files. The playlists determine what is to be played and the playlogs confirm return path information about what has actually been played. Standardized playlogs will make it easier for the customers of the digital signage operators, the advertisers, to interpret this information.

Figure 3.26 shows the fascinating possibilities that a media player located in a shopping cart might provide if combined with a positioning system in the shop. Then the media player knows its location and can present commercial messages accordingly.

Another quite fascinating but still a bit frightening way of knowing what to display on a screen is to use Radio Frequency Identification (RFID). RFID tags are small, passive devices that start transmitting an individual ID code if exposed to an RFID reader. RFID has been used for many years to identify goods in the retail industry, luggage at airports, and cars passing through highway toll booths. An exciting possibility is to use RFID tags in vehicles to know what message to show on outdoor billboards when cars of different brands are passing by.

Of course, from an advertiser's point of view, it would be interesting to have people carry RFID tags to know who is in the vicinity of a certain sign to be able to present a customized message to him or her. RFID tags could be placed in products from the start to be able to identify when people using a certain product are close to a screen. Although a fascinating use of technology, to some people it could bear a frightening resemblance to the iris detection systems used to identify people in science fiction movies like *Minority Report*.

Figure 3.26   A local positioning system in a shopping cart makes it possible to show advertising for a product as the customer approaches that product.

This chapter describes the basic digital signage elements shown on the screens and suggests some applications. Of course, it is necessary to know that the digital signage system you are considering has all the features needed for your purposes. The number of regions, layers, and tickers vary among systems just as the choice of computer hardware and operating systems does.

A good way to start is to evaluate the system based on the elements described in this chapter. You should also study the playlist functionality of each player. Can separate playlists be used for different regions or do the regions put restrictions on each other? Will that impact your application? Finally, different applications call for different requirements on the distribution of content. The choice of digital signage system is one thing; the choice of distribution is something else.

It is quite obvious that the out-of-the-home applications in stores and public areas will be the most important during the years to come. This chapter discusses some of the applications of importance today, but since files and streams carried by IP can contain any kind of information, there is no limit to applications for display technologies and media production.

4

THE MEDIA PLAYER AND FEEDING THE SCREENS

So far we have discussed what can be done with digital signage and we have looked at the variety of display systems that are available. Now we want to know how to fill the screens with content and how to create and distribute the content to the screens.

What is really fascinating about digital signage is that it is very easy to start experimenting on a small scale with this media. This is also the reason you find hundreds of digital signage systems in the market. Most of them started on a very limited scale and migrated toward a full-scale digital signage system.

To understand all this better, we will start with two small experiments that lead to some interesting conclusions about digital signage.

PERSONAL COMPUTERS AS MEDIA PLAYERS

The simplest of digital signage systems can be created using your desktop computer and basic software such as PowerPoint, Adobe Acrobat, or Macromedia Flash, or by using one of the many PC media players on the market today, such as QuickTime or Windows Media Player. These programs are well known to most people and the following sections might seem quite basic, but the special features that make the programs interesting for digital signage applications, such as playlists and looping, are not used frequently. With these features, we can apply these basic programs in completely new ways—the same ways that digital signage systems work. Some professional digital signage systems use these basic programs as parts of their systems.

PowerPoint

An easy way to create your first digital signage application is to use Microsoft PowerPoint, which is generally used for "manual" presentations where someone advances the slides as he or she illustrates something. However, PowerPoint presentations can be automated and used in a more stand-alone fashion. PowerPoint can also incorporate moving video clips, so it can function as a virtual TV channel as well.

The following example gives the simple steps for generating a "Bird" slide show from a number of video clips and setting it to run continuously in a loop. If you follow these steps, you will see the difference in picture quality among Windows media files with different bitrates. The "Bird" clip has been encoded at different bitrates and the clips are to be shown in sequence.

1. From the Insert menu, select Movies and Sounds; then from the File menu, select Movie (Figure 4.1). The video clip may be shown either as full screen (as in this example) or as a region.

Figure 4.1   Video clips can be added to a PowerPoint presentation just like any other kind of file.

Figure 4.2 Select Slide Transition.

2. After each video clip has been added to a slide, transitions will be used to show the clips in succession and loop the presentation.

3. From the Slide Show menu, select Slide Transition (Figure 4.2).

4. In the Advance Slide section, select Automatically after; then from the dropdown menu, choose the number of seconds to show each slide. This number should match the length of the clip, which is 7 seconds in this example (Figure 4.3).

5. From the Slide Show menu, select Set Up Show, and then select Loop continuously until Esc (Figure 4.4). This means the slide show will run until someone presses the Escape key.

We now have something that can replace the VCR as well as the DVD player. With PowerPoint, it is possible to create complex presentations with animations, video clips, and audio files. PowerPoint is popular because many people know how to use it and it has a lot of features.

So if you want to run a show on one screen, a PowerPoint presentation might do. The things you need are a computer that runs Windows and the free PowerPoint Viewer. You also need a computer with the complete PowerPoint application to create your presentations, but this is probably already available on your office

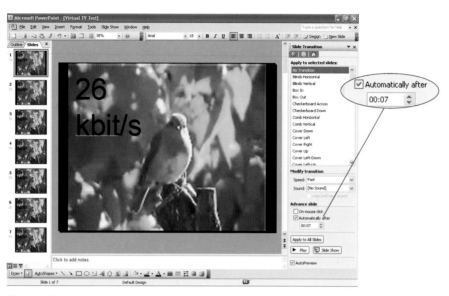

Figure 4.3 Select Automatically after. The transition will take place after the clip has run for the time you set here.

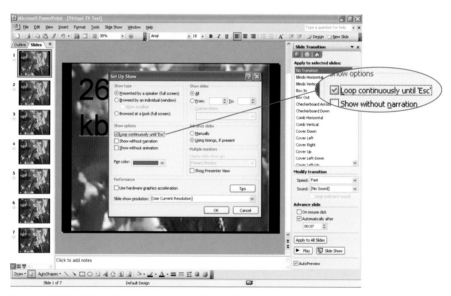

Figure 4.4 Select Loop continuously until 'Esc'.

computer. Note that the PPT file extension should be changed to PPS before using the PowerPoint Viewer.

By connecting a suitable screen to the computer, you have a complete digital signage display. You could even copy your presentation to many computers with the PowerPoint Viewer and have a complete digital signage system up and running in no time.

With a bit of creativity, you can also rotate pictures to portrait position and turn the screens to the same position. However, there may be restrictions in the software when moving to portrait position. For example, PowerPoint 2003 does not include the ability to rotate video clips. So, when using software that is not made for digital signage, examine exactly which features are included. Portrait position is a critical characteristic of digital signage.

Another critical characteristic of digital signage is the aspect ratio. The most common display device has a 16:9 widescreen flat-panel display that can be used in portrait or landscape orientation. PowerPoint easily adjusts the aspect ratios of the presentation.

Many professional digital signage systems are based on well-known software, such as PowerPoint, Adobe Acrobat, and Macromedia Flash. But even though these products have player features that can be used for professional applications, most people in the digital signage business tend to develop their products further and add features specific to their digital signage systems.

PowerPoint gives you the means to produce a digital signage presentation and feed it to a variety of screens ranging from the laptop computer screen to flat-panel TV sets and outdoor large-scale LED screens. This feeding process is still manual, however; you have to copy the presentation to each device that will show it. (Chapters 5 through 7 discuss automated distribution in greater detail.)

For this simple system, the presentation file can be burned to a CD or e-mailed if the display systems are, for example, for a chain of stores located far apart. If the computers acting as media players are connected through a local area network, they could read the file from a shared folder on the network and we would not have to install the file into each media player separately. Using other methods, the files also could be retrieved through the Internet, making it possible to have media players located everywhere.

Though this "Bird" virtual TV channel presentation wouldn't likely end up on an outdoor screen, this example shows how easy it is to set up a digital signage application on a single screen, whatever its

Figure 4.5 One computer can be connected to more than one screen, ranging from a small computer TFT to a large outdoor screen. Here the "Bird" slide show in Figure 4.3 is shown on a small and a giant screen, respectively.

size (Figure 4.5). This is only one of myriad ways to design a digital signage system. Now, we will discuss media players from a more general standpoint.

DIGITAL SIGNAGE FILE DISTRIBUTION

One quite severe restriction in this digital signage system is that it is based on using just one file to create the entire screen content. For many applications, this is not a problem, but combining regions, tickers, and layers in the media player rather than in the computer offers a lot of advantages. Now we will take a closer look at the differences between these two strategies.

By gathering everything in one single file using PowerPoint, Flash, or Acrobat, you can be absolutely sure of the final appearance of the screen content. It will most certainly look the same everywhere. In this case, you could say that the playlist is an integrated part of the file.

You will be able to work very much the same way that a TV station does. You produce one single file or stream that is used everywhere (Figure 4.6). The TV station produces one single TV signal at its play-out and that common signal is distributed to everyone.

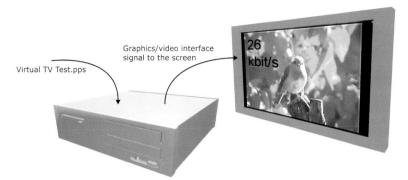

Figure 4.6 The media player is used to decode the information from one single PowerPoint file.

In the PowerPoint scenario, we have to transfer complete files to each media player every time a small change is made. By splitting the content into separate files, it is possible to update them and the picture elements separately. If you have screens containing news tickers, you have to update only the tickers using small files. Or, in gambling applications you have to update only the odds data or results using already downloaded background graphics or video clips. The same goes for stock market information and other rapidly changing information. This is much more efficient and reduces the bandwidth needed to keep the media players up to date.

Separate handling of files also means that it is easier to insert local information from files that are directed to specific media players. While one video clip might be standard regardless of where the media player is, another area of the screen might show the weather in that location.

Large libraries of video clips, animation and audio files and other heavy content can be reused and combined with new files easily just by issuing a new playlist (Figure 4.7). If the video clips can be handled separately by hardware decoding chips, the media player's processor is relieved of these tasks. This also means that the media player can be much more optimized to its task of being a media player. This is discussed further in the Dedicated Digital Signage Hardware section (see page 93).

Although single file systems are appropriate in some cases, they certainly do not represent the future of digital signage systems because they have limitations. We will focus on multiple file media players in the remainder of this book.

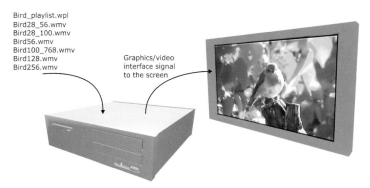

Bird_playlist.wpl
Bird28_56.wmv
Bird28_100.wmv
Bird56.wmv
Bird100_768.wmv
Bird128.wmv
Bird256.wmv

Graphics/video
interface signal
to the screen

Figure 4.7   The media player is used to decode the wmv
video clip files and to combine them into a graphics interface
signal according to the "Bird_playlist.wpl" playlist file.

PC-Based Media Players and Playlists

The heart of the multiple file digital signage medium is the playlist. Separate files with no control will result in nothing. The playlists
decide what content is to be displayed on the screen. Each region or
layer on the screen can be controlled by a playlist of its own.

In the earlier PowerPoint example, you could say that the playlist is
an integrated part of the PowerPoint file. There is most certainly a
playlist, but it is not a separate file and it is invisible to the user.

Here is another practical example that you can try. In this case, the
screen content will be a virtual TV channel created from a number of
video files that do not necessarily have the same format.

Probably you have already tried media player software in your
computer to play music, animation, or video files. You probably also
have received streamed video over the Internet using such software.
In most cases, you have probably used the media player just to decode
and view the files. But most PC-based media players also include a
playlist feature. The playlist feature enables you to create lists of MP3
files (or other kinds of files) to be played. The playlist is a separate file
that contains information about what songs to be played and in what
order. Some people use the playlist feature to automate the handling
of the music when they are hosting a party; the computer takes care of
the music throughout the night. Digital signage in stores or public
areas is a very similar situation—but using different kinds of files.

Figure 4.8 Software media players are very common and have many similar features.

There are many common PC-based media players, such as Windows Media Player, Real Player, Winamp, QuickTime, and VLC (videoLAN client), shown in Figure 4.8.

In Figure 4.9, I used Windows Media Player to create a playlist containing a number of Windows Media files (wmv files). In the upper right, you can see the files in the playlist. The video clips are played in sequence; pressing the Repeat/Shuffle button in the lower right repeats the playlist in a loop. Once the player is set in full-screen mode, we have a virtual TV channel up and running.

There is a significant difference between using Windows Media Player and PowerPoint to make a virtual TV channel. Doing the same thing in PowerPoint is possible but would have all the clips contained in one file without a separated playlist.

Using Windows Media Player, or other similar media players such as VLC (Figure 4.10), to do the same thing is based on separate video clip files and separate playlists. As a result, we can distribute a complete library of video clips to different locations and play different sequences of files at multiple locations using different playlists.

"Repeat" button

Figure 4.9   Windows Media Player plays a sequence of video clips using a playlist, visible in the upper-right corner. The file currently playing is highlighted in green.

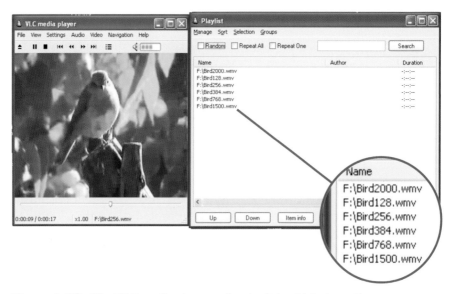

Figure 4.10   The VLC media player and a playlist, which stores the information in an m3u format.

In this example, I used a sequence of video clips with different bitrates and varying resolutions. This would never be done in a real digital signage application. Transitions between video clips with different bitrates and resolutions tend to be very poor quality, so all video clips used to create a virtual TV channel should have the same format and use the same bitrate.

To insert a commercial spot in the playlist, simply replace one of the video clips. This can be done easily without having to distribute all video clips once more in a single file. Video files are usually large and therefore it is crucial to be able to distribute them just once even though they are going to be used several times and in many ways.

The main issue with playlists is that they are not standardized. All media players have their own playlist file format. The Windows Media playlist format is wpl. Other playlist formats are pls, asx, and m3u. This may not cause any problem when playing music because you can convert playlists among the common formats. However, in full-scale digital signage systems, playlist formats are all proprietary and you must always build your system with equipment from just one manufacturer.

Decoding Live Stream Video

In these examples, we have been using PowerPoint, Windows Media, and the VLC player to play a sequence of video clips from files that are stored locally on the hard drive of the media player. Some of the players also can be used to decode an incoming stream of compressed video, essentially a file without a defined ending. This is really the same thing as IPTV, and we will return to this matter in Chapter 7. The two major tasks of a media player are to play various media files and to decode incoming IP streams of data. Software media players like the Windows Media Player, VLC, Real Player, Winamp, and QuickTime can all do that.

DEDICATED DIGITAL SIGNAGE MEDIA PLAYER SOFTWARE

To create more complex digital signage systems, we need to have more control over regions and layers. We also want to be able to automate the distribution of files and the handling of the media players.

Proprietary digital signage software often makes use of basic software media players so they can accept and decode standard audio, video, and image files. However, the files that control the media players—the playlists and scheduling files—are not standardized. There are several hundreds of digital signage systems in the world, and most of them use unique formats for their playlists. The ability to handle these two types of file is a key characteristic of a digital signage media player.

Decoding Picture and Video Files

The major task of media players is to include a large number of filters and decoders to be able to decompress and display a variety of video, animation, image, and audio file formats.

In television and radio broadcasting, the TV and radio broadcasting standards are the fundamental cornerstones of the media. In digital signage, the file formats for pictures, audio, video, and animations are the cornerstones.

Digital signage systems use existing standardized media file formats. Among these file formats, we find MPEG-2, MPEG-4, and Windows wmv for video; mp3, wma, and MPEG (Musicam) for audio; Macromedia Flash for animations; and common image file formats like JPEG and GIF for pictures. Adobe PDF files are also used to feed the media players in some digital signage systems. (Chapter 8 delves deeper into the file formats.)

The media player must be also able to handle streaming file formats. When you start to receive a live streaming file, you will not know its length and when it is going to end. However, these "never-ending" files are based on the same principles as the finite files.

The screen content may be created from a number of file and streaming formats (Figure 4.11), rather than from just one standardized television signal, as is the case for television. Media players may be even software upgradeable to support even more file and stream formats in the future.

Reading and Executing Playlists

The content in the different regions, layers, and tickers of the screens originate from files with common formats for audio, video, animations, and images. However, the procedure of fitting the content

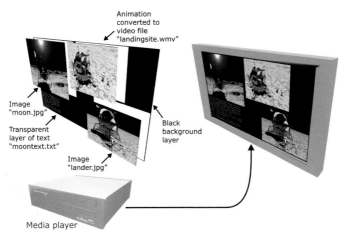

Figure 4.11 Two JPEG image files, one wmv movie file, and one text file have to be decoded and presented properly at the graphic interface of the media player.

together on the screen is done using playlists that are proprietary for each kind of digital signage system and media player.

The playlists do not just tell the media player what file is to be played and when it is to be played. The playlists also indicate where on the screen the video clip or image files should be played, if they should change size or move on the screen, and in what direction they should move. In text files, the playlists tell the fonts, the font sizes, and the colors to use.

Even though most content is played from files stored in the media player, an advanced player also has to be able to take care of live streams. In theory, live stream events may be addressed directly from the playlist.

Figure 4.12 shows the complexity of controlling which media player has to work when and controlling the content of the different regions. There might be one playlist for the entire screen or one playlist for each region. The X and Y coordinates define the regions for the media player. Regions that contain video clips are often produced by decoding video files using any of the PC-based media players discussed earlier.

An advanced media player must include a huge selection of software media players (or at least the codecs used in them) along with filters to import and decode many different image file formats.

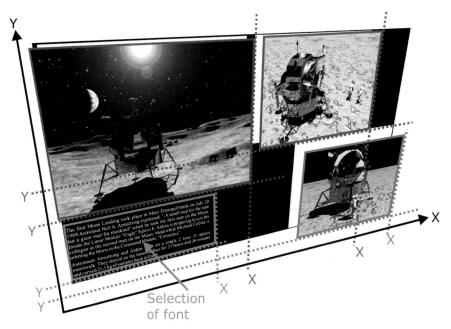

The first Moon Landing took place in Mare Tranquillitatis on July 20 1969 Astronaut Neil A. Armstrong expressed: "-A small step for the man but a giant step for mankind" when he took the first step on the Moon. Inside the Lunar Module "Eagle" Edwin E. Aldrin is preparing to join his colleague as the second man on the Moon. Meanwhile Michael Collins is orbiting the Moon in the Command Module "Columbia". Astronauts Armstrong and Aldrin moonwalk. They stayed on the lunar surface for 21 hours and 36 minutes and carried 21.1 kg of samples back to Earth.

Selection of font

Figure 4.12   The media player has to be able to interpret the playlists in order to present everything properly.

CHOOSING A DIGITAL SIGNAGE SYSTEM

The media player is, from a hardware and operating systems point of view, very similar to a computer. On the other hand, the media player is not used in the same way as a PC. A PC is manually given instructions by the user, who is actively searching for content. The media player spontaneously feeds a screen or other display devices with information; the user does not have to do anything except watch. This is, in many respects, the same kind of use as for a TV set. However, the media player allows limited interactivity so the user can make some requests to the media player about what is going to be presented by the display device. A media player could be regarded as somewhere between an Internet-connected computer and a TV set-top box.

The major differences among various manufacturers of digital signage systems is whether they offer hardware and software or just software. For some manufacturers, software is their core business and it is up to the user to select suitable hardware. Other manufacturers are hardware-based and their systems come with specific media player software. And if hardware is included, there are still two alternatives: preselected PC hardware or dedicated hardware that is designed specifically for media player use.

We will now take a closer look at the differences between these three strategies. Because digital signage is a very young and immature market, manufacturers around the world are trying all their new ideas to explore this new medium.

PC-Based Digital Signage Systems

The easiest way to get going with digital signage is to use ordinary PCs and conventional software like PowerPoint. This does not require very much product development and still there are possibilities to choose different elements of the hardware as you like. Computers have all the features needed to become media players. It is just the software that needs to be added.

When you use conventional PCs as media players, you have to stick to computer cabinets with power supplies with fans. When you use laptops, you get rid of the power supply fans but you cannot do without the processor fans even though they can cause noise that interferes with the digital signage viewing experience. The operational costs of PCs are high because of the many components, such as fans and hard drives, that eventually fail and require replacement (Figure 4.13).

Conventional PCs are made to do everything based on specific software run on very general hardware. This is very convenient in a PC where you want to do all your office work and much more. The same hardware could be used to make your own music studio, edit your own movie, or do whatever else you might want to do.

If you buy software separately, it is very important to select dependable PC hardware. One solution is to ask the software provider to recommend hardware that has worked well with their product. It may also be a good choice to buy the hardware from the software provider as a complete package.

Graphics Cards

Media player applications based on conventional PCs depend on software decoders for the video. This is a complex task that requires a lot of processing capability to deliver the video in a smooth presentation.

Processor Heat Dissipation

The major problem with using conventional PCs is the heat dissipation from today's fast processors that use high clock frequencies. As the clock frequency increases, the heat dissipation increases exponentially. This is the reason clock frequencies have not increased very much during recent years. It is also the reason for the introduction of the dual-core processors, which double the capability while just doubling the heat dissipation. However, dual-core processors require software that is multithreaded, so just as when the 32-bit programs were introduced, completely new software has to be developed.

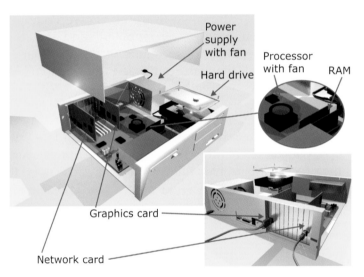

Figure 4.13 Media players based on standard PCs are easy to set up, from a hardware point of view.

One way to relieve the main processor is to use a high-performance graphics card. But this is a very expensive solution.

The choice of graphics card decides the kind of display interface you can use. Most display devices have a VGA input, so a simple graphics card might do. But if you intend to go for a high-quality digital interface, you have to choose a graphics card with a DVI or HDMI interface.

Remember that high-end graphics cards often contain very high heat-generating processors and have fans. This is something to take into account when it comes to long-term operational costs.

Later in this chapter we will take a closer look at the various graphic and video interfaces you might find on display devices.

Dedicated Digital Signage Hardware

Media players are devices that just take content from somewhere and display the content on the screens in a TV-like fashion. A PC can do this job, but it is not as convenient as using a TV set-top box, which is designed for specific tasks.

Still, media players are quite different from TV receivers and TV set-top boxes in that they may create a screen content graphical (video) signal from one or several files or from one or more IP streams of information. TV receivers produce screen content from just one incoming signal that has been completed at the playout of the program company. A media player has a tough task to fulfill.

One of the most important reasons for using dedicated hardware is to have separate chip sets handling the video decompression. Video decompression is the most demanding task of a media player. With dedicated video decompression hardware, the main processor does not have to handle this task. Most dedicated media players are intended for MPEG-2 or MPEG-4 and MPEG-4 AVC (H.264) decoding because there are lots of chipsets intended for TV set-top boxes that can easily be adapted for media player use. These formats are products of the broadcast world.

The competing format, the Windows Media Player, wmv, is used primarily in PC-based media players because Windows belongs to the core of the computer and Internet world.

Since it is not possible to make future replacements of the graphical or video interfaces of a media player with dedicated hardware, it is essential to know what you need right from the start. In a PC-based solution, you can replace the graphics cards if you have a limited number of media players.

Most dedicated media players have analog video along with VGA output. More advanced models often have a DVI or HDMI interface as well. Figure 4.14 shows the anatomy of a dedicated media player and Figure 4.15 shows one model currently available.

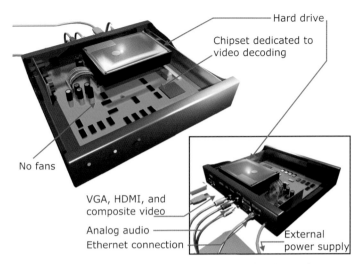

Figure 4.14   A media player with dedicated hardware functions as something between a personal computer and a TV set-top box.

Figure 4.15   Dedicated media player hardware with passive cooling and no fans from Swedish manufacturer MultiQ.

OPERATING SYSTEM CONSIDERATIONS

One thing of great importance is the choice of media player operating system. There is no absolute best choice. Windows, Linux, and Apple (Mac) (Figure 4.16) each have their advantages and disadvantages.

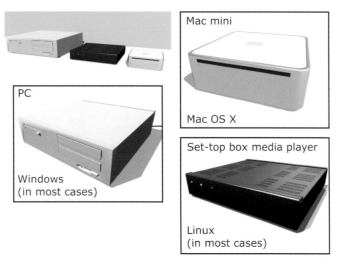

Figure 4.16   Windows is the most popular operating system for PC-based media players.

What to use depends very much on the applications and features that are most important to the user.

Windows

Windows is the most common operating system for PC-based media players. The main reason to use Windows is that it supports just about any file format. Advanced file formats like Adobe PDF with embedded QuickTime video clips can be easily used, as well as the Windows Media video format. Windows is well-known and many people like the easy-to-use interface and the development tools. It is very easy to handle graphics in Windows, which probably accounts for its popularity in digital signage applications. It is possible to buy embedded versions of the Windows operating system. In an embedded version, you can delete the unused parts of the operating systems to reduce the load on the hardware.

The major disadvantage with Windows Media Player is the licensing fee that has to be paid, just as on any Windows PC. Windows also requires a lot of processing power, so hardware requirements may require a more expensive computer. But there are exceptions, as in Figure 4.17, which shows a Windows-based dedicated hardware media player with passive cooling. This way problems associated with fans, such as noise and need for replacement of the fans, are avoided.

Figure 4.17 Although not very common, there are
Windows-based media players with dedicated hardware.
This device from German manufacturer Albrecht
Elektronik has passive cooling and the problems
related to fans are eliminated.

Linux

Linux is a free operating system—a great advantage if you are considering a system with a lot of media players. Linux requires more from the developer than Windows does, but still there are many Linux-based digital signage products on the market. Linux media players tend to become more like set-top boxes, where the operating system is more or less invisible to the user. Media players that run on dedicated hardware are often based on Linux, but Linux also can be used in PC-based media players.

Linux is often used in the content management and edge servers in the other parts of the digital signage systems (described in Chapters 6, 7, and 8).

Mac OS X

Apple's Mac computers have always been very good at handling graphics. The Mac Mini has a very slim hardware design and is quite popular as a media player. Mac OS X runs only on Mac hardware, which may be a nuisance to some but is regarded as an advantage by others. Standardized hardware has a tendency of being reliable.

A special thing about Macs is that you always buy the software and the hardware together. So if you choose Mac OS X for your operating system, you automatically choose Mac hardware.

LOCAL CONTENT STORAGE

Most media players for digital signage applications have local storage capabilities such as hard drives or flash memories in addition to the random access memory (Figure 4.18). Hard drives are very cheap and reliable, but still they have moving parts and a life expectancy of only three to five years. However the storage capacity of hard drives compared to price is unbeatable.

Flash memories do not have moving parts but there is a limitation on the number of times that data can be written to such a memory. Flash memories also have smaller capacities (only a few gigabytes) than

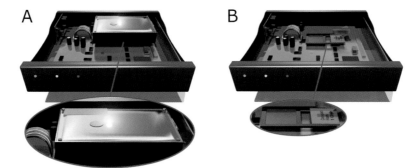

Figure 4.18 Local storage in the media players: **(A)** hard drive and **(B)** compact flash memory.

hard drives, though that is probably sufficient for most digital signage applications. Despite limitations in capacity and write access, a flash memory solution may be still quite favorable due to physical size and the limited dissipation of heat along with lower power consumption. But there are restrictions on what strategies are used when writing to the memories. There are no known limitations to the number of times that content may be read from a flash memory though.

OUTPUT INTERFACES

Media players provide an output signal that is fed to display devices. However, there are many different output video and graphics signals. We will now take a closer look at the options.

Media players are computers rather than television receivers. This means that they have more computer-related graphical interfaces. Some media players are intended to be connected to conventional TV sets. In most cases, however, there is at least a VGA connection intended for more high-resolution display devices than standard-resolution TV sets or monitors.

Digital signage is oriented to high definition since the content contains lots of graphic-heavy elements such as text, which requires more than the standard resolution of a TV set.

Analog Interfaces

Analog video and graphics interfaces are well established and there are many monitors, TV sets, and computer screens that support these interfaces. Although digital interfaces provide greatly improved quality, there will be a need to connect with existing display devices for many years to come. For this reason, even modern media players have one or more analog output interfaces. The most common are composite CVBS and VGA.

Composite CVBS Composite video is the classic SD video signal available from the RCA connectors of VCRs and satellite receivers and other TV set-top boxes (Figure 4.19). The technical quality is limited by today's standards, but still it provides an easy way to connect with SDTV sets. The disadvantage is that the resolution is limited to the standard TV resolution of 720×486 pixels (United States) and 720×576 pixels (Europe).

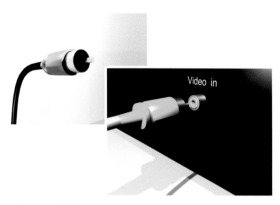

Figure 4.19 An RCA connector is part of the most common composite video interface.

Since this signal includes a color subcarrier, there is a risk of interference between the color information and the luminance information (cross-color and cross-luminance). Filtering the color and luminance components makes the resulting picture less sharp than it would be with other video interfaces that keep the signals separate throughout the transmission chain.

S-Video S-video was developed to improve the interconnection of analog video recorders and TV sets. On video tapes, the color information is stored at the lowest frequencies instead of at the highest, as it is in a composite TV signal. Therefore, the color information is treated separately in video recorders. To improve separation between the color (chrominance) and the black-and-white (luminance) signals, these signals are kept separated in the S-VHS interface. This gives better performance than the composite CVBS interface. The S-VHS connector includes only video and handles the chrominance and luminance signals on separate pins (Figure 4.20).

RGB SCART Connection In Europe, the SCART (Syndicat des Constructeurs d'Appareils Radiorécepteurs) connector (Figure 4.21) has been mandatory on all TV sets since the 1980s. The SCART connector has many pins, some of which are used to carry the separate analog RGB signals. This provides much better quality than the composite video and slightly better than S-VHS connection. For compatibility, the SCART connector also includes the video composite signal on a separate pin.

VGA The Video Graphics Array (VGA) is the traditional analog computer graphics interface. It can handle many resolutions and

Figure 4.20 The S-VHS connection keeps the color information separated from the luminance information.

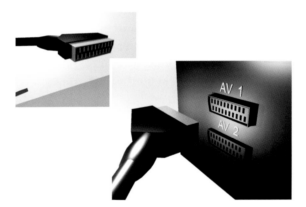

Figure 4.21 The SCART connector.

has no doubt been the most common interface in digital signage for a long time. Originally, VGA offered only 640 × 480 pixel resolution but has developed to support 1280 × 1024 pixels and is regarded as a high-definition standard. Although it does not belong in the broadcasting world, it fits well into the world between computers and TV sets, where digital signage resides. VGA is a low-cost solution that is also regarded as quite reliable (Figure 4.22).

Component Y-Pb-Pr   The most advanced analog video interface in the broadcasting world is the component Y-Pb-Pr interface (Figure 4.23). Using this interface for digital signage applications, it is possible to add progressive scanning as well as high-definition signals. However, still it is analog.

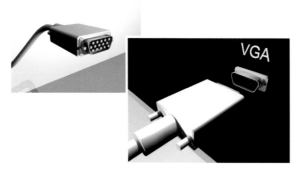

Figure 4.22 The VGA interface is probably the most common interface in the digital signage business.

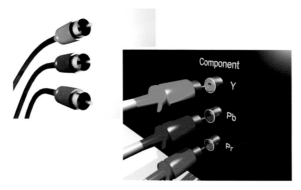

Figure 4.23 The Y-Pb-Pr component connection allows for analog high-definition signals and progressive scanning.

Analog Audio Interfaces

Even though digital signage is associated mostly with screens and display devices, audio may also play an important role in many applications. Audio can provide an atmosphere for the retail environment. And of course, no one would ever think about a home digital signage application that did not offer sound.

In a system with external multichannel amplifiers (or other external amplifiers), there is a problem related to the delay of the video signal as it is processed in the flat-panel display systems. The image must be converted between the transmission and the display resolutions. This requires processing power and time. Also, the process of

Figure 4.24   RCA analog audio connectors.

creating the addressing signals to the individual pixels on a screen requires some time. For this reason, the video signal will be undoubtedly delayed. The delay may be compensated for by delaying the audio as well. This audio delay may be added in the external amplifiers if such a feature is available. LCD and plasma monitors have internal delay systems that take care of this if the internal amplifiers and speakers are used.

RCA Connectors   The RCA connectors are no doubt the most common analog audio connectors (Figure 4.24). However, computers often use 3.5mm audio plugs, due to the lack of space for RCA connectors on the back plate of sound cards to be put into PCI slots in computers. There are simple conversion cables to connect the two kinds of connector though.

SCART Connectors   The SCART connector shown in Figure 4.21 includes analog stereo audio in both directions. In Europe, this is a very common way to connect audio and video devices.

Digital Interfaces

Digital interfaces offer optimum performance for digital signage systems. There are two main digital interfaces—DVI and HDMI—for video and computer graphics. The introduction of these interfaces has meant that HDTV set-top boxes and computers now use the same type of interfaces. Also, the difference between television and computer displays is beginning to disappear. Computers often use the widescreen 16:9 aspect ratio, which means that there is no longer any real difference between the worlds of computers and television.

DVI   DVI is the Digital Visual Interface that originally was introduced in computer graphics cards. It was developed by the Digital Display Working Group and exists in several versions. Depending on how the pins in the connector are used, it is possible to add the conventional analog VGA signals as well (DVI-I). This makes it possible to connect a computer screen with VGA using only a simple adapter.

DVI allows the use of either single or dual data links (DVI-D). With dual data links, the supported screen resolution increases to 2048×1536 pixels compared to 1920×1080 pixels for a single data link. 1920×1080 pixels will probably be sufficient for most digital signage applications for many years to come.

The interface only carries video signals and a separate audio connection has to be arranged either by analog or by using the S/PDIF digital audio interface. DVI (Figure 4.25) is compatible with HDMI but contains no audio. Mostly it is used in computer graphics cards.

HDMI   High-Definition Multimedia Interface (HDMI) is quite similar to DVI. The main difference is that the HDMI connectors are much smaller and also include digital audio.

HDMI also supports High-Bandwidth Digital Content Protection (HDCP) that prevents unauthorized copying of signals.

HDMI is probably one of the most important interfaces for digital audio and video for the future, and is likely to be the first widespread interface that is used for both computers and set-top boxes.

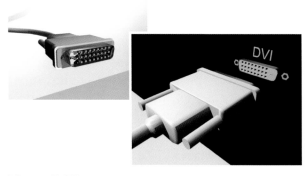

Figure 4.25   DVI is common in computers.

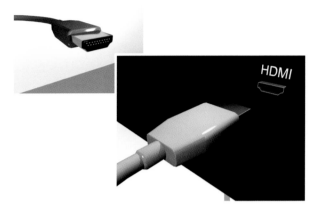

Figure 4.26   HDMI carries both audio and video.

Within a few years it will probably be the most popular interface for digital signage media players. (See Figure 4.26.)

More Advanced Digital Video Interfaces   There are more advanced digital video interfaces such as the SDI (Serial Digital Interface) and the HD-SDI (High-Definition Serial Digital Interface). These are the digital video interfaces used by TV stations. They tend to be too expensive in digital signage systems so they are very seldom used for these kinds of applications.

Digital Audio Interfaces

Digital audio has been with us for a much longer time than digital video. Only two common digital audio interfaces are used for digital signage applications. They are the S/PDIF (Sony/Philips Digital Interface Format) and HDMI, where the S/PDIF signal is an integrated part.

Sony/Philips Digital Interface Format   The most popular way to connect digital audio is the Sony/Philips Digital Interface Format, which provides multichannel audio as Dolby Digital and DTS, as well as linear two-channel stereo. The S/PDIF can be electrical or optical (Figure 4.27).

If S/PDIF is to be used, there is an S/PDIF audio encapsulator in the source device, such as a DVD player, set-top box for digital TV, or a media player. The audio must be decoded in a multichannel theater amplifier or in a display device with integrated decoder amplifiers

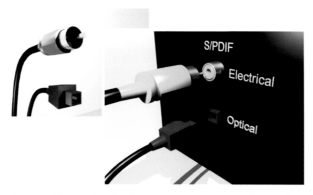

Figure 4.27 S/PDIF connectors are either electrical
or optical.

and speakers. This is covered in greater detail in the home theater
chapter of my book *Understanding Digital Television* (Focal Press, 2006).

RF Interfaces: Using the Aerial Input of TV Sets

In addition to analog and digital audio and video baseband interfaces, there is the possibility to distribute radio frequency (RF)
signals. RF signals can be analog or digital and can be distributed
quite long distances. This technique is similar to the one used to
distribute cable TV.

The aerial input of a TV set can be used to receive modulated analog
RF signals (Figure 4.28). In this case, you need screens with integrated
TV tuners. There are also flat-panel TV sets that include digital tuners

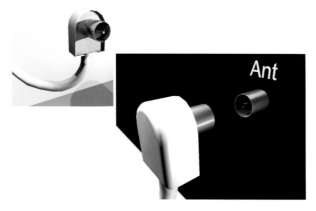

Figure 4.28 The TV set RF input (here with the
IEC connector).

but since it is still expensive to create modulated digital TV signals, these are seldom used for digital signage applications.

The only really efficient application for the RF inputs is to distribute the same message to a larger number of screens (discussed in the Analog RF TV Distribution subsection later in this chapter).

INPUT INTERFACES

One way to feed content into the media player is via a CD or DVD in the media player's DVD player. However, the most versatile interface is the network interface. The key element to all this versatility is the use of Internet Protocol (IP) packets to distribute the content to the media players. The IP packets are then encapsulated into Ethernet packets that can be carried in 8-wire twisted-pair cables (though not all of the wires are used today). The twisted-pair cables use RJ-45 connectors (Figure 4.29).

IP can be used to carry any kind of digital information, not just audio, video, and teletext or other metadata as in conventional digital television systems. In Chapter 5, we will take a closer look at how the media player can use the IP Ethernet interface to retrieve any kind of information, such as files from a server, or to receive streaming content.

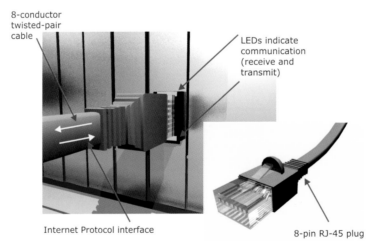

8-conductor
twisted-pair
cable

LEDs indicate
communication
(receive and
transmit)

Internet Protocol interface

8-pin RJ-45 plug

Figure 4.29 The twisted-pair cable and the RJ-45 connectors are the signature of IP carried by the Ethernet.

Using IP, we get an infrastructure that does not have to be changed when new transmission formats or standards are introduced.

THE INTERACTIVE MEDIA PLAYER

Another application for the media player is to become an interactive customer terminal, where the user can request information of interest. If nobody is interacting, the player will behave just like any other noninteractive media player and follow a preset playlist.

Since a media player is a computer, the RS-232, USB, or PS-2 interfaces can be used to obtain input from the user. The most popular input interface is, or will soon be, USB.

Any kind of input device can be used, such as a keyboard, mouse, or touch screen. For a touch screen (Figure 4.30), the application must have a coarse graphic structure because the finger is a wide pointing device (compared to a mouse cursor, for example). Using a keyboard or a mouse allows for more computer and Weblike applications but touch screens are more practical in public environments.

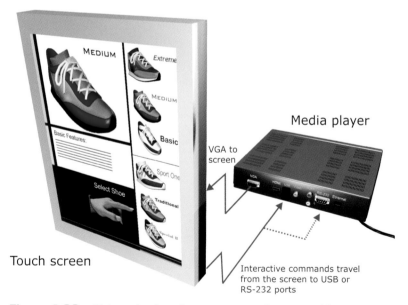

Figure 4.30 Using a keyboard, mouse, or touch screen adds interactivity to the media player.

SINGLE-CHANNEL VERSUS MULTICHANNEL MEDIA PLAYERS

If conventional PCs are used as one-screen (single-channel) media players, there will be at least one fan, one processor fan, and one hard drive needed for each screen. One way to reduce the long-term costs of replacing fans and hard drives is to have media players handle several screens with different content (multichannel media players). Such media players can be built with several graphics cards, each handling its own message channel (Figure 4.31). An alternative is to use a multiscreen graphics card (Figure 4.32), which reduces the number of computers, which reduces the number of fans and hard drives. The disadvantage is that the computer used as a media player has limited capacity for processing and decoding signals, so the number of regions available on each screen may be limited. You should carefully evaluate the need for feeding multiple screens with one player against the possible restrictions and problems.

In most cases, for a digital signage project a large number of media players are included. For this reason, average-performing computers are often chosen because they are at the top of the cost-versus-performance curve. For basic multiscreen applications, such as slide shows and simple animations, you do not need a cutting-edge computer. However the more complex the content, such as several live video regions or live video screens, the more expensive, top-of-the-line computers are required.

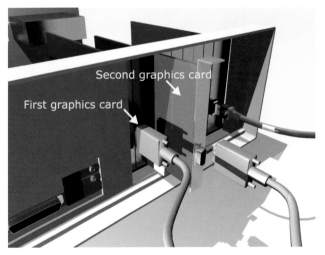

Figure 4.31 A PC-based media player with a second graphics card.

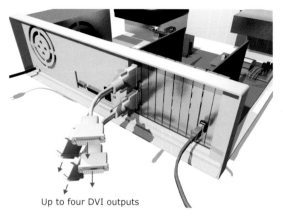

Up to four DVI outputs

Figure 4.32   Multiscreen graphics cards include special outputs to connect more than one display to the media player.

For example, an up-to-date dual-core-type computer is required to decode a full-screen HDTV signal. For these reasons multichannel media players might still be a quite expensive alternative compared to the single-channel players.

Finally, not all digital signage media player software supports multiscreen operation. The media player software has to be able to work as if it were several single-display media players, so it is essential to find out from the digital signage system manufacturer if multiscreen operation is supported.

FEEDING MULTIPLE SCREENS FROM ONE MEDIA PLAYER

In most digital signage systems, each screen has its own media player. This provides maximum flexibility and each screen can provide a specific message based on the viewer's location. However, there are situations where the same content is shown on more than one screen, and it may be an option to feed the multiple screens with one player. There are limitations to how this can be accomplished, depending on the type of output signal used by the media player.

Splitting the VGA Output Signal

If two or more screens are located close to each other and they are to show the same message, it is possible to split the computer video signal and feed both displays from one player. The VGA graphics signal may be split using a VGA splitter, but the cables must be shorter than

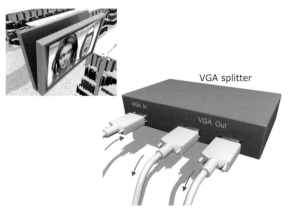

Figure 4.33 With a VGA splitter (*right*), one media
player can feed the same message to several screens
(*left*). This is a practical solution, especially if the
screens are close to each other, as in this figure.

30 feet (10 meters). One application might be two screens located
close to each other but facing in different directions (Figure 4.33).
There are also other splitters for DVI and HDMI signals.

Feeding One Message to Distant Screens

A single message can be fed to a large number of screens located
across a large area, for example, in a shopping mall or supermarket.
Truly, the best solution is to let each screen have its own media
player, but it may be cheaper to operate only one media player in this
scenario (Figure 4.34).

VGA cables have a limited maximum length, so the media player
video signal must be converted into other formats.

Analog RF TV Distribution No doubt, the least expensive way
to distribute video signals to a large number of screens is to use a
media player that provides analog composite video and analog audio
(Figure 4.35). These signals are fed into an external RF modulator that
produces a conventionally modulated analog TV signal that is fed to
TV sets or flat-panel displays with integrated analog TV tuners. A
coaxial cable network is required for the distribution of the signals.

There are both advantages and disadvantages to this method. The resolution in TV signals is limited to the SD format and the picture quality

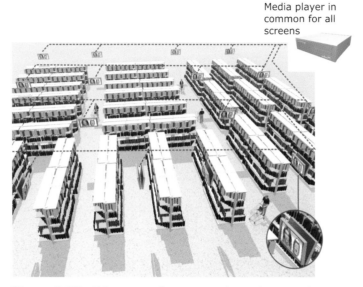

Figure 4.34   When several screens are located across a large area and the same message is to be on all screens, special means might be needed to connect them to a single media player.

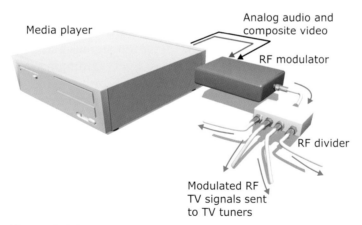

Figure 4.35   Distribution of signals using TV RF signals.

will be low compared to other methods. But the signals are easy to split and can be carried several hundred yards or meters, and amplifiers can be used if the signal should prove to be weak at some location. This method of distribution is borrowed from the analog cable TV business and is further described in my book *Understanding Digital Television*.

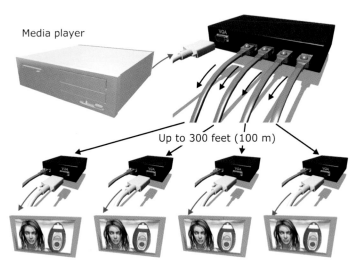

Figure 4.36   This transmitter can supply four receivers with VGA signals to feed four screens.

Twisted-Pair CAT5 or CAT6 Cables   To get more use of splitting the VGA signal, VGA to twisted-pair CAT5 or CAT6 cable converters may be used (CAT6, Category 6, is an improved cable). By converting the VGA signals to signals suitable for distribution via twisted-pair cables (not Ethernet signals), the video signals can be carried up to about 300 feet (100 meters). This is a very common way to distribute identical content to several screens in shopping malls. The cables can be reused for IP distribution if separate media players for each screen should be needed in the future.

DVI Cable Extension Systems   DVI signals are high-quality, high-resolution digital video signals. However, just as for VGA, DVI signals are not suitable to be fed through long cables. Matrox has developed a system called Extio, which is based on optical fibers and can feed four screens with four different messages at a distance of up to 820 feet (250 meters) from the media player (Figure 4.37).

THE SCREEN-INTEGRATED MEDIA PLAYER

A completely different—but very practical—way to handle the interface (more accurately, avoid the interface) between the media player and the screen is to integrate the two components. Combining the

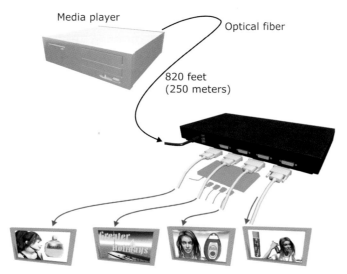

Figure 4.37 The Matrox Extio system feeds up to four screens with up to four separate DVI outputs.

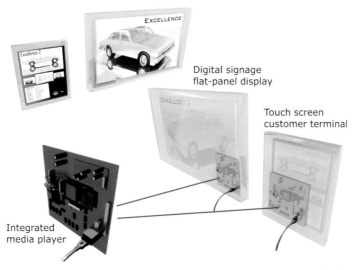

Figure 4.38 If the media player is integrated with the screen, multiple cables are not necessary.

media player and the display into one unit means that all video interfaces can be avoided and only one power supply and power cord is needed (Figure 4.38). These are small, practical details that are of importance in the retail environment.

However, there are some disadvantages. Integrated media players mean that it will be harder to integrate with any kind of display device. Using separate media players and screens also means that you can replace or upgrade the digital signage system without replacing the display units, while with an integrated system, if one piece breaks, the whole unit must be replaced. However, for large-scale systems, the savings in cabling and upfront investment may be large enough to justify this approach.

Using integrated media players certainly solves the problems related to the graphical interface and also makes it easier to do installation work. But sometimes you need to use a separate media player. Some manufacturers have tried to develop small media players that can be easily attached to the back of the screen. Figure 4.39 shows an advanced HDTV (1080p-capable) media player located on the back panel of an LCD screen. This may be an alternative to an integrated player if there are special demands.

We have come to the point where a media player is feeding video signals to a screen. This is fine as long as there is content in the media player. But to remain interesting, the content must be updated continuously. In the next chapter we will focus on how to get the content to the media players.

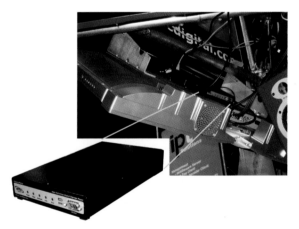

Figure 4.39 This HDTV media player from Adtec is small enough to be located on the back of the screen.

5

CONTENT DISTRIBUTION

There has always been a need to distribute advertising content to stores and other public places. The traditional way has been to send posters and other printed signs by physical mail to their destinations. Then the staff has to hang the advertising in the right place. People also have been necessary to set up outdoor advertising based on large printed posters.

Using electronic screens, such as TV sets, to replace the printed medium has introduced much more dynamic possibilities to advertise and to bring information to the customers. That has evolved into digital signage with even more distribution options.

MANUAL CONTENT DISTRIBUTION

Once, the only way to distribute electronic business media was to send VHS cassettes to the stores. Using VCRs and conventional TV sets, a retail outlet could show commercial spots at the point of purchase (Figure 5.1). One popular application still in use today is instructional videos showing how to set up and/or use the products.

The retail environment is completely different from the home because customers do not linger in a certain department of a shop for very long. In-store television is based on repetition of a short message, while television at home is most often based on providing new content.

But repetition in the retail environment means problems. VHS cassettes will not provide very good picture quality after a significant number of playings. As the tape wears out, the number of drop-outs increases and the tape becomes completely useless. But there is no doubt that VHS cassettes paved the way for the in-store electronic media advancements we enjoy today.

The move to DVD players for repeated in-store playback offered a great improvement. DVDs can play virtually forever without loss of quality, and it is easy to get the players to repeat the commercials without having to wait for a tape to rewind (Figure 5.2).

Figure 5.1 Introduced in the 1970s, VHS cassettes were the first in-store applications of visual electronic media.

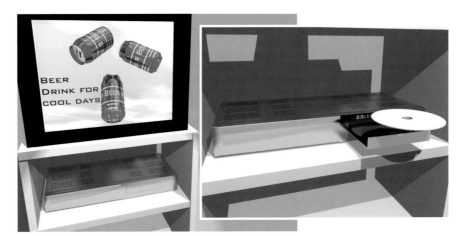

Figure 5.2 DVDs provide a large improvement over VHS cassettes when it comes to quality and maintenance.

Dedicated Production and Player Systems

Separating the content production from the player makes it possible to customize the devices for their tasks (see Figure 5.3). The creation tools are only necessary on the content creation and management computer, while the player can rely on media players included in the operating system (like Windows Media Player) or free players such as the PowerPoint Viewer or Adobe Reader. In Chapter 8, we will look more carefully into the different tasks of the content management server: content creation, content management, and content distribution.

The content on DVDs is really just files that are played according to a built-in playlist (played when you choose "Play All") or according to the choice of the viewer selecting chapters in the menu system. In a way, the DVD player may be regarded as the precursor to the media player.

The introduction of media players replaces traditional video recording techniques on cassettes and DVDs with conventional DVD audio and video content. The video DVDs have been replaced with CDs and DVDs formatted for common data file storage.

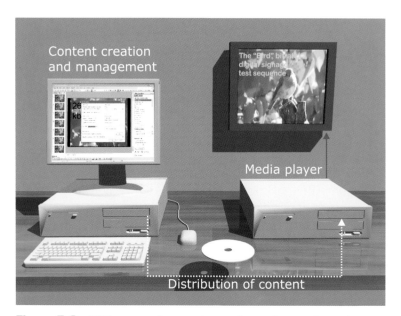

Figure 5.3   With a second computer used as a player only, we have both the first step toward a content management system and a prototype dedicated media player.

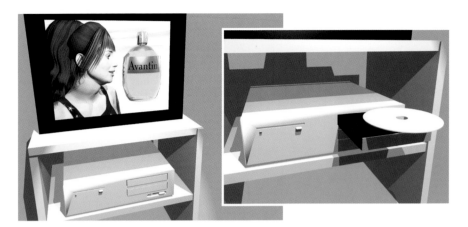

Figure 5.4 Media players, which are computers, offer much more flexibility than DVD players do.

Media players are computers that play back files in a much more flexible way than a DVD player does (Figure 5.4). Media players can use smaller image files, animations, audio files or video clips made in any format, as well as standard video files. Replacing the DVD player with a computer means a much more flexible way to play files because playlists can be edited to control the playback of the content files as desired.

Another advantage over traditional TV sets and DVDs is that computers use high-definition formats that facilitate improved reproduction, especially of text. You could say that computer graphics have been ahead of television for a long time when it comes to screen resolution.

CDs and DVDs can be used to distribute content to each computer-based media player. Files are copied from these discs to internal hard drives or flash memories (Figure 5.5). Both these options, combined with the internal memory of the media player, are ideal for repeated playback. As described in Chapter 4, there is a limitation to the number of times that information can be written to flash memory, though it does have an almost-unlimited number of playbacks.

In a system like this, the central content management server is used only as a main storage library for the content and to produce the CDs and DVDs that you send to the sites. A database, with all contact information and other details on the sites in the system also may be a convenient addition to the content management system. You also need dependable staff in each location to copy the new content to the hard drives or the flash memories once they receive the new content

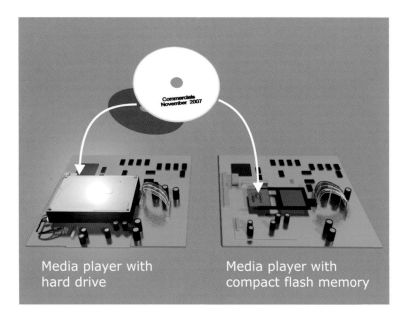

Figure 5.5 Data are downloaded manually to the media player and stored in the hard drive (*left*) or in the flash memory (*right*) before being used.

files. And of course, you cannot provide real-time or near-real-time updates this way.

This kind of distribution is quite similar to the distribution of printed posters and other commercial signs printed on paper. You have to rely on the people in the shop to do their jobs in getting the content to the media players, just as you had to rely on people in the shop to hang the posters or put out the promotional displays.

Digital Photo Frames with Built-In Flash Memory Readers

Digital photo frames are very simple and inexpensive display systems that are often used in homes as well as in public places. There are many new kinds of digital photo frame that have built-in flash memory readers and media players (Figure 5.6). These are essentially an electronic replacement of the printed poster or sign. The content can be distributed manually by copying files to the flash reader and installing it in the frame.

Digital photo frames are very simple and quite cheap display systems that are often used in homes as well as in public places.

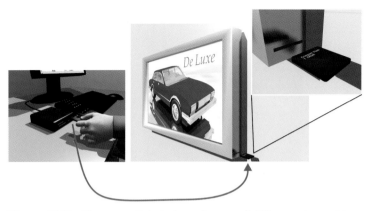

Figure 5.6 There are digital photo frames of different sizes with built-in flash readers and media players. The data are manually stored on a flash memory (*left*), which is inserted into the screen with a built-in media player (*center*) or into a digital frame (*right*).

INTERNET-BASED DISTRIBUTION

The next logical evolution in digital signage systems was to find a way to distribute the content more easily—a way that did not require duplication and mailing of DVDs or reliance on the staff to update each local system. Network solutions, whether the Internet or an internal file-sharing network, became the obvious development.

Manual Downloading and Updating

The least advanced way of using the Internet for content distribution is to manually download content from a central server to a computer in the shop, and from there, move it manually to each media player. If there is a broadband connection, the first step is to let the people in the shop download files manually from a File Transfer Protocol (FTP) server connected to the content management server (Figure 5.7).

First, someone uploads files and playlists to the FTP server (Figure 5.7, *left*). After that, someone in any of the signage locations logs in to the FTP server and downloads the files to a local computer (Figure 5.7, *right*) using an FTP client (see sidebar on page 122).

Neither the person in charge of the content delivery nor the person receiving the content has to be at the same location as the FTP server. Using an FTP site, many people at many locations can upload or

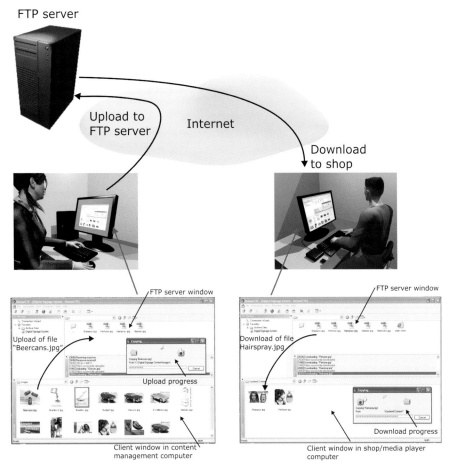

FTP server

Upload to
FTP server

Internet

Download
to shop

FTP server window

FTP server window

Upload of file
"Beercans.jpg"

Download of file
Hairspray.jpg

Upload progress

Download progress

Client window in content
management computer

Client window in shop/media player
computer

Figure 5.7 Introducing an FTP server to the content management process is a significant improvement for content distribution.

download content to the FTP server. This is one of the most interesting and most beneficial characteristics of digital signage: Most things can be done from everywhere.

Using the Internet to distribute content is a considerable improvement over sending out physical media. The distribution process to the signage sites no longer depends on physical mail and the production cost of the CDs and the DVDs disappears. Still, lots of manual work needs to be done locally in the shop. So you have to rely on your people in the shops. They have to bring the content from the

File Transfer Protocol

To use FTP servers, you must make a connection via a web browser (e.g., Internet Explorer, Netscape) or use special FTP software. For example, to gain access to an FTP server via Internet Explorer, enter ftp:// followed by the FTP server name in the address field. A preferable alternative is to use software known as stand-alone FTP clients. Several FTP clients are available for download on the Internet. Some of them are free, such as the DeLuxeFTP (used in Figure 5.7).

Most FTP clients give you an overview of the file structure in your own computer in one window and a similar overview of the folders that are connected to your account in the FTP server. To reach the folders in the FTP server you need three things: the name or IP address of the FTP server, a user name, and a password connected to that user identity. Some FTP servers also allow anonymous login.

If you have administrated a web site, you are familiar with the process of uploading the HTML and other files to a web hosting company. File transfers via FTP is done exactly the same way. As a matter of fact, you can use a normal web hosting account to manage a simple digital signage system. The only difference is that you only use the FTP server part to be able to store the content. In a normal web site application, you just use FTP to upload content and then the visitors use the Hypertext Transfer Protocol (HTTP) to access the web site. So FTP is a different, low-cost, and creative way to use a web hosting service.

local computer either using flash memories or the local network to the media players in the store.

Using FTP is not the only way to transfer files across the Internet. Another common alternative is to set up the content management server, using HTTP, as a web site where the content may be retrieved. The people downloading the content would copy the files from the web site just as they would from an FTP site. The automatic ways of handling content that are described in the next section work exactly the same as manual download is described here. FTP and HTTP are the cornerstones of content delivery to media players in digital signage systems.

Automatic Downloading and Updating

An even better, more reliable, way to make use of Internet-based distribution would be to have the media players automatically check for new content on the content management server as needed.

Each day or several times a day, according to a preset schedule, the media players can access the content management server to check for

Local Printing of Signs and Posters

A way to avoid sending the printed signs by standard mail is to distribute files through the Internet and have stores print them locally (Figure 5.8). Files can be e-mailed or transferred by FTP or HTTP. The only difference is that instead of downloading the image files to media players, they are printed.

This might speed the distribution process and reduce mailing costs, but still it requires the attention of the personnel and a dependable, high-quality printer.

This semi-digital concept is quite popular and may be regarded as somewhat in between traditional in-store advertising and modern digital screen advertising.

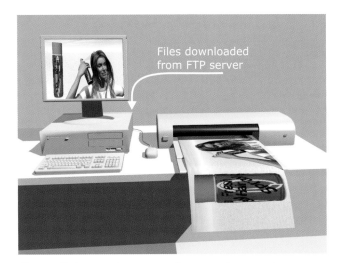

Files downloaded from FTP server

Figure 5.8 Local printing of signs and posters is a digital way of distributing analog media to the shops.

updated files (Figure 5.9). This relieves the store personnel of the task of updating the digital signage systems, and it delegates the responsibility of handling the content to the content management server. This saves time and money and also means improved control of what is being shown on the screens. Centrally updated content is greatly preferred over manual handling.

The media players either have to have the content manually downloaded (if staff are notified that there are new files) or they may be programmed to retrieve the files automatically from the FTP server. This requires some kind of connection to the Internet in the store. The most common way is via an Asymmetric Digital Subscriber Line (ADSL) modem that is constantly online.

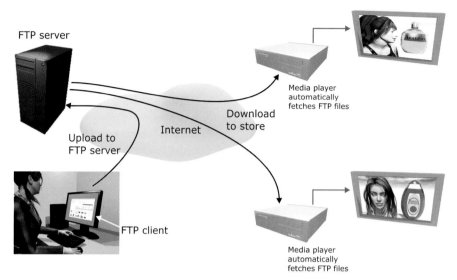

Figure 5.9   Media players programmed to retrieve content automatically from the central server provide many benefits to a digital signage system.

Theoretically, a dial-up modem would work for transferring content files over the Internet, but the file sizes tend to be so large that it is impractical. Mobile means of communication, such as GPRS or 3G, are often used for digital signage applications that use limited content. Dial-up systems may be of interest in some other situations, such as to establish a return path that is not very often used. This applies to systems that use one-way broadcast media that do not have internal return paths as is the case for broadband connections.

The ADSL Broadband Installation

Among the hundreds of digital signage systems that exist today, broadband through ADSL is probably the most common means for distribution. ADSL installations include an ADSL modem; a combined router, firewall, and switch; and a secondary switch that allows a larger number of computers to be connected to the system (Figure 5.10). This also enables the local computers to communicate with one another.

A very similar kind of installation may be seen in many homes where a broadband connection has to be shared by all the family's computers and media players. Nowadays, these home networks tend to be

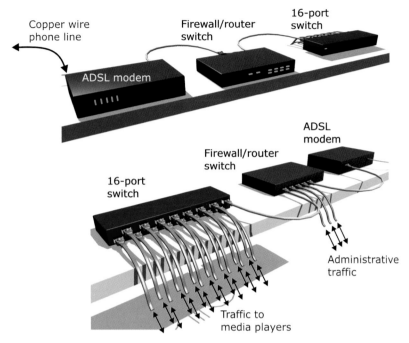

Figure 5.10 The most common broadband connection is based on an ADSL modem connected to a gateway consisting of a combined firewall and router with an integrated switch.

wireless. Of course, a network in a shop also may be wireless, but there are some disadvantages to using wireless LANs in public environments (described in Chapter 7). Otherwise, the most significant difference between home and public installations is the extra Ethernet switch that enables many more computers to be attached to the system.

As is shown in Figure 5.10, up to 15 media players might be attached to the system, and there are three ports to be used for administrative tasks such as the computer point-of-purchase systems, including the cash register.

The ADSL Modem An ADSL installation uses the conventional copper wire telephone line to get the signals the final mile from the local telephone station to the subscriber. ADSL can theoretically provide bitrates up to 24 Megabits per second (Mbps), depending on the distance to the telephone station and the quality of the lines. The maximum bitrate is, in most cases, around 4.5 to 5.5 Mbps.

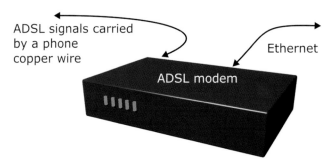

Figure 5.11   The ADSL modem makes it possible to use
copper wire telephone line for high-speed IP communications.

The ADSL signals are radio signals carried on top of the baseband telephone signals. At the telephone station, the Ethernet packets (including the IP) are adapted to the signal to be carried by the copper wire
using a DSLAM (Digital Subscriber Line Access Multiplexer). At the
other end of the line, an ADSL modem is required to demodulate and
retrieve the Ethernet signals (Figure 5.11). The ADSL modem has an
Ethernet connection that in principle can be connected directly to the
computer used for manual download or to a media player that automatically fetches content from the content management server.

However, a broadband connection normally has several users, rather
than being dedicated to the digital signage system. Other access
may include the computers used for administrative and sales tasks,
such as the store register system and more. This transaction traffic is extremely important and probably the reason for installing
broadband in the first place. After all, it would be no good to advertise products using digital signage if there were no cash registers at
which to purchase these products. As a result, there is obviously a
need to connect a number of computers to one ADSL modem, including the sales computers and the media players.

The Gateway Router/Firewall/Switch   Connecting multiple computers to an ADSL modem is done using a local area network including
a broadband firewall and a router/gateway. The router/gateway also
includes a simple switch. The router feature of this unit is extremely
important.

Every computer must have a unique *IP address* to communicate with
other computers. Your Internet service provider (ISP) may provide
you with either a fixed or a dynamic IP address.

An IP address consists of four, three-number groups separated by a dot, such as 162.117.114.201. Either this address is fixed, meaning it is the IP number your computer always has, or it is dynamic, meaning your computer will obtain an address as soon as you log on to the broadband connection. Dynamic IP addresses are obtained from a Dynamic Host Configuration Protocol (DHCP) server that administrates the IP addresses within that network. So, actually you only have one IP address that may be used to communicate with other computers on the Internet. But if you have several computers to be connected to the same ADSL modem, how do you solve this?

By adding the router/gateway and switch unit, you can create an internal, separate network that can contain several computers. (See Figure 5.12.) To the outside world, it will seem as if there is only one computer on the network. However, the router knows from which computer the specific IP packets come and with which outside IP addresses each computer communicates. This makes it possible for the gateway unit to route the correct packets to and from each internal computer or media player even though there is only one IP address for an ADSL modem used in a shop.

The gateway has several tasks to fulfill. Since it administers its own network, it must also contain a DHCP server to be able to provide local addresses to the units within its network. (For more information on IP addressing, refer to Appendix B.)

Figure 5.12 The gateway contains the router, DHCP server, firewall, and a four-port switch. The single IP address to the *left* (XXX.XXX.XXX.XXX) is provided by the ISP, while the internal router provides the private addresses within the network (i.e., addresses like 192.168.000.XXX).

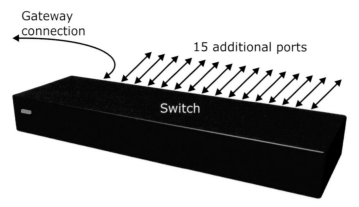

Figure 5.13 To get more physical ports, additional switches or hubs can be connected to the gateway. The gateway accommodates up to 254 clients (computers) connected to the network.

Hubs and Switches

The four ports on the router/firewall unit might be sufficient in a home network. However, in an office, shop, or other public area, more ports may be required to support more computers. The gateway administers its own IP addresses and can handle up to 254 unique private IP addresses within its network. By adding further IP switches or hubs, more physical ports are introduced and more computers can be attached (Figure 5.13).

The difference between an Ethernet hub and an Ethernet switch is that the hub distributes all packets to all its ports and the switch is selective and sends packets only to the port where the addressed computer is attached. In this way, using switches instead of hubs reduces unnecessary traffic in the local area network.

HOW COMMUNICATIONS ACROSS THE INTERNET REALLY WORK

Letting the media players retrieve the content automatically is a big improvement over duplicating and distributing physical media or requiring personnel to manually download content when it is ready. Now it is possible to build large networks of media players all over the world without worrying about the demands for human resources or the time it will take to get the new content to the various media players.

Broadband networks have two limitations when it comes to serving a lot of places: serving locations simultaneously and providing live coverage. This is because traffic on the Internet is based on IP unicasting.

IP Unicasting

IP unicasting means that a separate point-to-point communications session has to be set up between the content management server (in our example, the FTP server) and each of the media players. Packets are sent to their destination computer (media player). As they arrive, the receiving computer sends confirming IP packets in the other direction (Figure 5.14). If a packet is lost, it will be sent repeatedly until its safe arrival at the destination computer is confirmed.

This means there is two-way communication between the sender and the receiver. As a result, the content management computer will become busier handling all traffic as the number of locations to be served grows. Another problem is that the required capacity on its Internet connection will grow proportionally to the number of locations and the amount of traffic to each site. The return path traffic will also grow accordingly. (See Figure 5.15.)

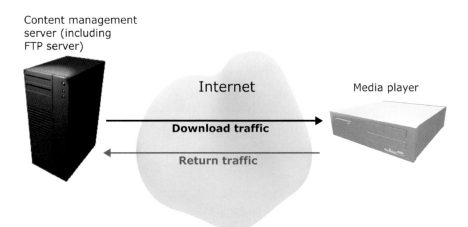

Figure 5.14   Unicasting means that a two-way communication session is set during automatic retrieval of content. For example, files (in packets) might be sent from an FTP server via the Internet to be downloaded to a media player, and the media player will send a message back to the FTP server to confirm the packets have arrived.

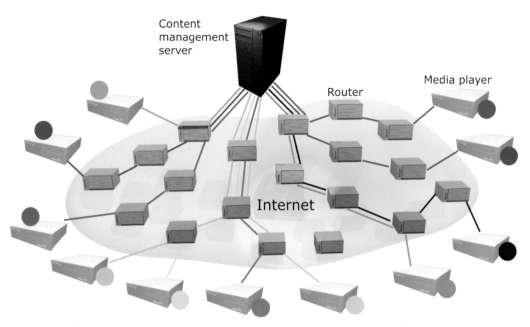

Figure 5.15 Unicasting means that all IP packets have to be sent separately to each receiving computer. So, the numbers of packets distributed will increase with the number of locations to be served.

The result is that the costs for Internet access and particularly the load on the content management server will grow, which may make this distribution method less favorable if the number of sites to be supported and the amount of content to be delivered increases.

The greater the load put on the content management server, the longer the time required to complete the transfer of data to all of the receiving locations. Therefore, transfer of files will not happen simultaneously and the possibility to provide near-real-time applications will be limited.

Streaming services using unicasting work the same way. The traffic received will have to be confirmed by the receiver and each location will require its individual stream of IP packets.

Unicast Streaming

Some would argue that still there is TV broadcasting on the Internet, and most certainly there is, to some degree. However, conventional

Internet television channels are not really broadcasting channels in a wider sense. If you want to watch a live TV channel on the Internet, you send a request to a streaming server asking for that channel to be streamed to your specific computer. This means that a communications session is set up between the streaming server and your computer. So there is two-way communication, with packets being sent back to the streaming server confirming that the packets received are without errors, just as in all unicasting communications.

Unicast video streaming is really quite similar to the traffic that occurs when you are downloading a file (Figure 5.16). The only real difference is that a streaming file has no defined ending. This also means that television on the Internet is quite limited since the streaming server can support only a certain number of simultaneously receiving computers.

In conventional broadcasting systems, this is not the case; an unlimited number of receivers may exist. The speed and quality with which your local television broadcast is delivered is not affected by the number of your neighbors who have televisions or who happen to be watching the same thing that you are.

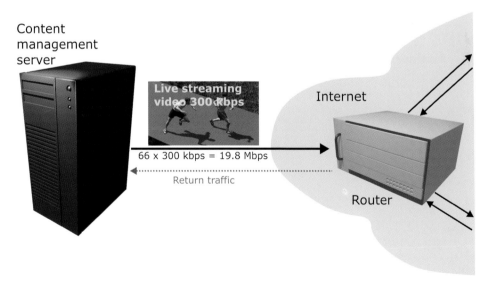

Figure 5.16 Unicast streaming means that only a limited number of receiving computers can be supported. If the server can provide 20 Mbit/s total, the maximum number of client computers to be served with a 300 kbps stream is limited to 66.

Unicast streaming is limited by the total bitrate that the streaming server may provide as well as the maximum bitrate on the connection between the server and the Internet backbone. The typical maximum streaming rate from a server ranges from 20 to 80 Mbps, depending on the server capabilities.

An example is a 300 kbps live Internet transmission. A 20 Mbps streaming server could provide IPTV signals simultaneously to 66 receiving computers. If increased to 80 Mbps, the theoretical number would increase to about 265. By using several servers, an even larger number of computers could receive the signals. Decreasing the bitrate is another way to increase the number of computers served. A typical figure of the maximum number of simultaneous receivers might be around 1,500. This is enough for many applications but still not adequate if it is a live event of great interest to many.

There are at least two ways to solve these distribution problems. One way is *IP multicasting*, which is the transmission of data via one stream to more than one recipient. But multicasting is not allowed everywhere. The Internet of today does not allow multicasting. There are two major reasons for this: one is the problem of assigning multicasting addresses, but the worst problem is that IP packets multiply in the routers when serving many users. This could cause the traffic load on the Internet to explode in an uncontrolled way.

Another way to limit the traffic load on the central server is to introduce in each store a local edge server that verifies that the same information is never sent to a store more than once.

In the next chapters, we will discuss how to introduce multicasting and how to use edge servers to get around these obstacles.

6

THE EDGE SERVER

Chapter 5 covered different ways of distributing content to media players: CDs, DVDs, flash memories, and broadband access. But each of these alternatives requires that each player be individually fed with files, either manually or by picking up new files from a central server using the Internet. Manual file handling through physical media such as CDs and flash memories is not practical. Because the task is so cumbersome, it is likely to limit how often the content is updated.

For these reasons, most digital signage networking uses broadband networks. Each media player checks the content manager for new content and instructions quite often, even up to several times an hour. As a result, there is lots of traffic if there are many media players in each shop. In this chapter, we will take a closer look at how to improve this. A way to limit the traffic is to have a local server that takes care of all traffic to the shop. This edge server also provides local storage of content that can be used by any of the media players.

We will start by analyzing how a number of media players can be used when individually connected to the Internet using a gateway/router and a local area network (LAN).

INDIVIDUAL MEDIA PLAYER UPDATING

Every media player at the site has to be connected to the Internet in one way or another. This may be done using a common ADSL modem and a gateway including a router that provides private IP addresses to a local area network within the shop. (See Chapter 5 for more detail on networking.) So there has to be local network including a switch and twisted-pair cabling (Figure 6.1).

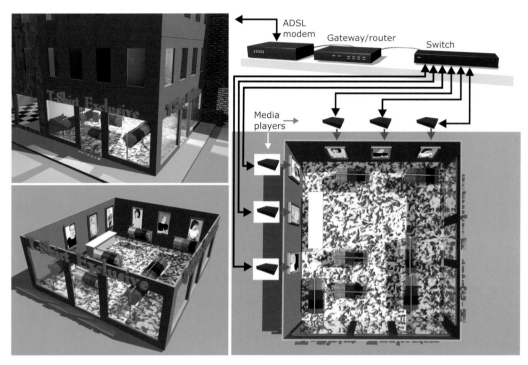

Figure 6.1 LANs are necessary to link several media players to the Internet. In this T-shirt store there are eight media players connected to the Internet using a local area network.

The gateway router, as shown in Figure 6.1, provides private IP addresses to be used within the network. These IP addresses will be dynamic—assigned each time they connect to the network—since all requests come from the media players in the shop and not the other way around. The content management server must, of course, have a fixed IP address so the media players know where to look for updated content (Figure 6.2).

Identities and Grouping

As can be seen in Figure 6.2, different screens in one digital signage network can show different messages. This means each media player must have an identity that is connected to a certain message. Digital signage is not like a television channel; it's more like a collection of television channels. Therefore, each media player belongs to a group of media players that should show a certain message. If a media

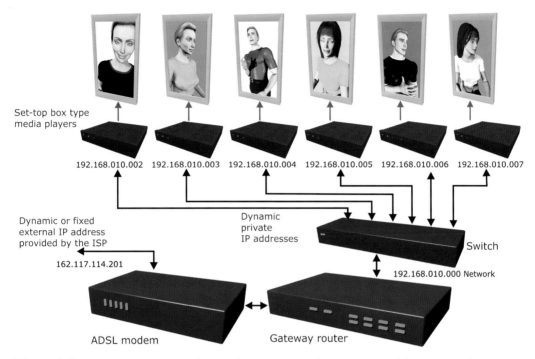

Figure 6.2 A gateway router with a DHCP server provides private IP addresses to each media player.

player is replaced or moved to another task, it has to change group identity to still be able to present the correct message.

In Figures 6.1 and 6.2, there are six messages in the same shop, so there must be six groups of media players, even though each group contains only one media player. In other franchises of the same retail chain, you will find a similar set of six media players, each of which belongs to one of the six groups and shows one of six messages.

Media Player Traffic

As digital signage applications develop, the number of media players at a site will increase. Their functionality might advance to include customer terminals. The customer terminals make a request of the content management server as soon as a customer makes some kind of input. This request could be avoided if enough information is stored in the terminal itself, but for more complicated tasks, there would probably be requests made to the central server anyhow.

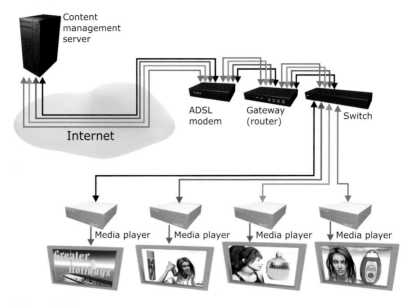

Figure 6.3 Each media player fetches its content from the content management server via a gateway, an ADSL modem, and the Internet. Four media players create up to four times as much traffic as one media player does.

All this traffic has to go long distance through the Internet. And as the network grows, the content management server will have to carry an increasing load (Figure 6.3). As we saw in Chapter 5, the bottlenecks of broadband distribution are the result of the capacity of the content management server and the connection from the server to the Internet backbone.

There are better, more economical ways to use the broadband connection. One problem is that the same files may be downloaded to different media players that are located in the same shop, duplicating the demand that the ADSL modem makes on the broadband connection.

THE EDGE SERVER

As the number of displays and media players increases, the content management server needs to be relieved of unnecessary traffic. Customer terminals are especially demanding because they may require the same traffic to be carried to the same shop or terminal over and over. One way to improve network efficiency is to install a common server for the site that will house all content required at the location. The common server is called the edge, or site, server.

With an edge server, only one computer has to communicate directly with the content management server and every file has to be fetched just once. Then all media players and customer terminals connect to the local edge server instead of the distant content management server (Figure 6.4). The edge server is one of the most important components of large-scale digital signage systems.

Since the content management server has to distribute files to only one computer at each location, the administration of the network is considerably simplified. The central content management server will have to keep track of storage in only one place for each geographical location of the network. The local handling of content within the store is handled by the edge server, the media players, and the customer terminals. There is much to be saved by distributing files, especially large files like video clips, only once into each shop.

Another advantage is that because more traffic is done on the local area network instead of the outside Internet, this system is less

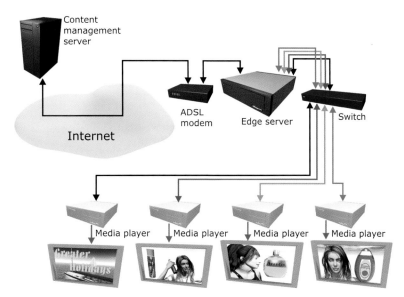

Figure 6.4 With an edge server, only one computer has to retrieve content outside the shop. The media players retrieve content locally from the edge server.

sensitive to disturbances in the broadband connection. The edge server can also have more storage capacity than the media players, which means more content can be available for a longer time. In systems with media players that use flash memories instead of hard drives, the storage capacity is limited; using an edge server would compensate for this.

Retrieving Content from the Edge Server

The edge server retrieves content from the content management server much as media players do in a system without an edge server (Figure 6.5). Edge servers use FTP or HTTP to make a connection to the content management server and request updated content. That content is either stored as files in the edge server or routed as a stream on to the media players. The content stored on the edge server may be requested by the media players as needed.

Since the edge server can house an FTP or web server application, the media players can retrieve files from the edge server as if they were communicating directly with the content management server—the media players won't know the difference. This makes it very simple to introduce edge servers in most digital signage systems.

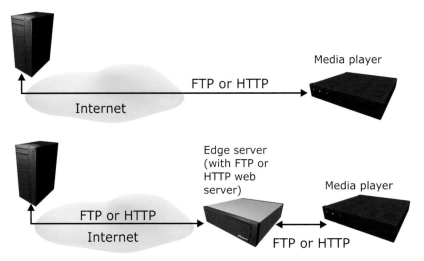

Figure 6.5 The media players can retrieve files from the edge server in the same way, using the same protocols, as they would to request content directly from the content management server.

However, FTP or HTTP are not the best ways to transfer files inside a local area network. It creates unnecessary logs in the edge server and requires a lot of bandwidth. This is a waste of capacity if the media players try to check for updated content once every minute or more. When an edge server is introduced into a local network, it's best to consider alternative file transfer methods.

Using Shared Folders or Network Neighborhood   If you have a local area network with a number of computers, the easiest way to transfer files is to use shared folders or to set up network neighborhoods (Figure 6.6). I will not go into the details of the protocols that can be used to communicate within a local area network—there are many networking books that do a more in-depth job.

As a quick overview, shared folders in Windows operating systems are based on the proprietary Server Message Block (SMB) protocol. However, SMB only works between Windows-based computers. There is an SMB-compatible protocol, Samba, that uses open source software. Thanks to Samba, it is possible to communicate between Windows-based and Linux-based platforms. This is significant, since digital signage systems often operate with Linux servers serving Windows clients or vice versa.

Linux computers also have their own file-sharing system, Network File System (NFS), which works similarly to SMB and Samba.

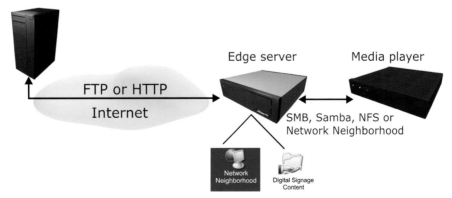

Figure 6.6   Shared folders or network neighborhoods are simple ways to handle local file transfer.

In the long run, most internal communication between edge servers and media players uses some of these file-sharing protocols. However, edge server systems are not currently as common as digital signage systems that have only media players.

Edge Servers with Dual Network Cards   If an edge server is introduced into a digital signage network, the edge server rather than the content management server will be the device with the fixed IP address. The fixed IP address makes it possible for the local media players to find the right server from which to download content (Figure 6.7).

With dual network cards, one network can face the local area network with the media players and the other one can face the external broadband connection (via the ADSL modem in Figure 6.7). This means the local media players will always use the same set of IP addresses, which simplifies the installation of digital signage as well as the ongoing network maintenance. The IP addresses in Figures 6.7 and 6.8 are an example. The private network IP addresses start with 192, which

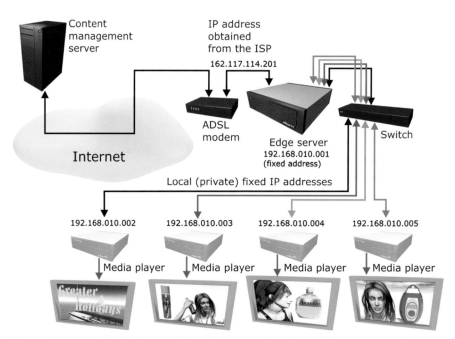

Figure 6.7   The logical connections in a network with an edge server. Media players retrieve content from the edge server at a fixed IP address.

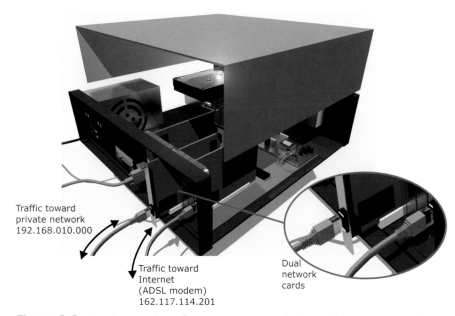

Traffic toward
private network
192.168.010.000

Traffic toward
Internet
(ADSL modem)
162.117.114.201

Dual
network
cards

Figure 6.8 Dual network cards in site servers make it possible to use a specific range of IP addresses for the media players.

means that this is a class C network, which allows 254 hosts to be attached to this network. Thus, the number of media players can be quite large. This configuration is not possible when the media players communicate directly with the content management server.

From an administrative point of view, using edge servers significantly simplifies a large network. All locations in a retail chain can have identical IP addresses for the media players and the ethernet port of the edge server that faces the local network.

Using dual network cards may also solve the problem of integrating with an existing local area network with a predetermined set of IP addresses. However, this will also make the setup of IP addresses in such a shop unique since it has to conform to that specific network.

Using a Gateway Router   A more common way to connect the edge server is to use a gateway router, similar to a home computer network. In most cases, however, the gateway router contains a DHCP server that provides dynamic IP addresses to the computers or media players within the private network. But remember, the edge server

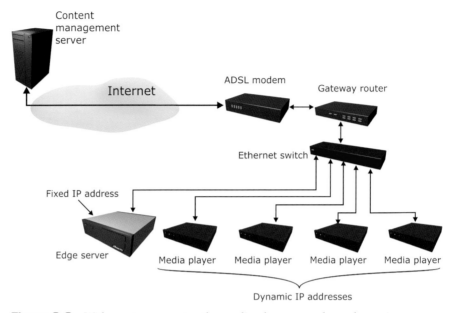

Figure 6.9   With a gateway router, the media players may have dynamic
IP addresses but the edge server must have a fixed IP address. Dynamic IP
addresses may be used, though, provided that the DNS is used and the edge
server and the media players have fixed names.

must have a fixed IP address (Figure 6.9). Otherwise, the media players would not know where to go to get new content. The central content management server must also have a fixed IP address so that the
edge servers can find it to get the content.

Edge Server Capacity   In many cases, one edge server can serve a
very large shop. If the tasks are not too data-heavy, the server could
even serve several stores or an entire shopping mall. The storage
capacity on the hard drive can be divided into folders or partitions to
serve several groups of media players.

If the edge server gets its content through multicasting (covered in
Chapter 7), there can be several proprietary digital signage systems
attached to the edge server. If the edge server communicates
through a unicast broadband connection to the content management
server, however, it is preferable that the edge server be a part of the
same digital signage system as the media players and the content
management server.

Names Instead of Numbers

Gateway routers contain a Domain Name System (DNS) server that enables you to configure your network with computer names rather than IP addresses. This means the edge server could have a dynamically assigned IP address as long as it had a fixed name to which the media players could refer. However, most digital signage systems rely on fixed IP addresses used by the servers and dynamic IP addresses used by the clients.

EDGE SERVER APPLICATIONS

Edge servers are especially efficient in network situations where the same content is used in several media players at different times. The edge server downloads the data once from the content management server and then distributes the content as needed to the media players on the local network. Here are a few examples where edge servers are the perfect solution.

Interactive Customer Terminals

Customer terminals mean lots of requests for information. People in different stores that belong to the same retail chain probably ask for about the same kind of information—whether it's a video demonstration of a specific car model's engine or the race history of a horse that a customer is about to bet on. These repeated requests from many locations for the same information make it impractical to rely on a distant content management server. An edge server can act as a local mirror of the content management server.

For example, imagine a video store where the customer can watch four movie trailers before deciding which movie to rent or to watch at the cinema (Figure 6.10). To serve multiple customers, there are five touch screens throughout the store. Using an edge server makes it possible to download the four trailers just once to the local network. If the customer terminals were connected directly through the Internet to the content management server, all four trailers would have had to be downloaded separately to each terminal. As a result, there would be five times as much load on the content management server and five times more traffic to be carried across the Internet.

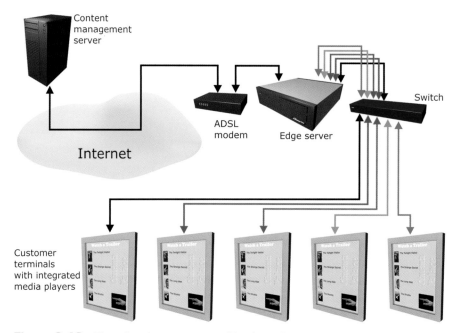

Figure 6.10   The edge server retrieves files from the content management
server and the customer terminals retrieve files from the edge server.

Handling large video files requires not only a lot of bandwidth but
also a lot of storage. Being able to store all the video clips in one place
in the shop also preserves space on the media player hard drives.

Complex Environments

Digital signage can be used in many ways in many types of retail
and public environments. Imagine all the ways to promote products,
inform the visitor/shopper, and provide valuable content, and you
can quickly imagine a very complex environment, where different
types of displays are providing different types of content with different levels of interactivity, network demands, and sound and video.

Cinemas are complex environments. There could be movie posters
and electronic menus running in the candy store and customer terminals where the cinema visitors may choose to watch movie trailers. In
an advanced scenario, preshow advertising and movie previews could
be a digital signage application. However, these many applications
can, to some extent, reuse the same content. It might even be suitable
to have one edge server intended for the preshow advertising and let
a second server handle the rest of the applications (Figure 6.11).

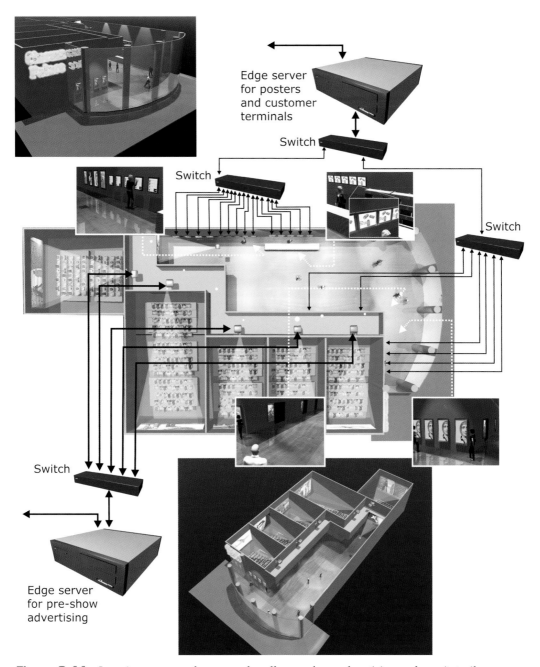

Figure 6.11 In a cinema, one edge server handles preshow advertising and movie trailers while another edge server handles posters and customer terminals. The same content may be used in several media players.

Streaming IPTV

Unicast streaming (discussed in Chapter 5) can be used to distribute video clips from the edge server to the media player. The media player requests a certain video clip from the site server and the edge server starts streaming the clip while the media player operates only as a decoder. The same situation applies to a customer terminal application where the customer requests a certain video clip. Then the edge server starts streaming the file to the media player.

An alternative is to download the video file to the media player before starting to decode it. The main disadvantage is that you have to save the file on the media player's hard drive, so the drive needs to be large enough to hold the content. When streaming from the edge server, you can make do with a simple media player without a hard drive or flash memory.

The main advantage in streaming from the edge server is that you do not have to stream all the way from the content management server. All streaming is done in the local area network only, so it likely will be faster and smoother than if the content were coming from the central server. And you may, as mentioned above, use simple IPTV boxes to decode the video.

In Figure 6.12, the video file is read from the hard drive of the content management server and downloaded to the media player, where it is

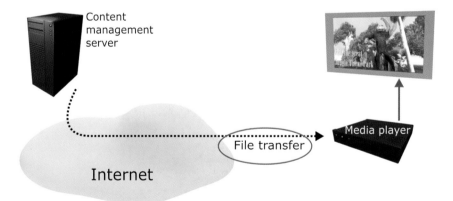

Figure 6.12 It is possible to download a file from the content management server to the media player's memory and then decode the file in the media player to display on a screen.

saved on the hard drive or flash memory. The media player decodes the content and presents it onscreen.

In Figure 6.13, the video file is read from the hard drive of the content management server as it is streamed to the media player. The media player decodes the incoming streamed file and displays it immediately. The media player does not store the file.

In Figure 6.14, the video file is downloaded to the edge server from the content management server. The edge server stores the content on its hard drive and streams the video file to the media player as

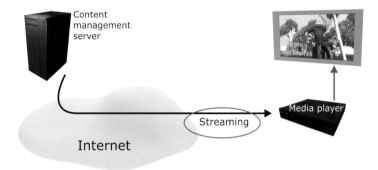

Figure 6.13 It is possible to stream data from the content management server to the media player, where they are decoded but not stored before being displayed.

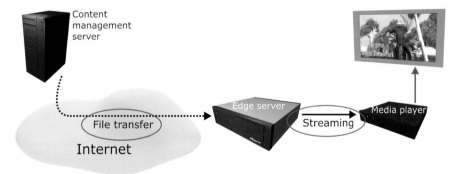

Figure 6.14 It is possible to transfer files from the content management server to the edge server and stream it from the edge server to the media player, where it is decoded but not stored before being displayed.

needed. The media player decodes the incoming streamed file and displays it immediately. The file is not stored on the media player.

In some applications, you may wish to simultaneously distribute an IPTV signal to several screens. One way to do so is to set up a number of unicast sessions and send one to each media player separately. However, if a huge HD file is to be distributed to a large number of screens, the load on the edge server may exceed its bandwidth capacity. Conventional smaller servers of today have a limit at about 20 Mbps when it comes to streaming. Multicasting (discussed in Chapter 7) is another way to handle simultaneous distribution where bandwidth is an issue. (Chapter 8 includes some practical streaming exercises.)

Using IPTV Boxes   If the edge server can stream IPTV signals, it is possible to use simple consumer IPTV boxes with modifications. These boxes cannot display still pictures; they require a continuous stream of moving content. With no hard drives or memory, they are what they are: TV set-top boxes.

Most IPTV boxes are made to fit proprietary IPTV networks. Therefore, there might be different, sometimes quite significant, adaptations required to use the boxes with the edge server. Even with the modifications, this kind of set-top box may be the most economic solution for some virtual TV channel applications. (See Figure 6.15.)

Using streaming video in wireless LANs (WLANs) in public areas might cause problems if there is interference from other wireless devices, such as Bluetooth phones. In IP networks, the files will be retransmitted if the receiving computer cannot confirm the signal as correctly received. This will cause an interruption that is quite disturbing to the viewer. In file transfer configurations, this is not a problem because the file is not played until it has been completely received. Streaming video should be used only in wired systems if there are IPTV boxes that depend on streaming signals (discussed further in Chapter 7).

IPTV boxes can be used with unicast signals but work even better in local area networks with multicasting signals. Then all boxes can share one multicasting stream and individual streaming to each IPTV box is not required. This relieves the edge server of a lot of its bandwidth requirements, and an unlimited number of IPTV boxes can be supported, provided that they are to receive the same stream.

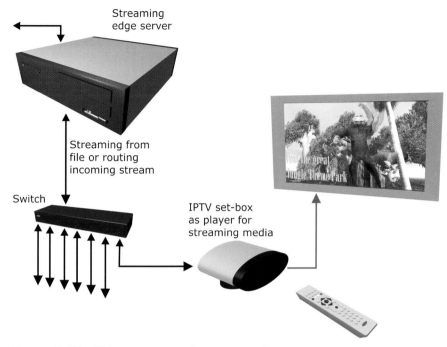

Figure 6.15 Using conventional IPTV set-top boxes (here Amino-type) may be an economical way of handling virtual TV channels in edge server systems.

Multimedia Thin Clients Hardware media players for home use are often "thin" clients, that is, very simple media players without content storage capacity. They depend very much on software that is installed in the supporting computer. These kinds of clients do not have the same versatility as digital signage system media players because they have very limited hardware and software capabilities. Simple retail or public digital solutions may be able to use thin clients, which are generally less expensive, since they have fewer features and fewer hardware components.

There are digital signage systems with the necessary adaptations to use this kind of media player. The thin client's supporting software must be installed on the edge server. Most consumer players of this kind require supporting software installed on a Windows-based computer.

Hauppauge's MediaMVP is a typical example of a home media player dependent on supporting software. The application running in the computer is controlled by the remote control of the thin client

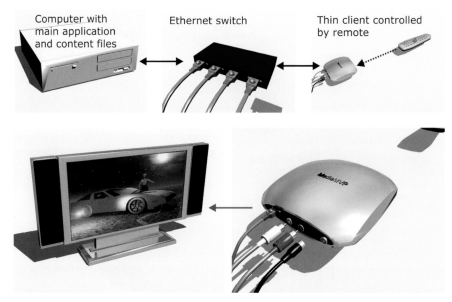

Figure 6.16   A thin client contains minimal hardware but depends on a supporting computer.

(Figure 6.16). The intention of devices like the MediaMVP is to overcome the geographical problem of the media files such as digital photographs, MP3 music files, video clips, and other content being stored in a computer that is not in the same room as the TV set. Up to 24 wired MediaMVPs or up to four wireless MediaMVPs can be connected to one single computer.

There are digital signage systems that use products like the Hauppauge MediaMVP to get low-cost media players. Since digital signage systems operate in a much more automated way than a home media player application, some adaptations must be made before this kind of client can be used.

Similar Home Applications

The digital signage systems that we have discussed here are all professional systems that include full-featured media players with hard drives or flash memories and that can retrieve content from a server in a very independent way. Today's home media players are, in most cases, not quite this robust.

As discussed in Chapter 1, media players in home applications normally pick up files from a PC that stores all the media content. The PC and the media players are all connected to a local area network through a switch or hub. (There might also be a stand-alone hard drive with network connectivity that could supply media files to the media players without a PC.) As seen earlier, there are many kinds of media players that can be used with the home local area network. These players include various devices for playing music, digital photos, video clips, and movies as well as devices for listening to Internet radio or for providing Internet access in the TV set. It is quite practical to be able to store all media in just one location in the home and use one Internet connection for all devices (Figure 6.17).

Another solution is to have a home theater PC (HTPC) connected to the TV set. This is a bit of going the other way around. Instead of separate media players fetching content from a computer with media files, the computer itself is used to replace the DVD players and recorders. A very good example is the Microsoft Media Center, which can be only bought as preinstalled software on computers that meet the hardware requirements. There are many other software packages based on a similar concept that you can use to build your own HTPC.

When combining a computer with audiovisual applications, you get very close to digital signage–like systems that combine Internet access with multifile handling on the same screen and temporary or permanent storage of media files. And of course, a media center can also be used by thin clients at other locations in the home.

In the long run, the media players used at home will become more advanced and resemble the professional systems you find in public installations. A big difference is that the consumer media players are generally handled directly by the users instead of by playlists and scheduling files, though there are already media players of this kind that include playlist features.

To be able to use digital signage at home in a similar way as today's applications in stores and public locations, there have to be content providers that can produce content suitable not only for real-time use but also for non-real-time and near-real-time applications. Many TV and radio stations as well as newspapers have extensive content

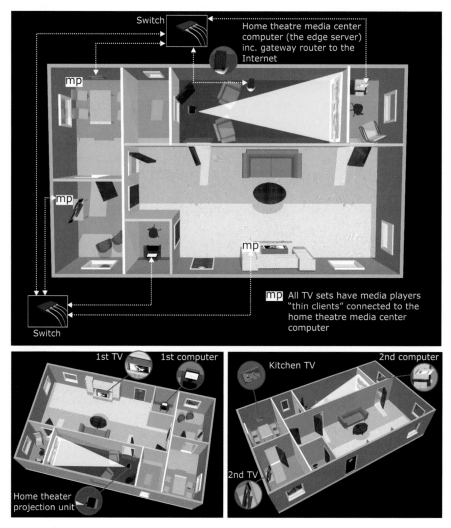

Figure 6.17   If we regard the computers as media players, connect thin client media players to the TV sets, and think of the home theater media center—including a gateway router to the Internet—as an edge server, the home LAN is really quite similar to a retail digital signage application.

on the Web. Such content is well adapted to non-real-time use. But playlists and other control files also have to be distributed by the content providers. Perhaps the media distributors already, without thinking about it, are on their way toward producing material for this new medium.

7

DIGITAL SIGNAGE BROADCASTING

No doubt, digital signage is something of the future for public and probably also for home applications. But to make this medium competitive with traditional television and other broadcast media, distribution must be efficient. Today, digital signage depends primarily on distribution by physical media or broadband. Physical media are certainly not realistic distribution methods for a signage system of more than a limited number of displays. Broadband provides much more efficient content delivery and can be automated and fairly well controlled. Also, broadband distribution is based on IP, which means the infrastructure can support any future developments in content files. IP handles file transfer and streaming from files, as well as live streaming.

But broadband distribution has its limitations. As digital signage grows to cover more and more sites and the amount of content to be distributed increases, more efficient media for delivery will be needed. Most users of digital signage will discover that they need a solution for distribution that is similar to radio or TV broadcasting.

UNICASTING

As described earlier, the old VCR playing a VHS cassette combined with a conventional CRT TV set is the predecessor to the media player. A similar application using ordinary TV sets is live, closed-circuit television used for gaming applications, such as horse racing and other sports that need to be covered as real-time, live events (Figure 7.1). Often, satellite is used to distribute this kind of event-based television.

Figure 7.1   Live coverage of sports events in betting shops was
the first use of use in–store, real-time applications.

As we shall see later on, satellite broadcasting still has a unique
position in providing real-time and near-real-time signals.

Internet communication is based on two-way communications. Every
received packet is checked at arrival to see if it contains errors and
the receiving computer confirms to the transmitting server that all
packets are correctly received. If it is detected that a packet contains
errors, a message is sent back to the originating server requesting
that the packet be sent again. This two-way, point-to-point handshak-
ing is called *unicasting*. Unicasting is a very reliable transfer of information because you always know that the transmitted information
is correctly received. Therefore, there is no real drawback as long as
you are communicating between two computers.

If you are trying to distribute the same content to several receiving
computers (Figure 7.2), however, the situation becomes very complicated. A separate communications session has to be set up with each
receiving computer, which means all information is sent separately
to each receiving computer. If 1 GB of information is to be distributed
to 100 places, the source server will have to send 1 GB of information
100 times, for a total of 100 GB transmitted. Since the server has limited capacity and the connection to the Internet backbone is limited,
this would take some time. With a connecting speed of 10 Mbps, it
would take 13.3 minutes to transfer to just 1 site. Transferring to
all 100 sites would take 1,330 minutes, or 22.16 hours. This is likely

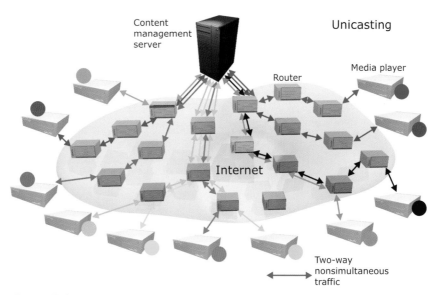

Figure 7.2   In unicast mode, the IP packets have to be transferred individually to each receiving computer.

too slow for weekly updates and impossible for a system where you want to send out daily updates.

PEER-TO-PEER NETWORKS

The increased load on the content management distribution server due to an increased number of media players to be served is a huge problem in growing broadband-operated digital signage networks. One way of controlling the traffic is to use edge servers as described in the previous chapter. Another way is to use *peer-to-peer networks (P2P).*

In a P2P network, every computer (media player) is involved in distributing content to all other computers in that network (Figure 7.3). This technique is well known from file-sharing systems such as Kazaa. In systems like this, the content management server and its backbone Internet connection are relieved from much of the load caused by distribution of content. Instead, the server works as a traffic control center, keeping track of the IP addresses in the network and directing the traffic among the media players.

Although many people consider P2P networks a solution and the capacity to some extent grows with the number of media players

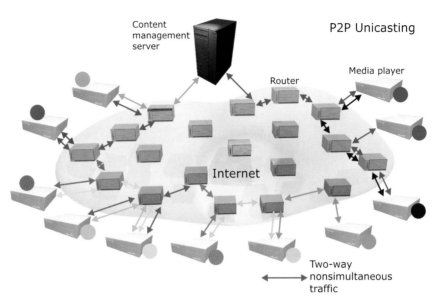

Figure 7.3 In a P2P network, all computers distribute content to one another, relieving the content management server and its backbone connection to the Internet.

connected, there are disadvantages. It is still quite difficult to control the traffic and to know in advance how long it will take to send a new file to the entire network. Another problem is that the load on the broadband connection in each store will increase in a way that is hard to control.

For these reasons P2P systems still suffer from many of the problems associated with unicasting distribution systems. P2P systems are very often discussed in the digital signage business. However, in practice they are not that common. Most digital signage broadband networks use a central content management server that handles the individual distribution to each site.

TERRESTRIAL BROADBAND MULTICASTING

The most efficient way to solve all distribution problems in IP networks that serve a larger number of sites with the same content is *multicasting*. IP multicasting would relieve the content management server, and its connection to the Internet, from the increased load

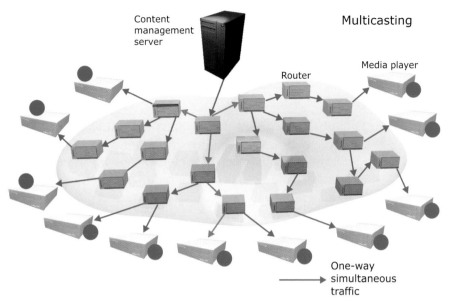

Figure 7.4 In IP multicasting, one message is sent simultaneously to a group of computers using only one-way communication.

caused by an ever increasing number of sites to be served. It also allows simultaneous distribution to all sites.

Multicasting means that the IP packets are sent just once from the source server. The packets make their way through the net, splitting up wherever necessary in the nodes (routers) of the network (Figure 7.4).

But terrestrial Internet operators do not like the "splitting up" effect since it could lead to an uncontrolled increase of traffic. Therefore, multicasting does not exist on the Internet and the routers used on the Internet are not enabled for multicasting. Multicasting IP addresses are recognized easily since they occupy the range between 224.xxx.xxx.000 and 239.xxx.xxx.255.

If multicasting had been allowed on the Internet there would also have been a problem how to assign the multicasting addresses. Multicasting addresses must be assigned to unique users since the packets could occur anywhere on the Internet. In order to use multicasting on the Internet, there has to be some kind of system for assigning the addresses to the users. Who is to use these addresses? The number of multicasting addresses is far fewer than the unicasting addresses.

The risk of running out of multicasting addresses is obvious. Ranges of unicast addresses are assigned to the ISPs who assign individual addresses to their subscribers. Doing the same with the multicasting address range is not practical since it is quite limited.

Private Network Multicasting

Though terrestrial multicasting is not allowed on the Internet, it can be implemented in local area and other private networks (Figure 7.5). Small private networks exist everywhere but it can be very expensive to build private networks on a national or international level.

If a satellite is used to handle multicasting on a national level (discussed next), LANs can act as the multicasting extension of the satellite feed to the media players. Therefore, on a local level, terrestrial broadband multicasting has its application.

The simple Ethernet switches used in smaller local area networks do allow IP multicasting. IPTV multicasting in local area networks is quite similar to analog and digital cable television. Everything that is broadcast can be received by anyone and by an unlimited number of receivers.

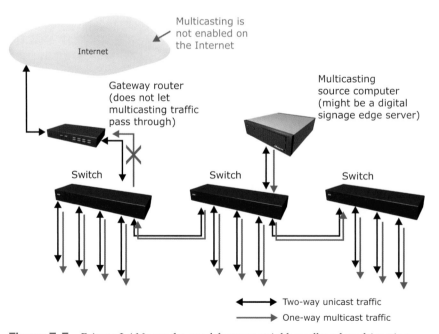

Figure 7.5 Private LANs can be used for terrestrial broadband multicasting.

Internet Group Management Protocol Join Request

There is one important issue to clarify. Multicasting means sending the same IP packet to a group of several computers in a network. IP broadcast means sending the same packet to all computers in that network. IP broadcasting is not very practical because not everyone wants to receive everything, and there is no use in sending packets in branches of the network where no one is listening. For this reason, the routers require that each receiving computer send an Internet Group Management Protocol (IGMP) join request before the multicasting path to that computer is opened.

Since the routers on the Internet are not enabled for multicasting, IGMP join requests are of no importance there. However, such requests are common in local area networks enabled for multicasting. Streaming computers and satellite modems also require an IGMP join request before providing a multicast IP stream. An IGMP leave request is sent when the receiving computer wants to leave the group.

The IGMP join and leave processes are carried out as point-to-point traffic (unicast traffic) between the multicasting source computer and the computer that is set to listen (Figure 7.6).

SATELLITE MULTICASTING

Radio and TV broadcasting, both digital and analog, are based on the assumption that the receiver is responsible for the quality of the received signal. Satellites contain transponders, each of which can distribute a number of TV channels. It does not matter if there is one receiver or 10 million. It still works.

Satellite Distribution

Most satellite communication is based on the use of geostationary satellites. These satellites are located in an orbit aligned with the equator at an altitude of 22,370 miles (36,000 kilometers) above it. This altitude was selected because it makes the satellites orbit Earth in 24 hours. As a result, the satellites appear stationary in the sky as seen from a location on Earth, if the satellites rotate east, the same direction as Earth. (See Figure 7.7.)

The satellites are located at fixed positions, relative to Earth, above the equator at a certain longitude. This longitude is referred to as

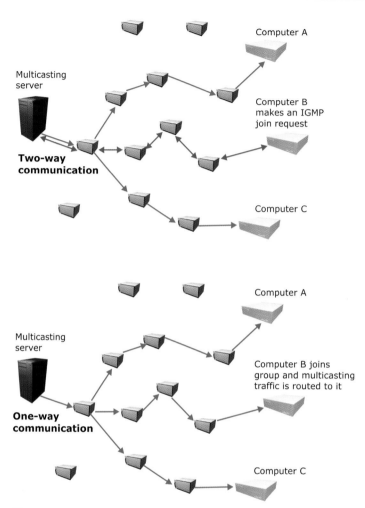

Figure 7.6 IGMP join requests avoid unnecessary multicasting traffic to branches of the network where there are no listening computers. In the top part of the figure, computer B makes a request (in unicast mode) to the multicasting server that it wishes to receive the multicast data. In the lower part of the figure, the multicast server has opened up the route to computer B that now can receive the multicast data.

the position, or *orbital slot*, of the satellite. The orbital slot of a satellite is chosen to provide maximum elevation angles (the height above the horizon for the satellite) for locations within the coverage area of the satellite (Figure 7.8). Therefore, most orbital slots are chosen to cover

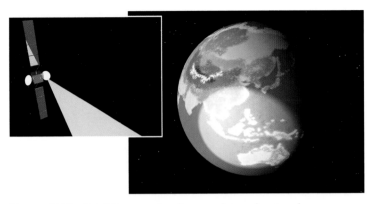

Figure 7.7 Satellites can simultaneously send a signal across continents to an unlimited number of receivers, such as across Southeast Asia and Australia in this example.

either the Americas, Europe and Africa, or Asia. There are also satellites optimized for trans-Atlantic or trans-Pacific traffic, though most satellite traffic across the Atlantic has been replaced by optical fibers.

Satellite communication uses microwave radio signals in selected frequency bands between 4 and 30 GHz. The signal from Earth toward the satellite is called the *uplink signal* and the signal from the satellite back to Earth is the *downlink signal*. As shown in Figure 7.9, the uplink frequency is higher than the downlink frequency. Uplinks in the 6 GHz frequency band correspond to downlink frequencies around 4 GHz (C-band) and 14 GHz uplink signals are downlinked at 11 or 12 GHz (Ku-band). Some uplinks operate in the 17 to 18 GHz frequency and the downlink signals are then also in the 12 GHz frequency band. There is also traffic in the 30 GHz uplink bands corresponding to about 20 GHz on the downlink (Ka-band).

The distance between Earth and the satellite is huge, and it takes about 0.25 seconds for the signal to jump from the ground to the satellite and back again. For example, if you are using a geostationary satellite-based phone line, there will be a delay before your voice is heard on the other side of the satellite path. This is quite disturbing, so most long-distance telephone providers have moved to optical fibers. This way, you cannot hear the difference between talking to your neighbor and talking to someone on another continent.

Because of the delay, geostationary satellite communication is mostly used for non-latency-dependent traffic such as distribution of television.

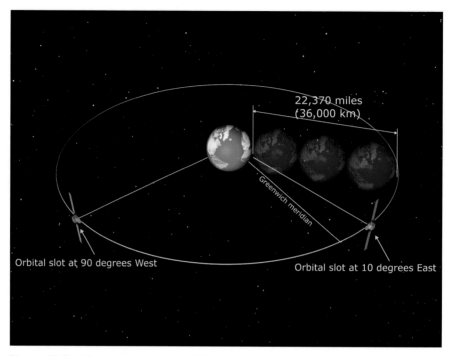

Figure 7.8 The geostationary satellites are located at orbital slots at a distance large enough to house three Earths between Earth and the geostationary orbit.

The uplink signal is produced by a satellite uplink station beaming an uplink signal that is received by an antenna in the satellite. First, the signal is amplified, then it is down-converted to the downlink frequency band and filtered to the transponder bandwidth. Finally, the signal is amplified using Traveling Wave Tube (TWT) amplifiers (or sometimes solid-state amplifiers). The signal is beamed back to the surface of Earth using an antenna that creates a beam that is shaped to fit the intended coverage area. Shaping beams is a way to optimize the satellite's output by reducing power that is unwillingly beamed toward unwanted areas such as oceans and countries not intended to be covered.

Each satellite is equipped with a number of transponders. A transponder is the equipment required to provide a radio channel with a bandwidth of about 30 MHz. Each transponder is also limited by its output power. The output power is given in a unit called Equivalent Isotropic Radiated Power (EIRP). The antenna diameter required (Figure 7.10) to receive satellite signals on the ground depends on the

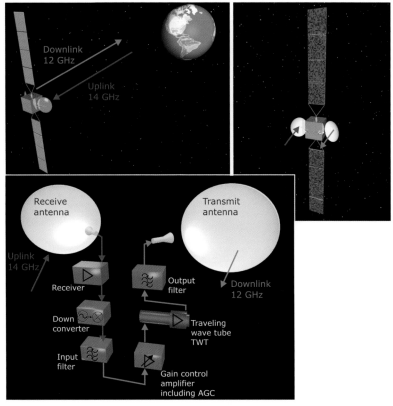

Figure 7.9 The uplink signal travels from Earth to a satellite, where it is converted to the downlink frequency, filtered through a transponder, and then sent back to Earth.

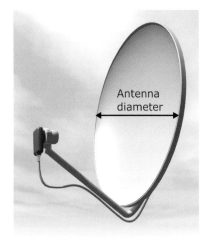

Figure 7.10 In offset antennas, the antenna diameter is the horizontal measure, as shown here.

Table 7.1 Relationship between the EIRP levels and antenna diameters* for satellites in the 12 GHz frequency band

EIRP (dBW)	Feet	Meters
41	6.23	1.90
42	5.54	1.69
43	4.92	1.50
44	4.40	1.34
45	3.94	1.20
46	3.51	1.07
47	3.12	0.95
48	2.79	0.85
49	2.46	0.75
50	2.20	0.67
51	1.97	0.60
52	1.74	0.53
53	1.54	0.47

*The diameters are for Ku-band reception (including rain margins for zones like Europe). In dry areas, dish diameters could be smaller.

output power of the satellite transponder to be received. Table 7.1 gives the relationship between EIRP levels and required antenna diameters for receiving signals from satellites operating in the 12 GHz downlink frequency band.

Most satellites used for direct-to-home distribution provide power levels around 50 dBW toward the primary coverage area. Within this area, antennas with diameters of about 2 feet (0.6 meters) can be used. Satellite footprints (also known as contours) can be found on the web sites of the satellite operators. Figure 7.11 shows three examples.

The geostationary satellites are located along a curve above the southern horizon when viewed from the northern hemisphere. In the southern hemisphere, the orbit is in the north. At the equator, the geostationary orbit is a straight line across the middle of the sky from east to west (Figure 7.12). To find a particular orbital slot, you have to know the elevation and azimuth angles of your reception site. Information on this can be available in the satellite operator's web

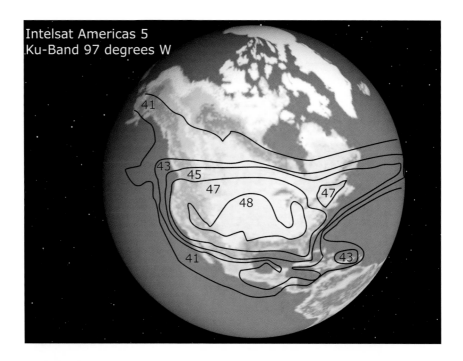

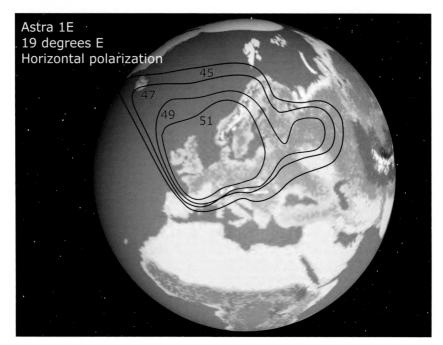

Figure 7.11 Satellite coverage maps with approximate EIRP contours (footprints) provide information about antenna diameters required. Here are one American, one European, and two Asian footprints. All are Ku-band.

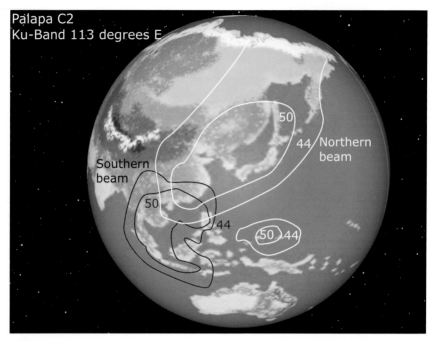

Figure 7.11   *(Continued)*

sites. In Figure 7.12, the uplink site is further to the north and to the east than the reception site.

Elevation and Azimuth Angles

When aligning a satellite dish or making the reconnaissance before a satellite installation, it is necessary to know the *elevation* and *azimuth angles* toward the satellite. The angles are defined in Figure 7.12. These angles can be calculated, but it is easier to use diagrams with precalculated curves. Figure 7.13 illustrates the elevation and azimuth angles for one satellite located directly on the Greenwich meridian, 0 degrees, facing Europe and Africa. Figure 7.14 shows angles for a satellite at 90 degrees east, facing Asia and Australia. The satellite in Figure 7.15 is facing the Americas at 90 degrees west.

In these figures, we can directly read rough figures for the elevation and azimuth angles. But what about other orbital locations—is there any way to have a diagram that covers them all?

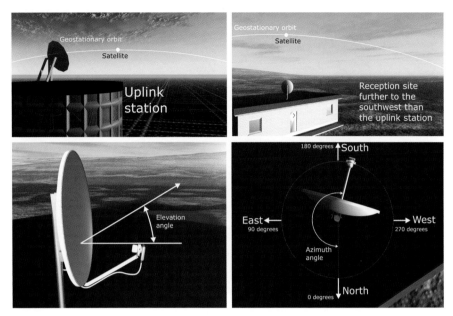

Figure 7.12 Viewed from the northern hemisphere, the geostationary orbit stretches across the southern horizon. To the left, is the uplink station feeding a satellite located straight south, meaning that the satellite is located at about the same longitude as the uplink site. To the right, the signals from the same satellite are received at a location farther west. Therefore, the satellite appears farther to the east in the sky than the uplink site. The reception site is closer to the equator, making the satellite appear higher in the sky than is the case at the uplink site. In this figure the elevation and azimuth angles used to find a satellite in the sky are defined.

Figure 7.16 looks different but is actually similar to Figures 7.13 through 7.15. In Figure 7.16 latitude and longitude have been included instead of a map. We need to calculate the difference between the longitude of our location and the longitude of the satellite. With Figure 7.16, it is possible to get rough estimations of the elevation and azimuth angles at any location on Earth for any orbital position of a geostationary satellite.

Here's an example. Our aim is to point a satellite toward the Echostar orbital slot at 148 degrees west using an antenna in San Francisco. San Francisco is at latitude 37.5 degrees north and longitude 122.5 degrees west. The angular difference between the satellite and the location's longitudes is 25.5 degrees (148 minus 122.5). The satellite is to the west relative to the reception site, and we are in the northern

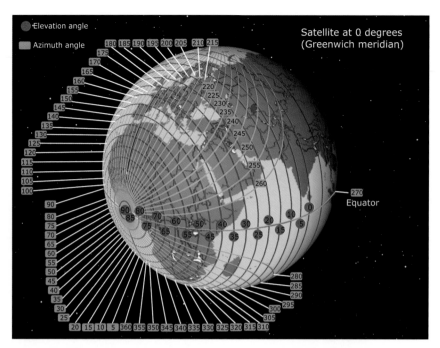

Figure 7.13 Elevation and azimuth angles toward a geostationary satellite at 0 degrees.

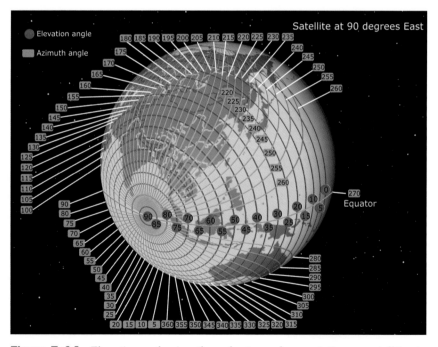

Figure 7.14 Elevation and azimuth angles toward a geostationary satellite at 90 degrees east.

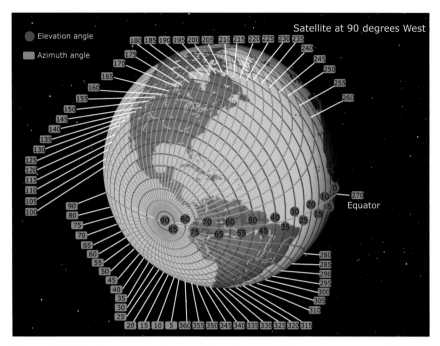

Figure 7.15 Elevation and azimuth angles toward a geostationary satellite at 90 degrees west.

hemisphere. So, the upper-right quadrant of Figure 7.16 should be used.

Using the white grid, find the location in the diagram where the latitude is 37.5 degrees and the difference in longitude is 25.5 degrees. Then estimate the elevation angle using the red curve. The correct elevation angle is 39.0 degrees. The azimuth angle is read using the orange curves and the correct value is 218.0 degrees. A diagram like this can be used only to make rough estimations of the pointing angles, but that is usually enough.

A second example is receiving Astra at 19 degrees east from Paris, which is at latitude 48.5 degrees north and 2.3 degrees east. In this case, the satellite is to the east relative to the receiving site. We are still in the northern hemisphere, so the upper-left quadrant should be used. The difference in longitude is 16.7 degrees (19 minus 2.3). Now find the right location using the white grid at latitude 48.5 degrees and the angular difference 16.7 degrees. The correct pointing angles are an elevation of 31.8 degrees and an azimuth of 158.3 degrees.

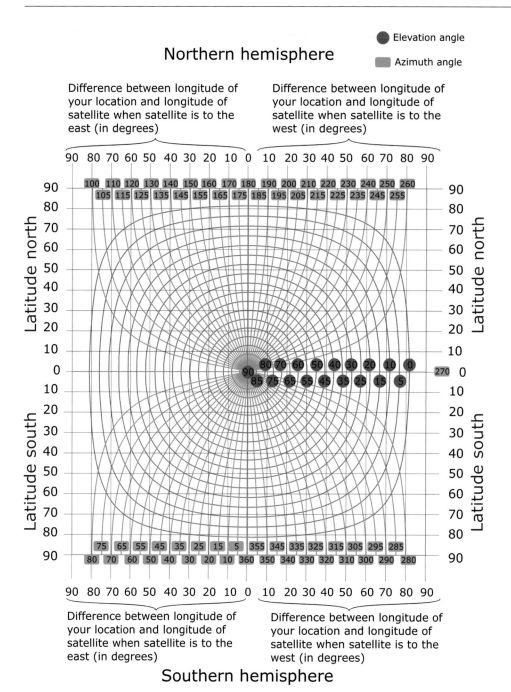

Figure 7.16 Diagram for estimation of the elevation and azimuth angles for any satellite and any location on Earth.

It requires some practice to read the diagram, but studying Figures 7.13 through 7.15 will help you understand better how the diagram is designed. The grid in Figure 7.16 is just "glued" to the Earth's surface for specific satellites. Figure 7.16 uses an invisible map that is defined only by the latitude and the longitude of your reception site.

Satellite Frequency Band Capacity

Most satellites transmit linear polarized signals. They can be vertically or horizontally polarized, and because the antennas used in the microwave frequency bands can achieve a very high level of isolation between the polarizations, the entire frequency range can be used twice (see Figure 7.17). An example is the downlink frequency band 10.70 to 12.75 GHz, which is used in Europe. From each orbital slot, a total

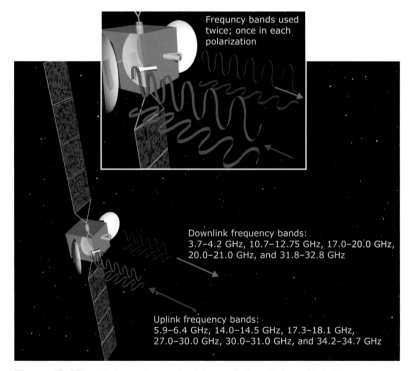

Figure 7.17 Various alternatives for uplink and downlink frequency bands. The 3.7–4.2 GHz uplink frequency band is combined with the 5.9–6.4 GHz uplink frequency band. The 10.7–12.75 GHz downlink frequency band is normally combined with uplink signals in the 14.0–14.5 GHz or 17.3–18.1 GHz frequency bands.

bandwidth of 4.1 GHz (2 × 2.05) is available. This corresponds to about 160 transponders from each orbital slot.

Satellite Signal Reception

Satellite signals are received primarily using parabolic reflector antennas. The received signal is concentrated in the focus of the antenna, where it is picked up by a low-noise block (LNB) converter. In the LNB, the signal is amplified and down-converted to a lower frequency (L-band 950–2,150 MHz) to avoid attenuation in the cable to the indoor satellite receiver set-top box (Figure 7.18).

Satellite signals can be horizontally or vertically polarized. By alternating the supply voltage from the receiver between 14 and 18 volts, the vertical and horizontal polarizations can be selected.

To receive a frequency range as wide as 10.70 to 12.75 GHz and to convert the signal into the L-band, the input frequency band has to be split into two parts. A common way to do this is to change the local oscillator in the LNB between 9.75 and 10.60 GHz. This is done by letting the satellite receiver send a 22kHz tone on the cable to the LNB. When the tone is there, the upper half of the frequency band is selected by using the 10.60 GHz local oscillator.

In the LNB, there is a control circuitry that detects the LNB supply voltage and determines whether there is a 22 kHz tone. An LNB with these features is called a universal LNB, common in Europe and other parts of the world.

Modulation is how to use a radio wave as a carrier of information. Altering the phase angle of the radio wave is one way. The most common way to modulate digital signals is quadrature-phase shift keying (QPSK). QPSK is used for most satellite digital video broadcasting signals. In each instant, the radio wave can show one of four phase angles and the receiver can detect the radio signal as having one of four possible states. These states symbolize one of four combinations of bits that are transmitted: 00, 01, 10, or 11 (Figure 7.19).

Digital Video Broadcasting

Most geostationary satellites are used to broadcast digital television signals. Most digital TV broadcasts use the digital video broadcasting

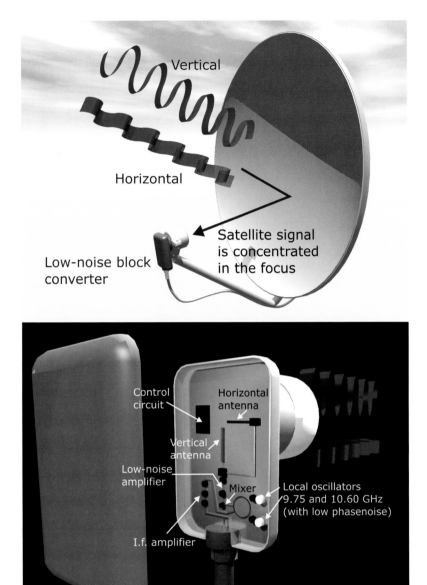

Figure 7.18 Satellite signals are received using parabolic reflectors with an LNB (*detail, bottom*) that amplifies and converts the signals into the L-band. Then the signals are fed to the satellite receiver set-top box.

Figure 7.19 QPSK modulation has four possible states.

(DVB) standard. Initially a European standard, DVB is now used in most other parts of the world as well.

Like IP, DVB is a packet-oriented protocol. Each packet has packet identification data (PID) that identify the signal to which the packet belongs. Different intensities of packets for different signals make it possible to mix high-bitrate signals, such as video streams, with less demanding signals, such as audio.

The first four bytes of a DVB packet are the header of the packet. This includes a synchronization word, the PID, and a counter that helps the decoder to get the packets processed in the correct order (Figure 7.20).

According to the DVB standard, each packet has an additional 16 bytes of data, that is, Reed-Solomon encoding data to provide error correction. So each transmitted DVB-S packet is actually 204 bytes. The Reed-Solomon error correction makes it possible to correct up to eight errors in a packet. If there are more errors, the packet will be rejected by the receiver.

In addition to the Reed-Solomon encoding, Forward Error Correction (FEC) is added to the stream. The level of error correction is chosen to fit the satellite channel. A very common FEC level is three-quarters, meaning that one-quarter of the transmitted signal contains bits added by the FEC. Using FEC half means that half the transmitted capacity is occupied by the FEC.

Standard-definition TV signals using MPEG-2 compression are often at about 4 Mbps, while a stereo audio multiplex may be 256 kbps.

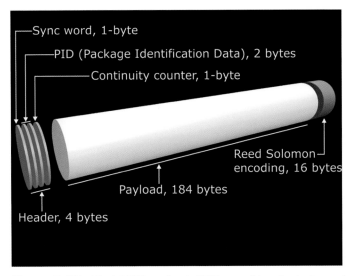

Figure 7.20 Each DVB packet is 188 bytes: 4 header bytes and 184 bytes of data payload.

A 33 MHz satellite transponder can carry a multiplex with a capacity of about 38 Mbps. Therefore, each transponder can distribute a number of TV channels (Figure 7.21).

Figure 7.22 shows a typical DVB satellite broadcast system. To fill one satellite transponder with one single carrier, a number of TV channels are multiplexed together, forming a combined DVB transport stream with a useful bitrate of 38 Mbps. However, portions of this capacity may be used for other purposes such as data channels.

A nice thing about DVB is that any kind of signal can be distributed. MPEG-2 encoding is slowly being replaced by MPEG-4 (H.264) AVC to carry HDTV. With DVB, the newer signal simply can be placed where the old encoding technology was used. This also makes it easy to use IP over satellite for multicasting to digital signage networks.

Internet Protocol via Satellite

Satellite is probably the simplest way to obtain IP multicasting capability, at least on a national or international level. Satellite IP broadcasting will probably be one of the most important ways to distribute content for digital signage in the future. Satellite operators are not

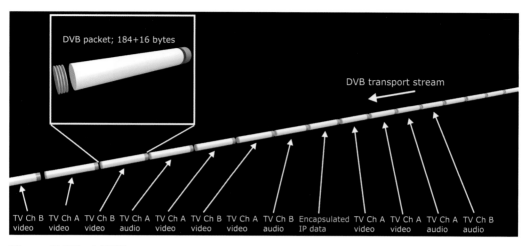

Figure 7.21   A DVB transport stream may contain a multiplex of various media channels—TV and radio channels and IP data channels.

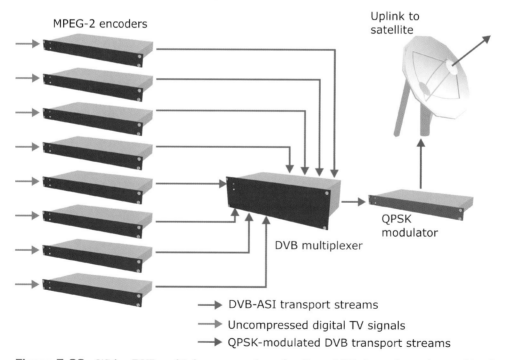

Figure 7.22   With a DVB multiplexer, a number of radio and TV channels can be combined into a single DVB transport stream.

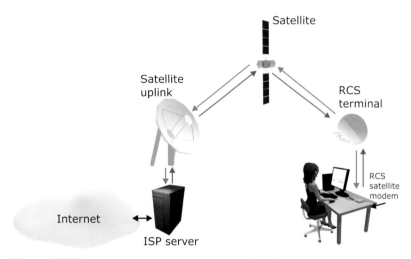

Figure 7.23 The most advanced version of satellite IP uses satellite in both directions, here using a satellite dish and an RCS terminal. The dish is actually a small satellite uplink.

afraid to offer multicasting because that is exactly what satellite broadcasting has been, right from the start.

Using satellite to distribute IP is nothing new. Similar techniques have been used to provide high-speed Internet access at locations where terrestrial broadband is not feasible. The most advanced way is to use two-way communications via satellite, called Return Channel over Satellite (RCS) (Figure 7.23). This is used in North America by StarBand and WildBlue and in Europe by TiscaliSat and Satlynx.

There is a more economical alternative where only the downstream is distributed via satellite and the return path uses a telephone modem (Figure 7.24). This way the terminal becomes much less expensive and is comparable to a direct-to-home digital satellite TV reception system. Of course, the return path will be quite slow and ties up the telephone line, sending requests to the ISP for files to be downloaded by satellite. This may also result in extra charges on the subscriber's phone bill.

Because of the delay of 0.25 seconds when the signal goes up to the satellite and back again, there are certain limitations on the services suited for satellite IP applications. Online games—dependent on the response times of the players—are not good for satellite distribution because a player with satellite connection will have his or her response

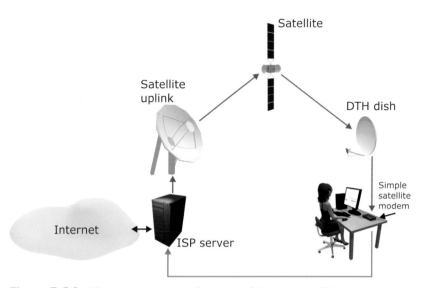

Figure 7.24   The more economical version of Internet satellite access uses a telephone modem as upstream connection to the ISP.

time increased considerably. However, for most Internet applications, other delays are more annoying than the satellite turn-around time.

We are used to distributing IP in a twisted-pair (TP) cable, and IP traffic can also be distributed in optical fibers or using satellite transponders. However, the signals always have to be adapted to the media to be used.

While there are hundreds of digital signage systems in use all over the world, there are only a handful of satellite multicasting systems to choose from. It is important to note that all these systems are proprietary even though they are used in conjunction with well-established systems such as DVB.

File Transfer   Internet Protocol is a very versatile way of distributing content, which makes it somewhat more complicated than conventional TV broadcasting. In radio and TV broadcasting, we always have a streamed signal continuously feeding the receivers with live content. In IP broadcasting, there are two possible ways of content distribution: file transfer and IP streaming. File transfer is used for non-real-time or near-real-time content and streaming is used for real-time live event distribution.

The basic distribution service for digital signage is file transfer. In most situations, this is a non-real-time service, like digital signage using broadband (described in Chapter 5). However, with multicasting, near-real-time file transfer is also possible. Quite a lot may be gained from this. Digital signs with content that needs to be updated continuously can be handled in an interesting and economical way. If the content contains text that needs to be updated, the updated information can be sent in separate text files, which will be very small because they do not have a lot of graphics or video. The backgrounds on the signs—more complex and larger files—can be sent in advance and do not have to be updated as often.

A multicasting server, in most cases, gets new files from an FTP server. The FTP server can be a separate server, as shown in Figure 7.25, or integrated in the multicasting server. This means that if the multicasting server is connected to an uplink, it is easy to reach the uplink from any Internet-connected computer in the world, provided that you have access to an account and a password. It has never before been so easy to reach a satellite uplink.

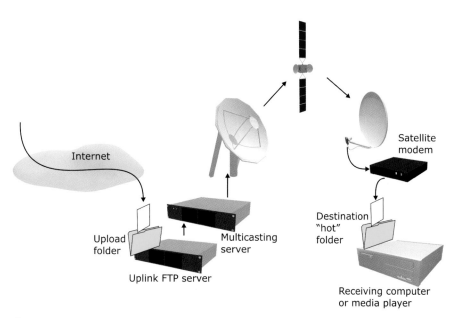

Figure 7.25   When a file is dropped into the upload folder of the FTP server, the file is automatically transferred to the destination "hot" folder of the selected receiving computers.

When a file is dropped into the FTP account upload folder, the file is automatically transferred via the satellite to the desired multicasting clients at the reception sites. In these receiving computers, there are destination "hot" folders where the files are stored for local use. A folder being "hot" means that it is online at both the origin and the destination side of the multicasting path.

The multicasting server does several steps of processing. First it detects if a new file shows up in the FTP server upload folder. If so, the file is transferred to the multicasting server to be inserted into a noncontinuous multicasting distribution channel (Figure 7.26). But before creating one or more multicasting IP channels, additional data are inserted, including error protection and data related to addressing of the multicasting streams. A checksum-based process is used to validate that the packets are correctly received at the other end.

In conventional unicasting traffic on the Internet, there is also a validation process; if this fails, the source computer is requested to send the damaged IP package again. In a multicasting system like this, we do not get requests back and retransmission cannot be done at the request of the receiving computer(s), unless there is a return path. For this reason, there must be a careful validation process at the receiving end and additional error protection might be needed.

There is error protection in the DVB distribution chain both as Reed-Solomon encoding and FEC. However, these means are intended for

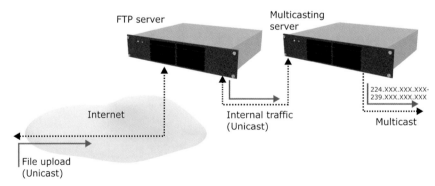

Figure 7.26 A multicasting server has the capabilities to send single or multiple files as a sequence of IP multicasting packets. The communication to the FTP and between the FTP and the multicasting server is unicasting.

continuous signals. Remember that an error in a file can be much more annoying than an error in a live TV signal. If some bytes are lost in a digital TV transmission, the result is just some pixilation or perhaps a second of blank screen. An error in an image file that is presented on a digital sign can be visible for a very long time, depending on how much and for how long that file is used. For this reason, the validation process of each file is important. At the very least, it prevents a damaged file from being used.

IP Streaming   The most common use of IP streaming is undoubtedly IPTV. The alternative multicasting source is a video encoder with an IP multicasting output. These encoders are very similar to DVB MPEG encoders and there are many encoders that can be ordered with DVB-ASI (Asynchronous Serial Interface) or IP multicasting outputs. In reality, these are just two alternative encoder output interfaces.

Hardware IPTV encoders like the one shown in Figure 7.27 are usually quite expensive, but that is because they must meet very high technical standards. (In Chapter 8, we will return to IPTV encoding using a freeware program, VLC, to make some experiments with streaming.) Using encoding and streaming software and a powerful computer is the alternative to dedicated hardware encoders. However, for most professional applications, hardware solutions based on appliances specifically made for their purpose are most commonly used.

Digital signage systems using terrestrial unicast broadband primarily use file transfer and only use streaming in very specific cases. You can

Figure 7.27   A video encoder with an IP multicasting output provides a continuous multicasting (IPTV) stream.

set up a unicast stream, but it has to communicate with all receiving computers separately. Therefore, there is always a limit to how many receiving computers can be served simultaneously. Stepping up to multicasting eliminates all these problems. To use satellite multicasting, however, we need to ensure that the IP streams can be encapsulated into a DVB satellite feed.

IP Encapsulation for DVB Distribution   One well-standardized part of the IP multicasting chain is *IP encapsulation*. IP encapsulation means using DVB packets to distribute the IP content. IP packets can be of various lengths but a common value is 1,500 bytes. Since each DVB packet has a useful data capacity of 184 bytes, each IP packet has to be divided into a number of DVB packets. This process is done using an IP encapsulator or IP gateway (Figure 7.28). In DVB systems, MultiProtocol Encapsulation (MPE) is used.

An IP encapsulator gets IP embedded in Ethernet frames on its input. These Ethernet frames contain information about MAC addresses (see Appendix B). Also there is checksum information that needs to be transferred to check the integrity of the IP packets when they arrive in the receiving computer. For this reason, there is some overhead added to the payload carried by the DVB transport stream packets (Figure 7.29).

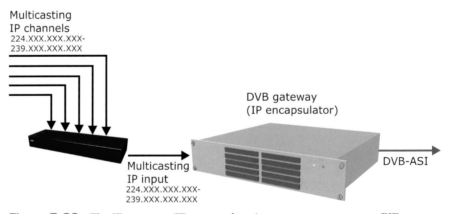

Figure 7.28   The IP gateway (IP encapsulator) can create one or more PIDs in a DVB transport stream. Each PID may contain one or more multicasting channels. An Ethernet switch may be used to combine the multicast channels that are to be fed to the DVB gateway.

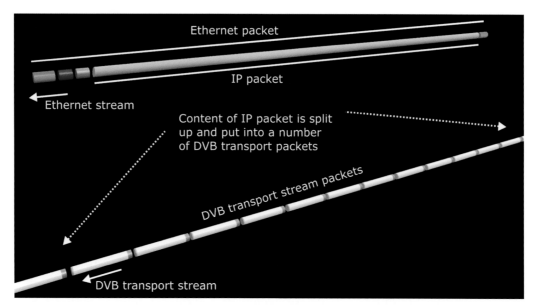

Ethernet packet

IP packet

Ethernet stream

Content of IP packet is split up and put into a number of DVB transport packets

DVB transport stream packets

DVB transport stream

Figure 7.29 The key to IP satellite broadcasting is using a multicasting server combined with an IP gateway (IP encapsulator). Some extra overhead capacity is required in each DVB packet in order to bridge MAC address information and checksums through the distribution chain (Ethernet bridging).

Digital Signage and Broadcasting Together

It is fascinating that files can be transmitted easily through the Internet. The content provider can be practically anywhere in the world. Non-real-time and near-real-time file delivery can use a conventional Internet connection to the FTP server at the uplink site. Delivery of live IP streams to the uplink station is a bit more complicated. Any kind of interruption in the transmission of a streaming IP signal is unacceptable; the quality of service (QoS) of the connection between the program provider and the uplink station must be guaranteed to be 100 percent. The contribution chain of an IP streaming service is as demanding as for any live broadcast channel.

In digital signage broadcasting, you are free to use file transfer in real-time, near-real-time, or non-real-time, in addition to using live streams. With multicasting, these various types of content can be combined in any way necessary for your digital signage configuration.

The other kinds of distribution, such as manual delivery of physical media and broadband over the Internet, have their limitations, especially when it comes to real-time applications and the ability to handle a large number of receiving sites simultaneously.

Figure 7.30 shows the full system with digital signage broadcasting integrated into a satellite DVB multiplex with six conventional MPEG-2 TV channels.

Receiving Satellite IP Signals

Satellite IP signals may be received via either a satellite modem or a satellite edge server.

Satellite Modems   The satellite modem has no way to process the received signal, other than to recover the multicasting IP signal and deliver it to an Ethernet port of the modem. In order to use the signal, the modem has to be connected to a separate computer that holds multicast client software. This software extracts the transferred files from the IP packets and loads them into a folder on the hard drive of the computer. This computer may also be a set-top box media player that carries the same facilities.

An alternative way to use a satellite modem is to connect it to an IPTV set-top box to receive a live IPTV stream. On the back plate of the simple satellite modem, there is an LNB input to connect the receiving satellite dish and an Ethernet connector where we can obtain the received IP that is to be sent to the computer. There is also a telephone line connection for the return path (Figure 7.31).

The simple satellite modem used for the one-way satellite Internet delivery system in Figures 7.30 and 7.31 is very similar to a digital satellite TV set-top box. In a real satellite modem, all the circuits are not as easy to see as they are in Figure 7.32, because most of the work is done by means of a processor and memory. But you would find a tuner at the input of the modem. Here the desired transponder is selected and the tuner also supplies the correct voltage to the LNB: 14 volts to receive vertically polarized signals and 18 volts to receive the horizontal. The tuner also injects the 22 kHz tone, if required, to switch between the upper and lower parts of the received frequency band if a universal LNB is used.

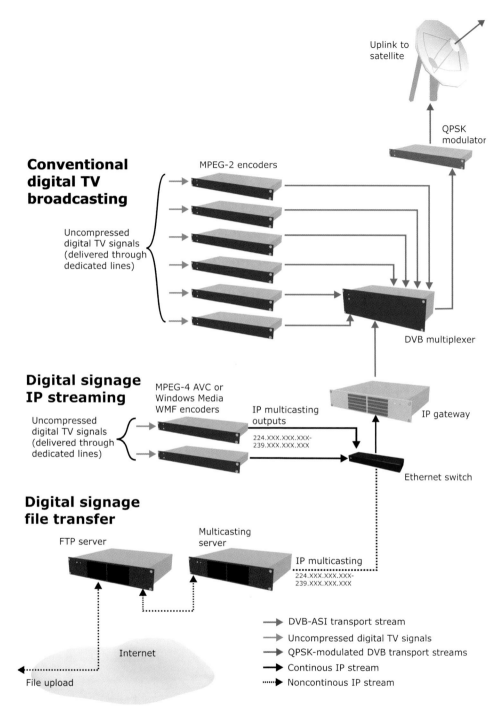

Figure 7.30 Digital signage broadcasting, where a DVB multiplex is shared with a number of conventional DVB MPEG-2 TV channels.

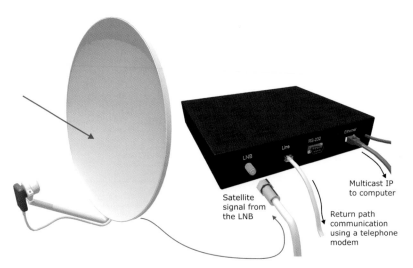

Figure 7.31 A simple satellite modem contains an LNB input, an Ethernet connection, and a telephone connection for the terrestrial return path.

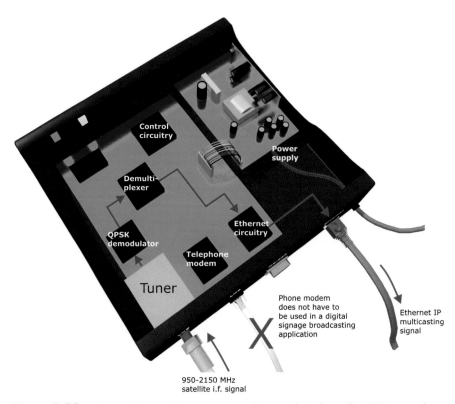

Figure 7.32 The satellite modem is very similar to a digital satellite TV set-top box.

The tuner is followed by a QPSK demodulator that retrieves the DVB transport stream that is sent to the demultiplexer. In a satellite modem, the demultiplexer is used to select the IP data PID (or PIDs) to be received. Finally, the IP is embedded in a new Ethernet stream that is available at the Ethernet interface. The received IP stream (or streams) is a multicast signal that does not normally require a response from the computer connected to the modem. However, sometimes the network interface of the modem requires an IGMP join request to be sent from the receiving computer.

Figure 7.33 shows how a satellite modem can be used to provide an Ethernet IP signal that can be sent to an IPTV set-top box or a computer for further processing. What may differ from one satellite modem to another is the number of PIDs that can be received. One PID can hold more than one multicasting stream but if the multicasting channels are on different PIDs, the modem has to be able to handle this.

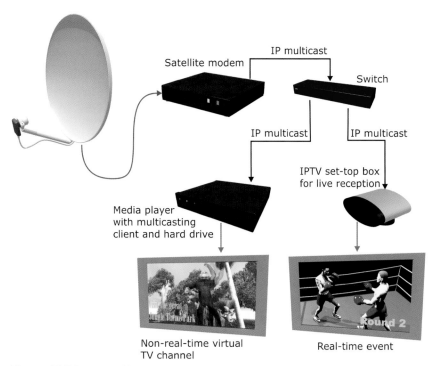

Figure 7.33 A satellite modem can be used to supply IP multicasting into a local area network with media players and IPTV set-top boxes.

Controlling the Receivers

A digital TV set-top box at home is controlled by the user. There might be automatic search features and the box might be preprogrammed one way or another, but there is normally no central control facility for the receivers even though there might be some limited ways to do this in some pay TV networks.

In stores and public locations, manual tuning is not acceptable if the satellite channel has to change the transponder or if other changes related to the distribution have to be made. Therefore, satellite modems and satellite edge servers are usually equipped with some kind of management system. The management system can send commands to single or groups of receivers to tune in on a different transponder or PID. This system can also be combined with some kind of encryption system when content is to be distributed to closed groups of receivers.

Of course, only one satellite transponder can be received at a time, since the modem only has one tuner.

A multicasting stream is defined by its IP address. However, the port number also may be used to identify specific file transfer services that are related to that IP address.

Satellite Edge Server By connecting a satellite modem to an edge server that carries a multicasting client, you could download files directly to the hard drive and media players in the vicinity could retrieve content from the server.

An even better idea would be to insert a satellite tuner card into the edge server itself. The result is a satellite edge server (Figure 7.34). The satellite edge server is extremely powerful not only as a streaming server but also as a router for received live streams and as storage for files that may be updated instantly using the satellite multicasting signal. The satellite site server is a perfect choice when it comes to providing multicasting services in local area networks (Figure 7.35).

Wireless LANs

Of course, a network in a shop also may be wireless. But, as discussed in the previous chapter, there are some disadvantages to using wireless LANs (WLANs) in public environments. A WLAN connection is a point-to-point unicast connection. This means that if packets are lost on

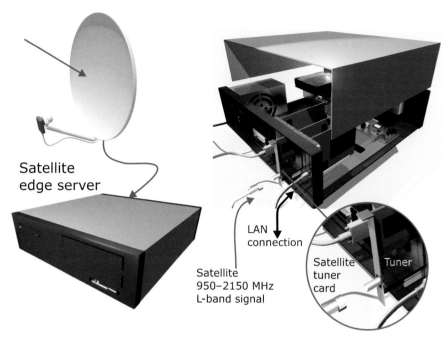

Figure 7.34 The satellite edge server is a computer equipped with a satellite tuner card.

the way to the receiving media player, they will be retransmitted. The shop environment is filled with interference, such as Bluetooth communications between cell phones; streaming video across such a connection might result in interruptions. Therefore, cabled LANs are preferable for IPTV streaming (Figure 7.36). However, for simple file transfer, a WLAN is a better choice. This way, any interruptions during the file transfer will only result in increased time for download to the media players.

Another problem in using WLANs is the risk for intrusion from outside. Media players usually always make a request to the edge server or the content management server. This is partially to withstand attacks from the outside but also to be able to use dynamic IP addresses. A multicast streaming session is set up by the media player or the IPTV set-top box starting with a unicast IGMP request to the source server. This way, the risks for intrusion, resulting in undesired multicast signals reaching the media players or IPTV set-top boxes, are minimized.

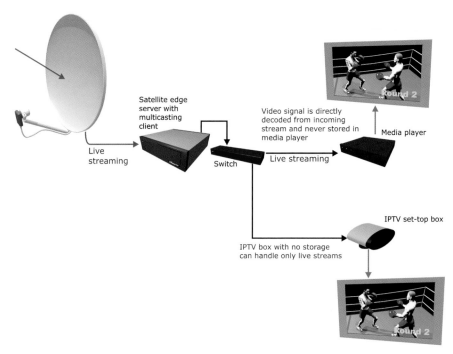

Figure 7.35   Live streaming channels and a satellite tuner card provide yet another way to use the edge server described in Chapter 6. The streams also can be stored in the server as files for later use.

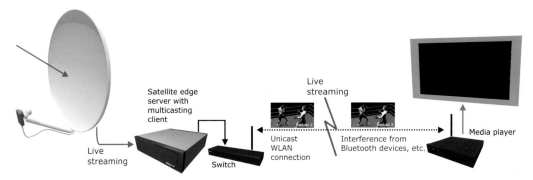

Figure 7.36   Cabled LANs are preferred to WLAN connections for IPTV streaming applications. Black screens or the frozen pictures might be the result if the WLAN connection is disturbed.

Other Ways to Use Satellite Transponders

Satellite IP multicasting so far has been described using broadcast transponders that also include conventional digital broadcasting TV channels. The advantage to using broadcast transponders is that they are operated in Automatic Gain Control (AGC) mode. The AGC ensures that the transponder is always saturated (providing maximum output power), as shown in Figure 7.37. Using saturated transponders makes it possible to use smaller consumer satellite dishes.

However, there is one disadvantage to using saturated transponders: A complete multiplex is needed to feed a transponder and all content for that multiplex has to be available at the same location. This requires bitrates of 38 Mbps using DVB-S and 50 Mbps using DVB-S2. This bitrate level is too much for today's digital signage networks. And if no TV channels are available to be using the same multiplex, it may be hard to fill up the transponder.

An alternative is to use transponders in linear operation. A transponder in linear mode contains several carriers linked from several locations. Such a carrier may have a low bitrate that is suitable as a digital signage distribution channel. There are, however, two significant disadvantages to using transponders operating in linear mode. The transponder cannot operate at maximum output power; it has

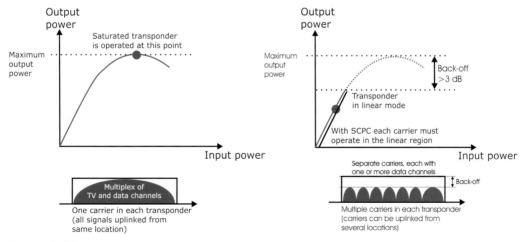

Figure 7.37 Transponders operating in linear mode allow low-bitrate uplinks at several locations instead of one single uplink for a complete transponder.

to be lowered to half or less of what may be achieved at saturation. Another disadvantage is that rain attenuation at the uplink site will affect the output power of the transponder since there is no automatic gain control in the transponder. As a result, larger antennas will be required at the receiving sites. Antenna diameters will increase by at least 50 percent compared to receiving broadcast transponders, as previously discussed.

Improvements Using DVB-S2

One of the latest additions to the DVB family of standards is DVB-S2, a toolbox of several modulation schemes, including 8PSK and 16APSK, improved filter roll-off factors, and error correction. With these improved error correction methods, it is possible to get more capacity from the satellite transponders. Introducing DVB-S2 makes it possible to increase the capacity of a standard 33 Hz satellite transponder, today operating with 27.5 MS/s and FEC = 3/4, from 38 Mbps by about 30 percent to almost 50 Mbps using the new tools. New TV set-top boxes are required to be backwards-compatible with DVB-S. This is not really an issue because people will have to get new set-top boxes for HDTV anyhow (discussed in Chapter 8).

Receivers for satellite IP signals will be affected in the same way. New satellite modems and satellite edge servers will be required as the new standards are adopted. However, DVB-S is very well established and it will be around for a long time. Most certainly, DVB-S2 will become a way to cut down on transponder costs, by up to 30 percent. In systems with many satellite modems, this reduction in costs may not compensate for the investment in new devices.

When adding an element of broadcasting to digital signage, we get a completely new medium that is capable of things that were never before possible. How can digital signage broadcasting be used now and by the content providers of the future? The next chapters will give us some of the answers and a glimpse into that possible future.

8

CONTENT AND CONTENT MANAGEMENT

This chapter and Chapter 9 look at digital signage from a content provider's point of view. It is my belief that today's TV stations, newspapers, and advertising agencies—along with all others working with media—will merge to form the media source of the future. These companies, not all of which are fully in existence yet, will provide media content to retail and public environments as well as to the home.

The example in Chapter 4 uses a media player (computer with Windows operating system) with PowerPoint software to create a simple digital signage system. You could say that the computer used to create the presentations worked as a kind of content management system. This is where we collected the files to go into the presentation and decided in what order to present the content (essentially, built a playlist). That same computer would probably have been used to burn CDs or DVDs to distribute the completed PowerPoint files. (Of course, we could use that computer to e-mail the files to the locations where they would be displayed.) The computer was used for content management, even though in a modest way.

In full-scale systems, there is a much bigger difference between the computers used for content management and media players. The content management server has to be able to do a multitude of things and the more management the server can do, the less functionality the media players must have. This means you can make the players simpler and less expensive. The content management server is also responsible for the distribution of content to the media players.

Chapters 5, 6, and 7 discuss transferring content and playlists from the content management server to the media players. But now we will focus on the content management server and how to collect content and produce the appropriate playlists. In Chapter 9, we will take a closer look at how to get the content to the content management server.

THE CONTENT MANAGEMENT SERVER

The digital signage content provider has to have somewhere to store content where the distribution chain to the players begins. The term *content management server* is used for the server where the content is originally stored.

If distribution is handled manually, the content management server only acts as an archive. Perhaps it also contains a database with facts about the signage locations and media players.

If the distribution is done automatically through broadband, the content management server is also responsible for the distribution of the content. For this reason, such servers are often referred to as content distribution servers.

In a satellite multicasting digital signage system, the content management server is feeding content to only the multicasting server at the uplink station. The multicasting server is the equipment actually doing the distribution part.

The content management server could be a simple device at the digital signage operator's premises or (more common) a professional, 19-inch, mounted device installed in a hosting company. The most common activities in today's hosting companies are web hosting.

The content management server can be located anywhere. The managing of the server is, in most cases, handled by Web clients, and the server can be operated from any computer connected to the Internet with a login account and a password (Figure 8.1). There are content management servers in the United States that serve media players in Europe. The most important thing is that the content management server is located in a safe place with an uninterrupted power supply (UPS) and trained personnel who can ensure that the server stays in operation at all times.

Very often, the content management servers are Linux-based servers that can be accessed through the web interface of Windows or Mac

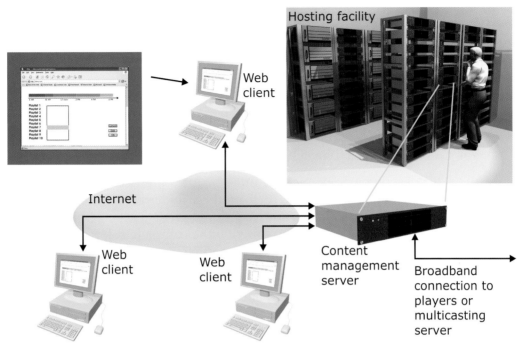

Figure 8.1 The content management server is the heart of the digital signage system.

computers. The web interfaces link the Linux and UNIX machines to the outside world of Windows and Mac clients.

CONTENT AS FILES

In digital signage, there are two basic types of content: content files and content streams. This also means that there are two kinds of distribution: file transfer and streaming. First, we will take a closer look at common content file formats and file transfer. At the end of the chapter, we will look at some ways to do practical tests with streaming.

In conventional broadcast media, which is a kind of streaming media, there are well-standardized audio and video formats. This makes everything fairly simple, compared to digital signage, where there is no such standardization. In principle, any known file format can be used in digital signage. This is a strong point as well as a serious weakness. Different digital signage systems have their favorite media file and stream formats. However, a careful and clever selection of file formats will offer advantages.

Image Formats

Images are built up by pixels, and each pixel is described by a number of bits. In grayscale pictures, each pixel is often divided into 256 shades of gray ranging from pure black to pure white. In order to describe brightness at 256 levels, 8 bits of information are needed. From this we get the 8-bit grayscale file formats.

To describe a color picture, three pictures are needed, one each for red, green, and blue. If each of these pictures is based on pixels divided into 256 levels and each level needs 8 bits, 24 bits of information will be required to describe the complete color picture. From this, we get the 24-bit color image format.

The size of a picture file depends on the number of pixels. The larger the picture, the more pixels, and therefore the larger the file.

Since digital signage systems are mostly based on computer graphics, picture file resolution must be high. This is quite necessary because most advertising applications involve text. Text requires a very high resolution because people tend to compare digital text with printed text and expect a similar level of crispness and clarity. This is also the reason computer screens reached higher resolution many years before television.

The most common compressed image format is undoubtedly the JPEG format (Joint Photographics Experts Group). This file format makes it possible to reduce the file to about one-tenth of its original size without significant loss of quality (Figure 8.2).

Video Formats

Video clip and video stream formats vary. Various kinds of MPEG (Moving Pictures Experts Group) formats are used. MPEG-2 and

Color Printing Formats

Another format, the 32-bit CMYK format, is used for color printing. This format is used because each of the C, M, Y, and K components (8 bits each) describes one printing layer. *C* is for the cyan component, *M* is for magenta, *Y* is for yellow, and *K* is for black.

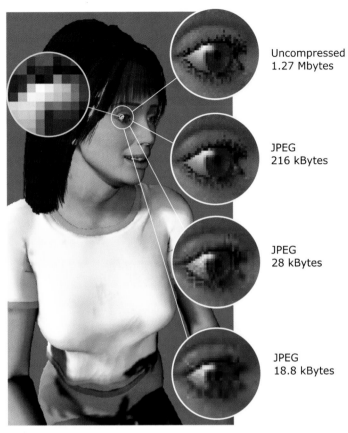

Uncompressed
1.27 Mbytes

JPEG
216 kBytes

JPEG
28 kBytes

JPEG
18.8 kBytes

Figure 8.2 A sample image compressed in several levels using the JPEG format.

MPEG-4 (H.264/AVC, Advanced Video Coding) as well as Windows Media (WMF) are the most common. MPEG-4 has the potential to be twice as efficient as MPEG-2, and WMF files have about the same compression capabilities that MPEG-4 will have when fully developed. In the long run, an MPEG-4 file will be half the size of an MPEG-2 file that contains the same video clip. This means it will be possible to stream MPEG-4 at half the rate of streaming MPEG-2 while maintaining the same subjective quality level. However, MPEG-4 compression software and hardware encoders have not yet reached their optimum performance. MPEG-2 had similar problems in its early days. In general, MPEG-4 will have the most support among broadcasting people, and WMF is widely accepted in the world of computers and telecommunications. Digital signage is somewhere between these worlds.

The main idea behind video compression is to avoid distributing the individual pictures that make up a moving image. Instead, the differences between two consecutive pictures are extracted. This results in significantly less information to transmit than if these two images were transmitted in their entirety (Figure 8.3). Pictures are divided into *groups of pictures (GOPs)*, and one complete picture is sent in the beginning of each group. The rest of the pictures are calculated from the first picture, and the difference data, which require far fewer bits than the complete pictures, are distributed. Even the picture sent at the beginning of the group is compressed as a JPEG file (MPEG-2). The length of

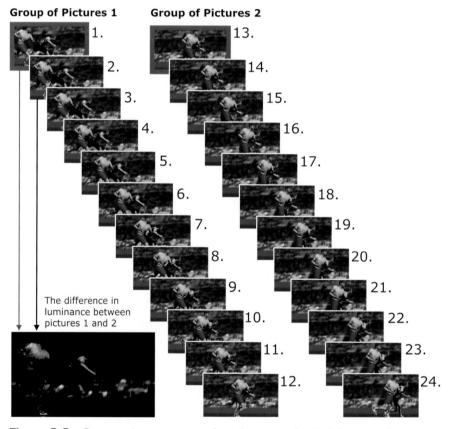

Figure 8.3 Compression systems are based on several principles, one of them is using similarities between pictures. Only the first picture in each GOP is distributed as a JPEG image. The black areas in the luminance difference picture do not contain information. Only the bright areas contain information that has to be transferred.

a GOP may vary, but 12 pictures in each group are quite common. Each time there is a new scene, the content of the picture changes more than between two consecutive pictures within a scene. For this reason a new GOP has to start with each change of scene.

By using this kind of compression, the bitrate of an uncompressed standard-definition TV signal can be decreased from 170 Mbps to about 4 Mbps when using MPEG-2. WMV and MPEG-4 allow a further decrease of the bitrate.

When presenting video clips in smaller regions, a lower bitrate is required than for full-screen applications. This is one way to keep file sizes and bitrates in streams at acceptable levels.

Animation Formats

As an alternative to pure video files, flash animations are somewhere between live motion video and still pictures. The major difference between video and animation clips is the way they are produced. Video clips are produced primarily with video cameras and editing systems, and animation files mostly contain completely computer-produced moving graphics.

The most popular animation file format is the Flash format, and some digital signage systems use the Flash format for everything.

Audio Formats

Common audio file formats are WAV, MP3, and WMA. In most cases, the compressed audio is embedded in video clip files, but nothing prevents the use of separate audio files (as if the digital signage system were transmitting radio), though it's not common in digital signage applications.

STORING THE CONTENT

Different kinds of content are stored in the content management server. Some of the content is long-lived video files or background images, while other content is more short-lived, like advertisements or promotions that last only a week. There are even very short-lived content scenarios, such as news ticker text files, stock market figures, or gambling odds data.

The content management server must contain all content currently in the digital signage system. In most cases, the content management server also contains all content ever used. So it also acts as a kind of archive, which means there is a mass storage problem to solve with redundant hard drives such as RAID (Redundant Array of Independent/Inexpensive Drives/Discs) systems.

Knowing What Content Is Where

All content is supposed to be available in the content management server itself. This may be comparable to the archive parts of a content management system used in a broadcasting company. There you will find everything that has ever been broadcast. In real-time distribution systems, such as television, you only have to keep track of what has left the playout. Once content has been broadcast, it disappears and exists only in the archive. As a result, the amount of information in the digital signage content management server can be very extensive.

In digital signage systems, we need to know what content is presently stored at locations within the system other than the content management server itself (Figure 8.4). The media players may have hard drives or flash memories where content is stored and, in larger installations, there also might be edge servers that contain content. Of course, the

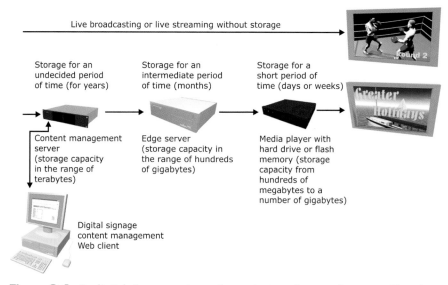

Figure 8.4 In digital signage systems, the content can be stored at several locations along the way to the media players.

content contained at these locations may not be there forever—they are designed to hold only the content that is currently in use.

It is necessary to keep track of what is stored where so that if content is missing anywhere, it can be distributed again to that location. It is also important to be able to track the capacity of the local storage media to ensure they are not getting filled up. (This calls for different kinds of maintenance procedures, further discussed in Chapter 10.)

The principle of storing content automatically along the way from the content provider is one unique feature of digital signage systems. This minimizes the amount of content that needs to be distributed in the network because everything, in most cases, needs to be distributed only once. Another advantage is that the content can be used in a different way at every location; this will be the major feature in future consumer applications for digital signage at home.

CONTENT MANAGEMENT IN PRACTICE

Let's take a closer look at handling digital signage content from a practical perspective. Since there are hundreds of digital signage systems out there and standardization is scarce, I have chosen to illustrate the different procedures in handling a content management system by creating a simplified demonstration.

Creating the Playlists

The content management server stores the playlists in addition to all the content. Playlists are created manually using the Web clients, often following the principles shown in Figure 8.5. The system needs to accommodate the ability to update playlists whenever needed, and the ability to create very complex playlists and schedules (which are essentially playlists that handle playlists).

Creating playlists is similar to producing TV programs. You choose the content, which can include video clips, still images, sound effects, and tickers. In some systems, you can split the screen into regions and have one playlist running for each region, with different types of content in each region.

To make it simple, we will describe here the handling of a virtual TV channel playlist with four video clips (Figure 8.5). First, the horror. mpg clip is played and then the show.mpg, shoes.mpg, and park.mpg

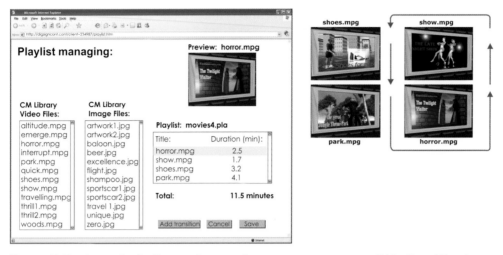

Figure 8.5   A sample playlist creation page in a content management Web client. Here four video clips are scheduled to play in a loop of 11.5 minutes.

clips are played in sequence. In the playlist managing menu, we can see the length of each clip. By looping the playlist, the content is repeated every 11 minutes and 30 seconds (sum of the time for the clips). Figure 8.6 shows a more advanced playlist that contains still images and video clips.

The length of display for a video clip or an animation file is set by the file, but when selecting still image files we also have to decide how long each file should be played.

Transitions   Of course, it is important to have suitable transitions between the video clips, animation files, and still images. The transitions are not handled by the content management server; instead, this is a feature included in the media player. The transitions, however, are decided by the person who creates the playlist, and he or she includes the command to use a certain transition in the playlist.

Scheduling   Scheduling is quite similar to making playlists, though at a higher level. While building a playlist can be compared to editing a TV program, which is one small portion of a TV broadcast, creating a schedule is more like compiling a collection of TV programs into a full day's worth of programming. Here the timeline is of extreme importance. The daily, weekly, or even monthly schedule contains

Figure 8.6 In most digital signage applications, there is a mix of video clips and still images. Here a still image (beer.jpg) is included in the playlist of video clips.

information about when the different playlists are to be played and which regions of the display are to be used. In a digital signage broadcasting system that allows live distribution, even live events can be included. During that distribution, instead of using a playlist, the media player is changed into a live stream player for a certain amount of time.

Scheduling files are created manually using a Web client, just as playlists are, and they control which playlists are used at certain times. Timeline tools are often used to facilitate the scheduling (Figure 8.7).

Figure 8.8 shows an example from an aerospace museum. Five regions are controlled by three scheduling files. Controlling multiregion screens means several scheduling files have to be created, but then each region can be run independently. The mix of content in the multiple regions makes it possible to use one configuration of messages at several locations in the museum, thus promoting the movies or making text-based content anywhere there is a display. Still there is a possibility to include information that is specific to the individual screen in any of the regions.

Controlling the Media Players

Both playlists and schedules can be activated by being downloaded to the media players and overwriting earlier playlist and schedule versions with identical filenames.

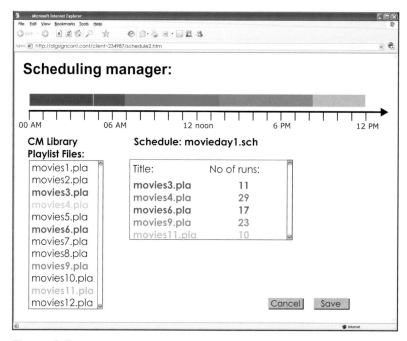

Figure 8.7   Schedules are playlists that control playlists.

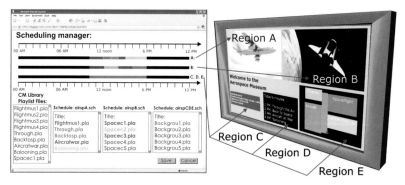

Figure 8.8   A scheduling manager. Region A shows that trailers to
promote the movies in the museum theater are shown at different hours
in the afternoon. Region B shows content that is not related to region A.
Regions C, D, and E contain background material that does not change
frequently; they are controlled by a very simple common scheduling file.

It is essential to note that in a broadband-based digital signage system, the files are not actively sent to the media players by the content
management server. Instead, the media players retrieve the files from

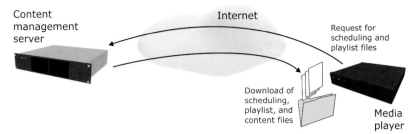

Figure 8.9 As scheduled, a media player requests content from the content management server. A simple way to control the content stored in the media player is to download new playlists and schedule files with the filenames of files they are to replace.

the content management server. The media players are programmed to contact the content management server at specific times to check for new instructions (Figure 8.9). It may do so as often as several times a minute or as rarely as once or twice a day. This depends on the purpose of the content. Media players are much more active than conventional broadcast set-top boxes, which simply wait for signals to be fed from the outside.

To call the content management server, the media players need to know the IP address of the content management server as well as the path to the folder that holds the content on the server. Using the same filenames for the scheduling and playlist files and overwriting previous files is one way to keep the number of files stored in the media players at an acceptable level.

Digital Signage Message Channels Each media player must have an identification number. A media player is assigned to produce a video signal that will feed a screen that is there for a specific message. So, in a location with more than one display, we will have to keep track of which media player is used with which screen.

One way to handle this is to assign a task number to each media player unit. In such a system, the task number is connected to the message that is to be distributed on the screen.

Imagine a retail chain where six different messages are displayed on six screens in each store. Assume that there are 300 stores across North America, and we want to control these screens accurately.

If two screens show the same message in one store, we miss the opportunity to promote the product that was supposed to be featured on one of the screens.

In this scenario, six different digital signage message channels would be created. Each media player in each location is programmed to one message channel. As in Figure 8.10, every store would have one media player listening to channel A, one listening to channel B, and so forth. The message channel is like a TV or radio channel that broadcasts its message to the devices that are "tuned in."

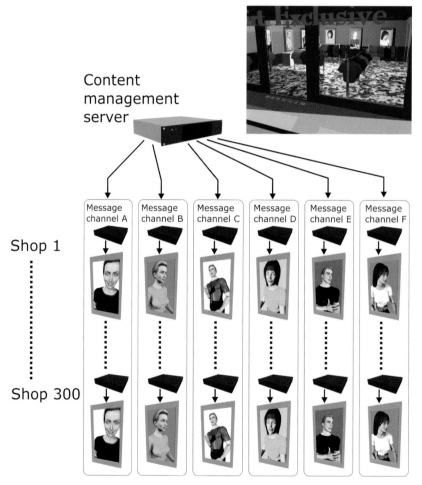

Figure 8.10   Digital signage message channels control what message is broadcast to each media player in each location.

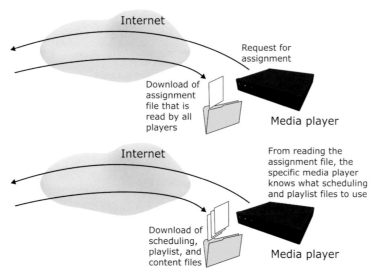

Figure 8.11   Assignment files control the playlists, scheduling, and content files downloaded to each media player.

If a media player should fail and have to be replaced, the installer has to reprogram the new media player to receive the correct digital signage message channel.

An alternative way of handling message channels is using an assignment file (Figure 8.11) containing a list of all media player identities and the corresponding scheduling files to be used by each player. All media players in the system must be programmed to find and read the assignment file to know their tasks. In this case, the system installer has to report back to the content management system which media player ID has to be used to present which message channel; the assignment will be centrally controlled.

Keeping Track of the Media Player Population   An important part of content management is creating groups of media players that should contain and display specific content. In the T-shirt store scenario described in Chapter 6, all the media players that listen to channel A would be grouped together to make digital signage systems manageable (Figure 8.12). That way, when the message on channel A changes, the new content can be distributed to all the media players in group A. Or, if using a system with assignment files, the grouping can be created

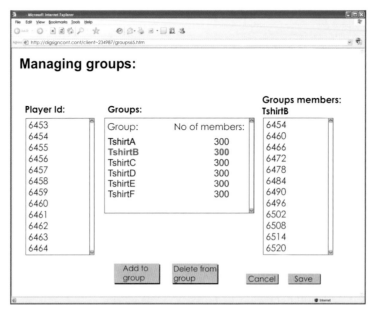

Figure 8.12 Grouping the media players makes larger digital signage systems manageable.

easily by giving several media players the same assignments in the control assignment file.

The content management server must also keep track of all the media players' locations. In many cases, the media players display local content, so they must be treated as individual players in addition to as members of a certain group. Most content can be downloaded to a large number of media players, but the playlists may be individualized for use by just one media player. Also, in systems that have a return path, the identity of a specific player is used when receiving alarms and playlogs.

Monitoring the System The content management server is responsible for monitoring the status of the media players when it comes to alarms and for collecting logs generated by the individual units. But there is also the task of monitoring what is shown on the screens. The quality of television broadcasts can be monitored by simply watching the final tape or file with the program. However, the digital signage broadcast does not take on its final appearance until all the elements are processed and displayed by a specific media player. One way to monitor this is to simulate the final screens in the Web client that controls the content management server using the actual content files and playlists. Theoretically, this is the most efficient way of handling the monitoring problem. However, in practice it may be hard to rely on this kind of solution.

The best, though complicated, way to monitor the final appearance of the digital signage message channels is to have a set of media players receive the files and to display the final result on screens. This may be done both in advance to test new playlists and content but also to monitor ongoing operations in a digital signage system.

There is room for many innovations when it comes to monitoring digital signage systems.

Alarm Handling If something goes wrong with a media player or an edge server, there are two ways of getting the content management server to attend to the problem. If it is a minor problem, the media player can send an alarm to the content management server. However, this will not work if the media player fails in a way that prevents it from sending alarms (for example, if the power goes out and the media player is completely shut down). A way to get around this is to program the media players to call the content management server frequently. If the content management server has not been in contact with a certain media player for a set period of time, it will assume that the unit is faulty and needs attention.

The media players also can be used to monitor the condition of the screens and to send status data back to the content management server.

Playlogs One way to know if the digital signage system is operating properly is to review the logs generated by the media players. These files include statistics such as what content has been shown on the screens, what requests have been made by customers using customer terminals, and so on. With a return path established, these playlogs can be sent to the content management server for administrator review. This means that directories and file management practices must be implemented to ensure that the playlogs are properly handled and stored.

In broadband digital signage systems, there is always a return path available. In digital signage multicasting systems, just as in any other broadcasting systems, the availability of a return path is not that evident. A separate unicast-based return path would be necessary (covered in more detail in Chapter 9).

Content Management for Edge Servers and Satellite Multicasting Systems

Broadband-based digital signage systems are administered by the content management server only, as shown in Figure 8.13. Things get a little more complicated when an edge server is inserted into the chain (Figure 8.14). But still, everything is controlled by the content management system alone. Digital signage multicasting systems can, however, be administrated on more than one level.

As mentioned, there are hundreds of digital signage systems in the world but there are only a handful of satellite multicasting systems. This makes it necessary to interface broadband digital signage systems

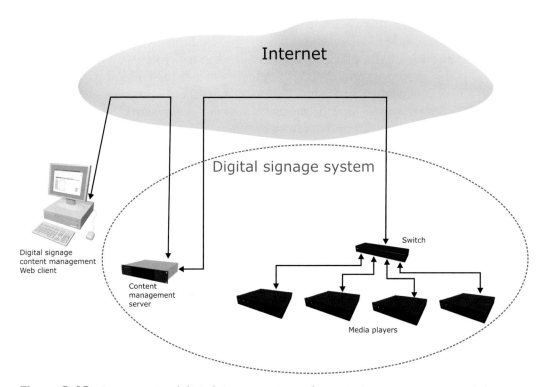

Figure 8.13 In conventional digital signage systems, the content management server is in direct control of the media players.

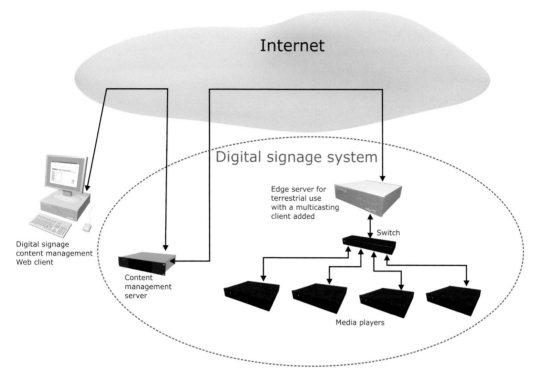

Figure 8.14   If edge servers are used, the content management server must keep track of the content and downloading of files to these servers as well as to the media players.

with satellite multicasting platforms. Satellite multicasting systems also have their own administrative tools. So, in order to download files to specific satellite edge servers, groups or individual edge servers or computers must be defined to receive the files. For this reason, some features will be doubled when the systems are combined.

However, if used strategically, the administrative tools of the satellite multicasting platform can complement the digital signage system. The best way to split the tasks between the satellite multicasting platform and the digital signage system is to let the satellite multicasting platform take care of the transport tasks like directing the receivers to the correct satellite transponders and PIDs. The satellite platform might also include some kind of encryption or a database containing the authorized receivers.

On the other hand, the multicasting platform database might take care of which receiving multicasting clients are allowed to download what files to the hard drives of the edge servers. Then the digital signage system should take care of the same tasks it does when used in a terrestrial broadband system, basically controlling the media players. Figure 8.15 shows how to interface a satellite multicasting platform with a digital signage system.

A satellite modem can be used to feed an edge server intended for terrestrial broadband use (Figure 8.15). Some digital signage systems primarily intended for terrestrial broadband use have edge

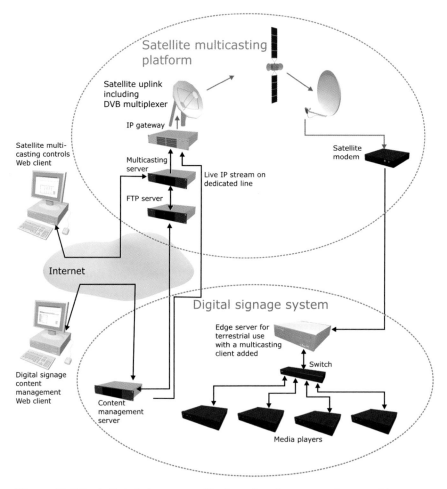

Figure 8.15　A digital signage satellite broadcasting system is created by combining a satellite multicasting platform with a conventional digital signage system. In this case, the edge server belongs to the digital signage system.

servers, and in this case the edge server is controlled from the content management server rather than from the satellite multicasting server. The edge server has to have a multicasting client installed that does the same job as the multicasting client of a satellite edge server.

An alternative is to use a multicasting platform that includes satellite edge servers (Figure 8.16). In this situation, the media players have to retrieve files from the satellite edge server using FTP, HTTP, or any of the shared folder protocols (discussed in Chapter 6).

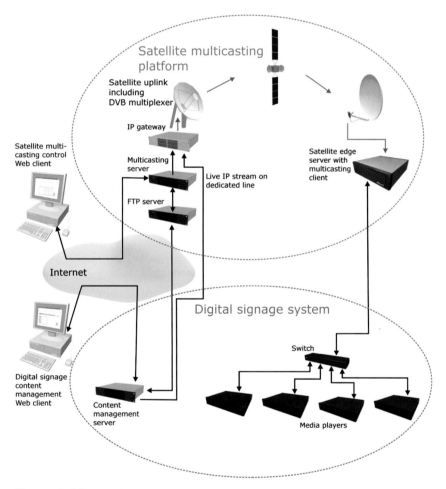

Figure 8.16 Satellite servers can be used in more specialized satellite multicasting digital signage systems. Here the satellite edge server belongs to the satellite multicasting system.

Controlling the System

To summarize, the content management server has to be able to deliver the content files to the media players and edge servers. The scheduling and playlist files needed to control the use of the content files are downloaded the same way. Special-assignment control files, read by all media players, can be used to let each player know which scheduling files to use to provide the correct digital signage message channel on the screen.

In a broadband-based digital signage network, the media players request content and administrative files from the content management server. So the only thing the content management server has to do is to stand by for the files to be retrieved by the media players. System security is the primary reason to configure the network this way. The media players in most systems will not accept a connection request from outside. This means the content management server will be receiving connection requests fairly frequently. If several media players call on the content management server simultaneously and there is a collision, mechanisms built into the system will make the media players issue a repeat request to the content management server after a short waiting period.

In a multicasting digital signage broadcasting system, however, the content management server has to actively deliver the files to the FTP server of the multicasting platform, which then forwards the files to the edge servers (if any) and the media players. So, in a multicasting system, the content management server will act in a much more "broadcast"-like fashion. The media players still "fetch" their instructions and content, but in this case from the edge server.

If the multicasting client is embedded in the media player, the situation is quite similar to ordinary broadcasting. The files are directly downloaded into the hard drive of the player itself. This alternative is shown at the bottom of Figure 8.20. Downloading files by satellite to a single media player is most appropriate to systems with one screen only. Such cases may be single outdoor screens at locations that have no broadband connection or other applications where a more economical single-screen solution is desired.

Figures 8.17 to 8.20 summarize how the media players are controlled by requesting scheduling, playlist, and (if applicable) assignment

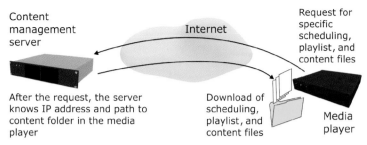

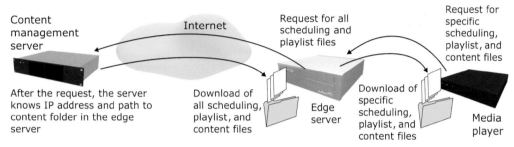

Content management server

Internet

Request for specific scheduling, playlist, and content files

After the request, the server knows IP address and path to content folder in the media player

Download of scheduling, playlist, and content files

Media player

Figure 8.17 Basic broadband-based digital signage system that consists of only a content management server and media players.

Content management server

Internet

Request for all scheduling and playlist files

Request for specific scheduling, playlist, and content files

After the request, the server knows IP address and path to content folder in the edge server

Download of all scheduling, playlist, and content files

Edge server

Download of specific scheduling, playlist, and content files

Media player

Figure 8.18 Broadband-based digital signage system with an edge server.

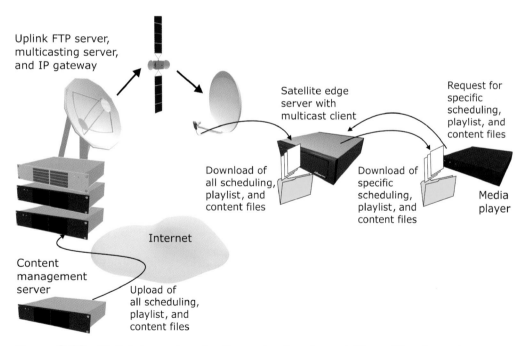

Uplink FTP server, multicasting server, and IP gateway

Satellite edge server with multicast client

Request for specific scheduling, playlist, and content files

Download of all scheduling, playlist, and content files

Download of specific scheduling, playlist, and content files

Media player

Internet

Content management server

Upload of all scheduling, playlist, and content files

Figure 8.19 Digital signage broadcasting system based on satellite multicasting and satellite edge servers.

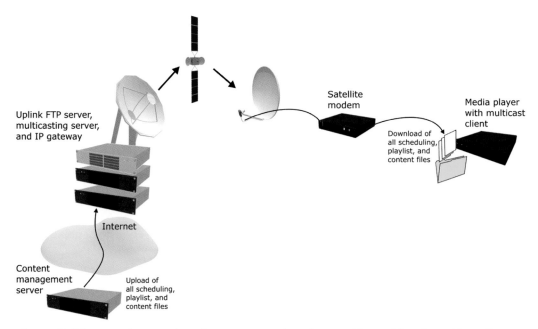

Figure 8.20   Digital signage broadcasting system based on satellite multicasting with media players having integrated multicasting clients.

files from the content management server. First, in Figure 8.17, we have the traditional broadband distribution network, where each media player retrieves content directly from the content management server. Second, Figure 8.18 shows the edge server alternative, where the edge server fetches all content needed at the location (that may include a large number of media players). Third, Figure 8.19 shows the satellite multicasting solution, where the satellite edge server is automatically loaded with files from the content management server. The content management server does not respond to requests and is not affected by the number of locations to be served. It just serves one location—the uplink station FTP server.

The media players, however, request and retrieve files from the satellite edge server. In the fourth alternative, shown in Figure 8.20, the media player is fed by a satellite modem and has its own integrated multicast client. The media player does not request anything from anywhere. You could say, though, that the media player software requests and retrieves files from the download hot folder that resides in its own hardware.

STREAMING REAL-TIME AND LIVE CONTENT

Chapters 5 and 6 describe the distribution of live streaming signals. In Chapter 7, the important concept of multicasting digital signage content, digital signage broadcasting, is introduced. Now we have all the important tools needed to explore the various ways to distribute live streams as IPTV.

From a content management system point of view, streaming media is quite simple, as long as it is not stored along the way to the players. Mainly, content management takes place at the content provider's facilities just the same as for conventional television. However, there is one important command to be sent to the media player: the command to switch from playing file content to decoding of the live stream.

The VLC Player as a Streamer

The VLC software is open-source freeware so anyone can contribute to the project. It is used primarily as a media player, but it is also a very versatile streamer. It is a real gold mine when it comes to studying streaming media. By putting one VLC player on one computer, acting as streaming source, and a second VLC player in a second computer, it is possible to set up a complete distribution chain between the two (Figure 8.21).

The VLC is a full-featured re-encoding machine that lets you encode a wide selection of video compression formats, including MPEG-1, MPEG-2, and MPEG-4 (even H.264). It also offers a number of audio encoding formats. It is fascinating to try different bitrates for the audio and video streams, to evaluate the picture and audio quality when using various compression formats (Figure 8.22).

Streaming between two computers on the test bench or in your home is easy in multicast mode. However, if you intend to stream to another location, you have to use the Internet, which makes unicasting the only way to perform streaming.

The VLC software contains menus to set the audio and video compression formats as well as the bitrates to be used for each (Figure 8.22). You also have to define the multicasting IP address and to tell the program which elementary streams to use. An elementary

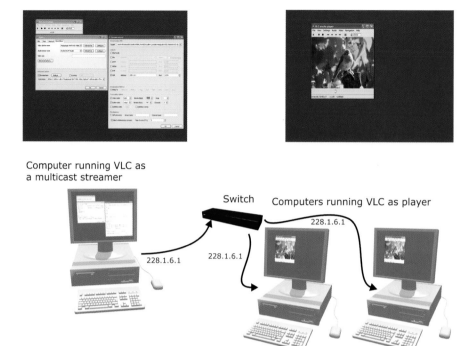

Computer running VLC as
a multicast streamer

Switch   Computers running VLC as player

Figure 8.21   With a VLC player as a streamer (*left*) and one or more computers with VLC as players (*right*), it is possible to set up a complete IPTV streaming test system.

stream is the separate compressed audio or video stream. By selecting "Select all elementary streams," you get the audio as well as the video streams. Another interesting parameter is TTL (Time-To-Live). TTL is a counter inside the IP packet that defines the number of routers that the IP package is allowed to pass before being eliminated. Every time a router is passed, the TTL value is decreased by one; at zero, the packet will stop being forwarded. The purpose of setting TTL is to avoid IP packets to be sent through IP networks forever. This is quite important to be able to handle traffic on the Internet.

Live Streaming in Full-Scale Broadband Networks

The only way to do streaming across the Internet is to use unicasting (Figure 8.23). This means that an individual connection has to be set up between the streaming and receiving computers. As just described, VLC can be used for unicast streaming as well. The

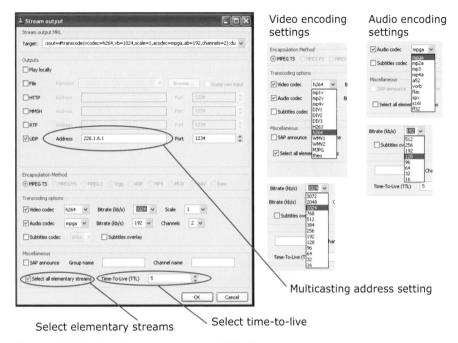

Video encoding settings

Audio encoding settings

Multicasting address setting

Select elementary streams

Select time-to-live

Figure 8.22 Sample menus to use a VLC player as a streamer.

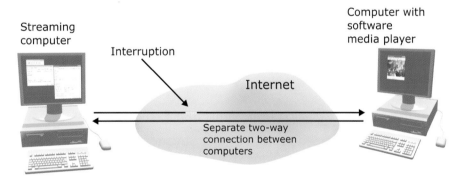

Streaming computer

Interruption

Computer with software media player

Internet

Separate two-way connection between computers

Figure 8.23 Streaming over the Internet must be unicast streaming and requires a separate connection between the streaming computer and each receiving computer. The risk of interruption makes the Internet less suitable for live streaming.

problem is that it is a point-to-point connection and a separate connection has to be set up with every receiving computer, since IP packets received have to be confirmed to the streaming computer.

Another problem with using the Internet for live streaming is the quality of service (QoS). The Internet does not provide a 100 percent reliable connection because the resources on the Internet are always overbooked. This means that there is a risk that we lose the contact between the computers for a while, which will require information to be sent again later. Interruptions are not acceptable in live streaming—anyone who has tried to watch TV over the Internet has experienced the frustrating messages of "Net congestion . . . buffering . . .," and so on.

The only real way to be sure that live streaming will work is to use a 100 percent dependable connection. But dedicated terrestrial lines are expensive and can be only used either for smaller local area networks or between a limited number of locations on a national level. In the next section, we will look at an interesting alternative: using satellite in combination with local area networks (LANs).

Streaming in Local Area Networks

As shown in Figure 8.21, we can do multicasting streaming in any local area network if the Ethernet switches are configured to allow for this. Simple 4-, 8-, or 16-port Ethernet switches usually have a default setting that lets the multicasting packets pass through. However, routers must be specifically enabled to do so.

It is very easy to build a LAN that can be used for multicast distribution. But as soon as we have to use the Internet to get to other networks, we get into problems.

Streaming with Satellite and Multicast LANs

As discussed previously, live streaming can be done easily by satellite. Satellite can provide a 100 percent guaranteed connection between the streaming computer and the receiving sites. To do live streaming of IP on a larger scale, satellite can be used to distribute the live multicast signals to LANs where multicasting is allowed. In this way, very large national coverage multicasting systems can be created.

To set up simple IPTV applications, VLC is a fantastic tool. For more professional use, however, there are special encoder appliances that may be used to produce the multicasting stream. These are more or less the same thing as the encoders used for digital TV broadcasting. The major difference is that instead of a DVB-ASI output, which is the signal format for digital television, the appliance has a multicasting ethernet IP output. The connection from the streaming source to the satellite uplink station has to be a dedicated line that is secure against interruptions. If an Internet-based connection is used, the content has to be uploaded to the uplink in advance and streamed from there. This might be acceptable for some services but is not a way to perform distribution of live events.

At the other end of the satellite link, LANs can be used to forward the live multicasting IP streams to media players that are in live decoding mode or alternative IPTV set-top boxes (Figure 8.24). Of course, all this is similar to traditional cable television where satellites distribute signals that are then carried to the final destinations through local cable TV networks. However, in this case we use IP streams instead of conventional television signals.

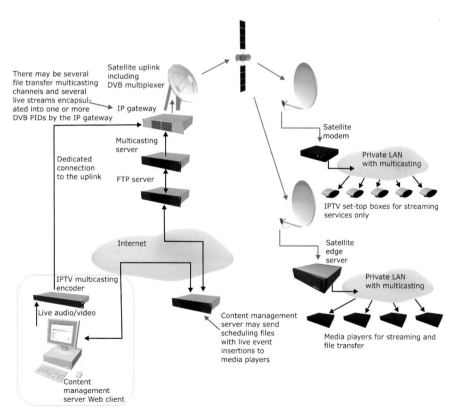

Figure 8.24 Multicast streaming on a national or international level can be done over satellite to local area networks that allow multicasting.

Live Streaming Systems

One of the more spectacular possibilities of multicasting (compared with unicast mode) is the ability to broadcast live events using IP. But IPTV is really quite similar to conventional digital television. The main difference is that IP is used to carry the digital television signals instead of the dedicated television protocols such as pure DVB-S.

Quality HDTV Capacity Requirements   Content for digital signage is often based on commercials made for TV. Since the beginning of digital signage, in the VHS VCR demonstration tape era, standard-resolution TV signals have been used. But the introduction of HDTV for home reception means that consumer awareness of quality will increase. HDTV signals will therefore most certainly become an important part of digital signage content.

It appears that the HDTV display devices and interfaces, as well as the HDTV transmission standards, are all in place and ready for use in digital signage. However, there are always two sides of a coin: how to choose the appropriate balance between quality and distribution capacity.

Satellite operators have longed for HDTV. This would mean that the broadcasters will have to use SDTV and HDTV dual illumination for quite some time. This is quite similar to the situation before analog broadcasting was shut down and most channels were distributed as digital as well as analog.

On the other hand, broadcasters do their best to reduce the need for bandwidth. There are a number of HDTV transmission standards based on either 1280 × 720 pixels or 1920 × 1080 pixels. These standards require more information to be transmitted than the conventional TV systems did (Figure 8.25).

HDTV is consuming a lot of capacity and two ways to deal with this problem are emerging in the world of broadcasting: DVB-S2 and MPEG-4.

These solutions also make things easier for IPTV services used in digital signage systems. By using smarter fault-protection algorithms, DVB-S2 increases the useful bitrate of a conventional transponder from 38 Mbps to about 50 Mbps. All services benefit from this.

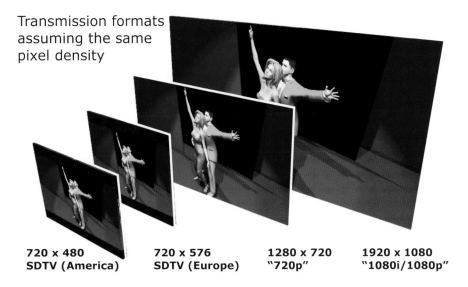

Transmission formats assuming the same pixel density

720 x 480	720 x 576	1280 x 720	1920 x 1080
SDTV (America)	SDTV (Europe)	"720p"	"1080i/1080p"

Figure 8.25 HDTV will most certainly become an important part of the digital signage content.

MPEG-4 increases the required bitrate for both SD and HD signals. But compressing TV signals is not easy, and people get choosy.

When introducing higher-resolution display devices that are larger than 32 inches, people quickly see the differences in distribution quality between the channels. Most SDTV MPEG-2 channels use bitrates around 4 Mbps for the video. This choice has been mainly based on subjective tests using "normal" TV sets, that is, "forgiving" CRTs with screens smaller than 32 inches. When these signals are displayed on 40-inch or even larger LCD or plasma screens, the MPEG-2 artifacts, such as blocking effects and color jumps, become a nuisance, and the picture becomes mushy. The problem becomes even more evident with HD projectors that produce even larger pictures. People tend to keep their regular viewing distance when buying new and larger TV sets.

The solution to these problems is high-definition signals. However, it is essential to note that increasing the resolution is only one way to improve quality. By increasing the bitrate or using the latest MPEG-2 encoding equipment, quite a lot can be done to improve SD signals as well. There are SD DVDs available that use increased bitrate and the movie needs to be stored on two DVDs. These products are targeted at home theater enthusiasts who wish to deal with these quality problems using SD DVD players and other SD equipment.

The HDTV Satellite Distribution Capacity Problem The aim of MPEG-4 H.264 (Advanced Video Coding, AVC) is to reduce the required bitrate to 50 percent of what is required using MPEG-2 while maintaining the subjective quality of the TV signal. MPEG-4 will require new receivers, but this is not an issue if it is introduced at the same time as the new set-top boxes with DVB-S2 and HD capability.

Subjective tests have proved that MPEG-4 does not yet fulfill the goal of reducing the bitrate requirements by 50 percent. This is probably because it takes a few years to perfectly implement any new standard. MPEG-2 only held four TV channels in a satellite transponder when introduced in the mid-1990s. Today, that same transponder can carry up to 10 channels. Of course, in the mid-1990s, four channels per transponder was still a great achievement compared to being able to distribute only one analog channel per transponder. MPEG-4 will eventually be able to fulfill its promise.

Since digital signage of today is based on computers, IP is always used for distribution. However, using MPEG-4 is still more economical than MPEG-2, and DVB-S2 will provide more capacity even when encapsulating streams of IP. So both television as well as digital signage will benefit from these advances. Digital television and digital signage will continue to develop alongside one another when it comes to improvements in resolution and other quality aspects.

Digital signage broadcasting systems are store-and-forward systems that add the dimension of time and storage to conventional broadcasting. Content management in these systems is complex and we are still just in the beginning stages of development of these new technologies. But content management also includes gathering of content from other sources. This may also be completely automated, as will be shown in the next chapter.

9

CONTENT GATHERING AND CUSTOMER BILLING

All the discussion of the content management server and managing the content distribution to the media players is meaningless without suitable content for the signage system. Introducing digital signage in a retail chain—as a complement to newspaper distribution, cinema chain, or news agency—means exploring a new media. The information age went through a similar change when the World Wide Web was introduced.

Only the future can tell which media outlet—newspapers, TV and radio stations, advertising agencies—will be among the best content providers. I expect many types of companies will try to build a business around this, and not all will succeed. This chapter describes some alternatives for establishing a digital signage content provider.

Building an operational digital signage system requires a well-planned strategy for the content. To be successful, the content has to be much more dynamic than is the case for printed advertising, whether it is produced in-house or by an advertising agency. Therefore, much more content—and content with a different approach to delivering its message—is required to work with digital signage. Still pictures and text will not be enough; you will need to include animations and probably video clips as well (Figure 9.1).

If live content is to be used, you also have to use dedicated connections from the scene of the event to the distribution system.

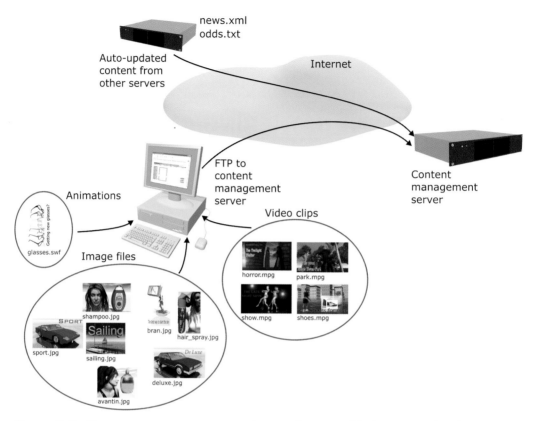

Figure 9.1 The content management server is not only responsible for content distribution; it must also gather content from various sources.

GATHERING THE CONTENT

Printed media is, for natural reasons, based on static messages, while TV commercials and Web content are dynamic. Therefore, one way to get more dynamic media to the screens of the digital signage system is to pick up the content from TV station archives or web sites. To a large extent, these kinds of media already meet the requirements of interesting and dynamic content.

One of the first things to do when establishing a digital signage system is to check for content that is already available. Most newspapers also have web sites, and some of them own and run television stations as well. TV and radio stations, in addition to their regular broadcast content, also have web sites. Retail stores have web sites and also use TV commercials. Sports betting sites use both the Web and sometimes live, closed-circuit TV. The list goes on and on. Most companies considering a digital signage system probably have lots of content on their web site or elsewhere that could be repurposed.

Manually Uploading Content

We have already seen that most content management servers used for digital signage are Web based. This means that content can be manually fed into the system from anywhere in the world. This is essential, because it does not matter where the advertising agencies or news reporters are located. They can always upload content as well as scheduling and playlist files to the content management server from anywhere. Web interfaces also make the content management server available to any mobile Internet-connected device. (See Figure 9.20.)

Automated Fetching of Files

When looking for content for your digital signage network, start on your own web site. The content probably has to be converted to one of the native formats for the media player, but that can be automated and handled in a batch process. This kind of conversion is mostly done with news, weather, sports results, odds data, stock market updates, and other rapidly changing information.

To reduce the work required to provide content to the content management server, it should have a feature to retrieve content from existing web sites. This process—detecting changes of data at these sites and updating the content management server—is often automatic (Figure 9.3). There are different ways of doing this. One is by using *RSS*, an XML-based file format that is really three different format standards: Rich Site Summary, RDF Site Summary, and Really Simple Syndication. One common way of using RSS in digital signage applications is to get updated information to news and stock market tickers.

You do not necessarily have to go to the Web to find content. You can also fetch data from the same databases that the Web-based content management system does. The important thing is to avoid manual

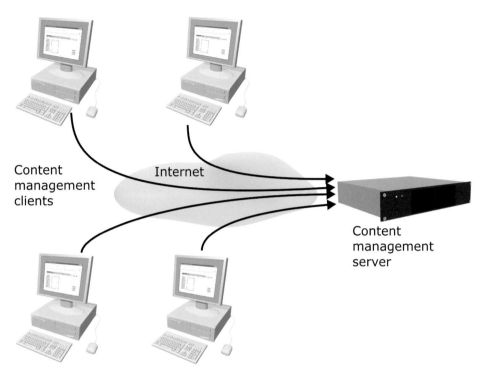

Figure 9.2   Manual input to the digital signage system is easy to do from anywhere in the world using any computer with Internet access.

work for the editorial staff when transferring information from the web site to the digital signage system.

Handling Various File Formats

An important question is if the digital signage system can use all file formats on the Internet and other types of content creation. The answer is definitely yes. But in many cases, it is not practical to use and distribute every file format in use. It is better to use a consistent set of file formats that can be handled easily by the media players in your digital signage system. Besides live streams of video, there are four basic kinds of files of interest for digital signage applications:

- Video clips such as MPEG, WMV, and other video file formats. Audio files are also included in this category.

Existing URLs
on the Internet

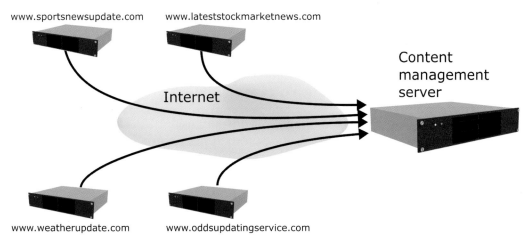

Figure 9.3 Content management servers can produce news tickers and other near-real-time digital signage content by automatically checking web sites for updates.

- Still image files of various kinds. Animation files also can be included here though they are a cross between video and still image files.
- Smaller files, such as text and XML files, used primarily for data that have to be updated on a near-real-time basis.
- Files where the authoring work has already been done to combine media files, such as Adobe PDF and PowerPoint.

TV Commercials in Virtual TV Channels

An easy way of getting content to virtual TV channels in digital signage systems is by reusing TV commercials. These are expensive to produce, so using them in digital signage will maximize the investment and provide valuable content in the stores. However, TV commercials—like all other TV content—are moving toward HD, and the files sizes are increasing. This will have an impact on the choice of the distribution system to ensure that the bandwidth and storage capacity are sufficient. Existing HD content may need to be rescaled before distribution to digital signage systems.

Developments within HDTV broadcasting will also affect digital signage in virtual TV and live streaming applications. Therefore, we will now take a closer look at HDTV transmission formats.

There are a number of transmission formats. The most demanding transmission systems are the 1080p50 and 1080p59 (59.94) systems. These systems will probably be used mostly on DVDs in home theater systems and should be avoided for digital signage systems, especially if distribution capacity is limited.

Even the interlaced 1080i/50 (Europe) and 1080i/59 (59.94) (United States) systems require about four times as much capacity as standard television does. There are also the 720p systems that require less bandwidth than the 1080p systems, but it is at the cost of less resolution.

Interlaced or Progressive Scanning   *Interlaced scanning* is the traditional way to scan a television picture. Scanning the TV picture starts on top and moves down the screen, scanning every other line and then going back to the top to scan the skipped lines. Interlaced scanning was invented in the 1930s to prevent flicker in the picture. In those days the ambience of the zinc sulfide that was hit by the electron beam had a tendency to fade before the electron beam swept the same screen location if scanning the entire picture top-down. This would make parts of the screen get dark before the electron beam returned during the next scan. This caused a flickering effect.

In interlaced scanning the image is divided into two frames, and only every other line is horizontally scanned during each vertical scan. A vertical scan will be accomplished in 1/60 of a second compared to 1/30 of a second according to the American television standards or 1/50 of a second compared to 1/25 of a second in Europe. Flickering is reduced considerably when using interlaced scanning.

Since a certain amount of time elapses before the second frame of the scan is completed, the vertical contours of the picture with fast horizontal movements (like a sporting event) may become a bit jagged. This is called a weaving effect. Weaving effects have been accepted by TV viewers for decades but today *progressive scanning* is preferable since the old CRT fade-out problems have been resolved. In progressive scanning, the lines are scanned consecutively from top to bottom and there are no weaving effects. Computer screens have always used progressive scanning.

High-Definition TV Files   Digital signage networks, at least those that use broadband for distribution, have limited capacity if a large number of sites are to be covered. In those cases, it might be best to use standard-definition signals. However, widescreen-format SDTV signals are necessary to fit the 16:9 flat-panel displays. With the exception of computer TFTs (which have an aspect ratio of 1.25:1), the general standard in digital signage is the widescreen 16:9 format.

Today nobody can say for sure what the bitrate requirements will be for HDTV in a few years. This depends on the development of MPEG-4 and other compression techniques.

The MPEG-2 standard requires a bitrate of about 4 Mbps for an SDTV channel. An MPEG-2 HDTV channel in the 1080i format requires about four times as much, 16 Mbps. In the long run, MPEG-4 is intended to require only half the capacity of an MPEG-2 signal, so 2 Mbps will be required for an SDTV channel and about 8 Mbps can be used for an HDTV channel using 720p50/59 (59.94) or 1080i50/59 (59.94). The 1080p50/59 (59.94) format would require about twice that much, 16 Mbps.

For broadcasting to homes, it seems that 6 Mbps is the long-term goal for HDTV using 1080i50/59 (59.94) or 720p50/59 (59.94) signals. However, this requires implementation of the full potential of the MPEG-4 standard and probably also making a compromise when it comes to quality. Together with DVB-S2, this is believed to be the most economical trade-off for direct-to-home broadcasting of HDTV. The quality level chosen for direct-to-home broadcasting might pave the way for the selection of a quality level for HDTV in digital signage networks as well.

The major SDTV and HDTV systems are illustrated in Figure 9.4.

In digital signage, the file sizes as well as the bitrate are important. Therefore, it is important to understand the number of bytes required

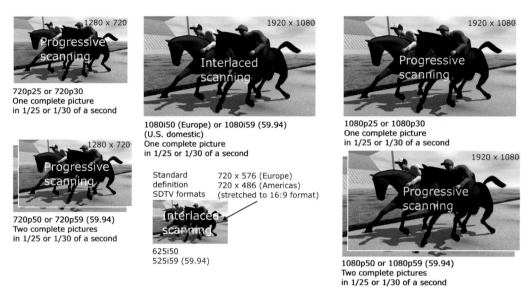

Figure 9.4   Some of the common SDTV and HDTV formats for television and digital signage.

per minute at different bitrates, as shown in Table 9.1. It is obvious that there is a careful optimization to be done when selecting the format to distribute HD video clips in digital signage systems. Please note that these are rough estimates, and you should always perform subjective tests before choosing bitrates for specific applications.

Animation files can be regarded as a type of video file, though they are produced more in a graphical manner directly in a computer. The result is a sequence of pictures experienced as a kind of movie. Video clips are produced using cameras and video editing software.

Video Files for Cinema Applications   Using media players where playlists decide how to cut the video clip commercial spots before the main movie is much more efficient than using conventional film. E-cinema is (using MPEG-2 compression) 4 to 20 Mbps, while D-cinema is more than 30 Mbps. DVD quality (which is about 4 or 5 Mbps) might suffice for preshow advertising, but it is often regarded as a low-end E-cinema application. If a performance similar to analog film is desired, the best format to use is the 1080p/25 format or rather the more unusual 1080p/24 format. Analog film runs at 24 pictures per second and progressive scanning at 25 pictures per second is as close as you can get

Table 9.1 Video clip file sizes compared related to various bitrates

Bitrate (Mb per second)	File size (MB per minute)
1	7.5
2	15 (MPEG-4, SDTV)
3	22.5
4	30 (MPEG-2, SDTV)
5	37.5
6	45 (goal of MPEG-4, HDTV)
7	52.5
8	60 (MPEG-4, HDTV 1080i/50,59 and 720p/50,59)

to conventional film. If done properly, the audience is not likely to notice the difference.

Image Files

When using image files, it is essential to use files that are optimized for the resolution and quality level that is expected to be on the screens and nothing more. There is no use in having more resolution in the image files than can be presented on the screens. This would result in less economic distribution and unnecessary use of processing power and storage in the media players. (As a general rule, this applies to all kinds of files.)

So, efficient distribution starts off in the content production stage. In television, smart encoding appliances are used to encode the audio and video signals in an optimum way. Once configured, this is all done automatically. However, when handling individual image and other kinds of separate files, we have to make a lot of decisions by ourselves. The major point is to use the appropriate image resolution and compressed standard formats, such as JPEG or GIF.

Small Data Files for Continuous Update

Continuous update of data requires a more or less continuous flow of data files. This is the real art of optimizing files. Smaller files have much better capabilities than larger ones to reach their destinations quickly. In digital signage systems, there might be queues (described in more detail in Chapter 10), and the smaller the files are, the more likely they are to outrun larger files. The most popular file format for these kinds of files is XML (Extensible Markup Language). XML is perfect to distribute data in an organized and structured way. However, there are other kinds of text file formats that can be used for this kind of information.

Combined Media Files

PowerPoint and Adobe PDF files are examples of files that combine image, video, and other kinds of files into a single presentation file. These kinds of files are produced somewhere outside the content management server. The major advantage is that they are very common file formats, and the development tools are almost impossible to beat. The major problem is distribution when near-real-time updating is desired. The entire combined file will have to be updated and redistributed, increasing the amount of time and bandwidth required to keep the content up to date. But there certainly are ways of combining the best of both worlds, as will be described later.

CONTENT CREATION

Creating the content is not really a part of the digital signage system. Content is mostly created using conventional tools on another computer and delivered to the content management server in any of the file formats mentioned above. Much digital signage content is actually created for some other media and then adapted to be used in a digital signage system. Therefore, you should not consider content creation as a part of the digital signage system itself (even though some components can be added there as well). Nevertheless, many digital signage systems contain tools for creating text and adding transitions between images, animations, or video clips. These tools are often used when authoring the appearance of the digital signage screens.

Authoring

Authoring is the process of compositing the various elements of a screen, combining the content in the different regions and layers to an attractive final appearance (Figure 9.5). The creation of playlists and scheduling is sometimes also considered a part of the authoring process.

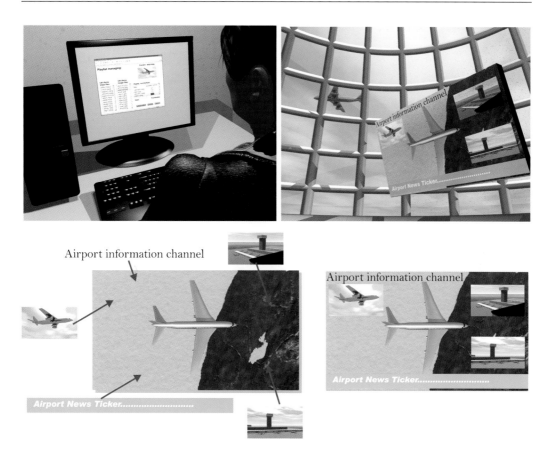

Figure 9.5 Authoring is, in part, bringing all elements together in regions and layers.

With combined media files such as PowerPoint or Adobe Acrobat, the authoring process, except for the scheduling, is handled in a separate system. As a result, updating the content means updating the combined files, which can be very large. This has deep implications on the kind of distribution to be used and the capabilities required of the media players. (See the section "Single File Format" later in this chapter.)

THE RENDERING SERVER

It is obvious that there is a great need for converting files between formats, changing resolutions in images, and rerendering video files to achieve an optimized digital signage system. As noted in

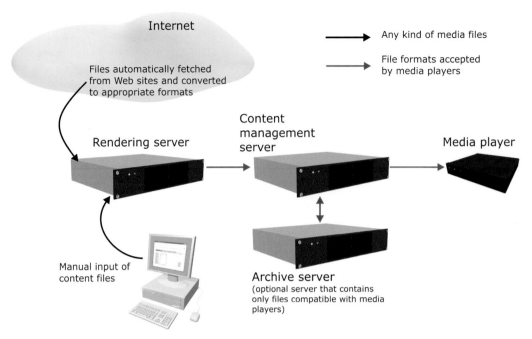

Figure 9.6   The rendering server converts files into a limited number of formats read by the media players.

Chapter 8, to ensure smooth transitions, it is essential that all video files in compressed video clips use the same video format (picture resolution) and bitrate. However, there is probably no digital signage system in the world that can handle all existing file formats and screen resolutions. But there is an advantage to having the right tools to prepare the media files for the content management system. In Figure 9.6, a rendering server is introduced to the system, ahead of the content management server. The rendering server handles the conversion from most file formats into the specific formats selected for distribution in the digital signage system. It may also do automatic rendering tasks when using online content.

It is, of course, advantageous to use the right formats from the start when doing manual input of files. This reduces the load on the rendering server. Another aspect of using consistent and optimized file formats is that money can be saved by using simple media players. Using fewer image, video, and audio formats means the media player hardware and software can be simplified.

Ideally, HDTV content is converted when produced. Delivery of commercials should be done in both standard and high-definition format. Converting HDTV content into SDTV format in the rendering server is probably not the best choice, at least not in today's rendering servers. It is better to have the production company do this, because it has the best equipment to do so.

Obviously, it is crucial to carefully optimize the specification for file formats to be used in the digital signage systems.

When studying current digital signage systems, there are two basic strategies to handle the file formats for distribution: single file format distribution and multiple file format distribution. There are also systems that operate somewhere between these strategies but these are the two basic philosophies.

Single File Format

The principle of always using the same file format for distribution means that all content has to be converted into that particular format. The combined files, such as PowerPoint or Adobe PDF files, can include all the elements required in a digital signage application, such as video clips, images, audio, and all kinds of graphics. There are also digital signage systems based purely on the Adobe (Macromedia) Flash animation file format.

Using one file format is comparable to conventional radio and TV broadcasting, where everything is converted into a standard distribution format before transmission. In this case, the rendering server is actually doing the conversion of files into the selected format and—even though the screen is divided into regions and layers in the production process—the media players will treat it as one region and layer, as if they are TV set-top boxes. There is no local handling of regions and layers in the player.

In systems that operate according to this principle, the files have to be merged by the rendering server (Figure 9.7). This process may be quite complicated and may also require manual handling, although certain things also may be done automatically.

A big advantage is that it becomes very easy to preview and test the final result before it is distributed. Because the one file contains

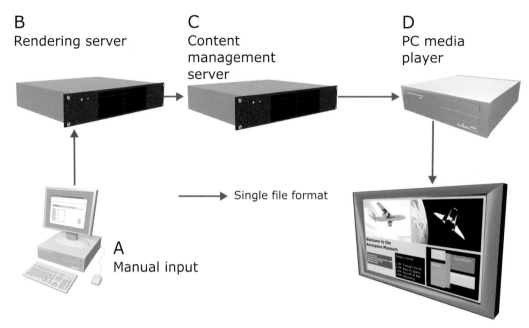

B
Rendering server

C
Content
management
server

D
PC media
player

→ Single file format

A
Manual input

Figure 9.7   Single file format. The rendering server converts all files into a single file format before they are distributed to media players, which handle the content as one region and one layer. **(A)** Content files and authoring content in a single file format are input manually into a computer with a Web client. **(B)** The rendering server converts content files into a single file format or keeps the original single format. **(C)** The content management server adds only scheduling and control files. **(D)** The media player is a PC that handles the content as one region and one layer.

the content for the entire screen, you can review the file and see exactly what is going to be placed on the screen and where.

A disadvantage to this method is that handling these kinds of single file formats, such as Adobe Acrobat and PowerPoint, requires a lot of processing power. In most cases, a Windows computer is required, which means that dedicated hardware media players can not be used. This is especially important if video clips are embedded in the files. Then the main processor has to have enough power and the right features to handle video decompression.

Another disadvantage is that if even just a tiny detail on the screen has to be updated, the entire file has to be redistributed. This results in an increase of distribution capacity. Using a single file format is not a practical strategy for signage systems that require frequent updates, but it

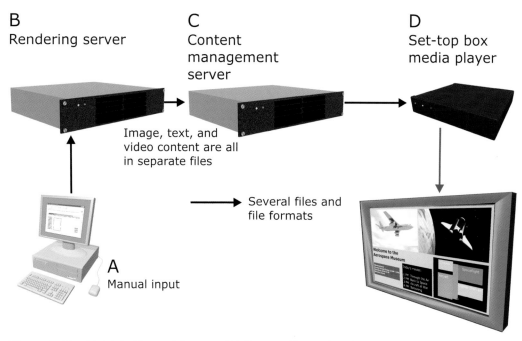

B
Rendering server

C
Content
management
server

D
Set-top box
media player

Image, text, and
video content are all
in separate files

Several files and
file formats

A
Manual input

Welcome to the
Aerospace Museum

Figure 9.8 Multiple files and formats. **(A)** Content files and authoring content are input manually into a computer with a Web client. **(B)** The rendering server converts content files but maintains separate files for video, images, and text. **(C)** The content management server handles a number of file formats and adds scheduling and control files. **(D)** The set-top box media player decodes, with dedicated hardware, the video files and handles regions, layers, and tickers separately.

might work in a situation where monthly sales promotions are sent to all the locations of a retail chain, for example. Virtual TV channels are another good example of single file format digital signage applications.

This strategy may be used if it is not important to reduce the required processing power in the media players. These kinds of combined files are often selected in systems with conventional computers used as media player hardware where it is considered as an advantage to use software like Adobe Reader or PowerPoint Viewer.

However, it should be remembered that even if only Flash, PDF, or PowerPoint files are used for the content (with embedded playlist files automatically created by the authoring software), we still need to add scheduling files and control files, such as assignment files, to be able to control the media players in a longer time frame.

Multiple File Formats

The basic idea of using several files—instead of having all content embedded into a single file—is that different kinds of files can be treated separately. A video file is much easier and faster to decode in a specialized chip than by a software decoder in a shared processor. Small text or XML files are most certainly easier and quicker to update individually than a larger file that combines text, graphics, and video files. If the files are handled separately, the system can reach a greater level of optimization.

In this case, the rendering server focuses on converting the incoming files to a limited number of standard file formats. These file formats are used by the media players to create the screen content (Figure 9.8).

This strategy has two major advantages. Video clips can be decoded using dedicated hardware, which is more efficient and favorable to hardware-oriented media players. Another advantage is that it is possible to update only the portions of the screen content that have changes, instead of having to distribute the complete screen content over and over. This also applies to customer terminals where local interactivity is involved; content divided into files is easier to reuse and adapt to input from the customer.

The major disadvantage of this strategy is that it is difficult to preview the final result before distributing the content to the network of media players. A monitoring facility is necessary to reproduce what will happen at the media player end to check for errors and see that everything is placed just right.

Just as in single file format use, the multiformat distribution chain requires converting to the file formats that are best suited for the media players.

Splitting a File into Several Files

The principle of using separate files to form the screen content has obvious advantages when it comes to distribution bandwidth and possibilities to construct dedicated and efficient media players. However, content creators and people involved in the authoring process may prefer to use their ordinary software tools, such as Adobe Acrobat and PowerPoint. Is there a way to use these tools and still be able to distribute content separated into individual files? To achieve efficiency, it is particularly important to be able to use separated playlists and video clip files.

With some authoring software, it is possible to combine the convenience of producing in well-known tools with a method of distributing the content in the most efficient way. In this case, the rendering server takes the single file created by the authoring software and converts it into separate files for the various regions and layers of the final digital signage display (Figure 9.9). With the ability to break single files up into multiple files, any web authoring or desktop publishing software tool could be used.

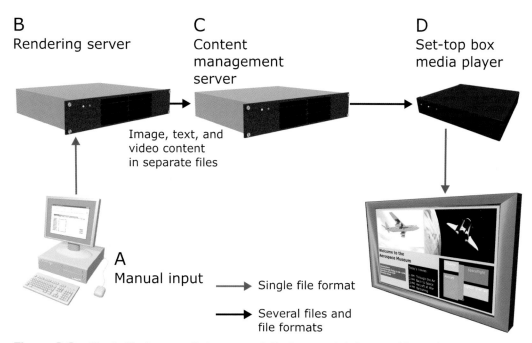

Figure 9.9 Single file format split into several file formats. **(A)** Content files and authoring content in a single file format is input manually into a computer with a Web client. **(B)** The rendering server splits the files into separate files for video, images, and text. **(C)** The content management server handles a number of file formats and adds scheduling and control files. **(D)** The set-top box media player decodes, with dedicated hardware, the video files and handles regions, layers, and tickers separately.

To be able to split into several files, the details of the combined file formats have to be known to the digital signage system designers. They also need to know how to extract information to create playlists.

Higher-Level Content Management Systems

All companies and organizations that handle media want to be able to archive and use their content in a convenient way. Many of them also want to use several publication channels. Just about every media outlet today has a web site as a complement to its core business. Therefore, there is a trend toward creating content management systems that are interconnected or completely integrated to handle all publishing channels (TV, radio, print, and Web) for the same content (Figure 9.10).

Of course, digital signage should and will be one of the publishing channels in future systems. Such an integrated content management system is a necessity to make digital signage media channels for home consumer use (described in Chapter 12).

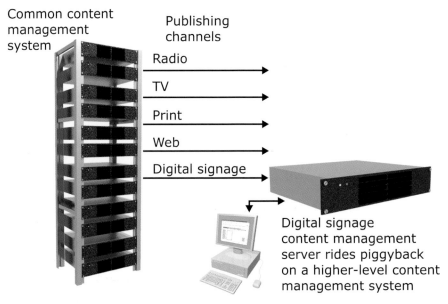

Figure 9.10   Content management affects more publishing channels than just digital signage.

OUTLETS FOR DIGITAL SIGNAGE

There are three major business ideas for advertising space in digital signage:

- Retail chains and other sites that have their own digital signage networks for their own use. In this case, the billing and customer relations management (CRM) systems are of little or no importance. The cost of the digital signage should just improve sales and other income.
- Companies that have a network of digital signs or billboards where the advertising space is leased. These kinds of networks are extremely dependent on the CRM system to sell advertising space and to prove to their customers that the bills are correct.
- Individual shops or hotels and others that have digital signs where they let others advertise. This fragmented market is very interesting. It may be hard for individual owners of single or a small number of screens to find advertisers, even though there is always a local market if the signs are strategically located.
- One way to get more advertising on a national scale might be to provide advertising to the screens against a payment. This is very similar to Google's concept of putting commercials on web sites and charging customers per click for the display of the advertisements. In this case, the billing is handled centrally by the Google advertising server that controls the distribution of advertisements to the screens.

Customer Relations Management Systems

Of course, operators of digital signage systems want to make money out of their business. This can be done in several ways. A retail chain might invest in a digital signage system to maintain more efficient contact with its customers and promote specific items. Betting companies may want to make gambling more interesting and dynamic to set themselves apart from their competitors. These companies use their digital signage networks by themselves.

But some digital signage operators use their networks to sell advertising space. For this reason, yet another system is needed behind the scenes, the *customer relations management* system (Figure 9.11). You could say that the CRM system is the link between the content management system and the handling of customers' commercials. The CRM system keeps track of what commercials and advertisements are available in the content management server and sees that the content matches the content that was ordered to be displayed. It also keeps track of logs, proving that the content actually has been displayed accordingly so billing can be done.

A similar system can be used for planning of advertising campaigns and content management for internal digital signage systems. However, in these cases, the billing feature is of less importance.

You will find similar systems in TV stations that sell commercial slots. Such systems have been around for a very long time. However, in television advertising, it is all about the amount of time that is sold and when it is sold. TV networks can also sell local advertising slots, so there also may be a geographical component in planning and billing.

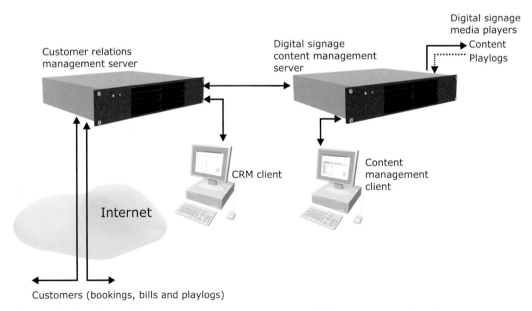

Figure 9.11   Behind the content management server, a CRM system is used to plan, insert, and sell the advertising space on the digital signs.

Digital signage is slightly more complicated. It is not only a matter of how much time on the screens is sold; it is also a matter of how much surface of the screen is sold. A commercial can be located in a small or large region or can be just a layer or a piece of text in a ticker. Audio commercials also can be included.

Customer terminals are a challenge. The advertising space on such a terminal can be used in a very powerful way because the customer actually tells the terminal about his or her profile. Customer input may drive the terminal to provide directed advertising suited to that particular customer. How to assess that kind of advertising? One way might be to use it for Google-like pay-per-clicking. Another possibility might be to create click statistics that can be used to decide the preferences of the customers.

Another important pricing factor for digital signage systems is the geographical location of the screens. Pricing strategies for digital signage applications may keep advertising sales people occupied for years.

The CRM system has to do more than keep track of the orders that come from the customers. It also has to be an advertising space planning tool and, as mentioned, it must be aware of what content is available in the content management server. If content is missing, the CRM system requests the right version of a particular advertising video clip, animation, or image.

Finally, the CRM system is used for billing the customers according to how much advertising capacity they have used.

The Playlog: A Necessity or Not? An interesting subject related to advertising sales and billing is the playlog. The playlog is a log that confirms what has been shown on each screen. The playlogs are gathered in the content management server and then fed to the CRM server to be sent back to the customer along with the bill, to show that the advertising was truly displayed. As an alternative, customers might be able to log in to an account on the CRM server to check the playlogs themselves.

Handling playlogs in larger systems may be quite extensive. The main challenge with playlogs is that a return path must be available. In digital signage networks based on broadband distribution, there are always return paths. In very large systems handling huge capacities, one-way multicasting may be used for distribution (see Chapter 7). In this case, the return path might have an extra cost. In many mass media, such as television, there is no return path. Digital signage might develop in the direction of being a one-way media, when the number of receiving sites reaches a critical volume.

The return path is different from the forward path in many respects. One difference are that the data going back to the content management system are much less demanding than the distribution of media files and possible media streams in the forward direction. So, far less bandwidth is necessary. Another difference is that traffic on the return path could be scheduled during off-peak windows—the return path information is generally far less time sensitive than the forward distribution of real-time content.

There is a true conflict between using the broadband connection in a store for media content delivery and other prioritized transactional purposes, such as the register transactions, price updating, and credit card blacklist updating. These things are all happening during regular store hours and place demand on the system's bandwidth.

However, the required return path traffic of a digital signage system does not have to claim that much capacity if the digital signage system is strategically designed.

The traffic required from the media players to the content management server includes playlogs, keep-alive signals, and alarms. If a media player or an edge server should fail, it might or might not be able to send an alarm to the content management server. If there is a serious issue, the device might have problems in producing the alarm. A simple way to avoid this is to send *keep-alive (or heartbeat) signals* at certain intervals. If a device does not call in to the content management server, an alarm can be initiated by the server.

Digital Signage System Return Paths   Digital signage systems that use broadband for networking always have a return path. As a result, most digital signage systems have highly developed return path features. Sometimes, this return path capacity is wasted or ignored because it is considered free in a broadband environment.

However, in multicasting systems, such as satellite IP broadcasting, it might be worthwhile to design a low-bitrate return path. In this case, the existing broadband connection can be used without interfering with other traffic. Also, means of broadband connections besides ADSL, such as wireless GPRS or 3G UMTS (Universal Mobile Telecommunications System) modems, can be used.

It is usually very inexpensive to use GPRS if only a few megabytes are required each month. And a few megabytes might be sufficient in the return path to keep a high-performance system up and running if the digital signage system is designed to take capacity into account. Using satellite for content delivery and GPRS for the return path makes it possible to build completely wireless high-capacity and high-performance digital signage networks. Using a separate GPRS or 3G return path also has the advantage of not interfering with the broadband connection used for transactional traffic to the shop. Therefore, it also can be used at any time.

There are digital signage applications where even content delivery is done using GPRS and 3G modems, but this is only applicable for limited amounts of content. If video clips and other larger files will be transferred, the bitrate and costs related to these mobile systems are not acceptable. GPRS and 3G techniques are based on unicast, point-to-point communication, just as any broadband connection using the Internet.

Figure 9.12 shows a full-featured digital signage broadcasting system with content delivery provided using satellite multicasting and a return path on either an ADSL broadband connection or a GPRS or a 3G wireless modem. The wireless modems are used to connect to the Internet. Knowing the IP address of the content management and multicasting servers, the satellite edge server can contact the multicasting server while the media players can stay in touch with the content management server. The traffic in the return path is limited if optimized properly. Really, there is not much information created by the media players and edge servers. As a result, we get a system without compromises, where unlimited media distribution capabilities to an unlimited number of sites are combined with a return path for safe and monitored operation.

On top of this, completely wireless systems could be built at locations without landlines, such as digital billboards on highways or hotels and other locations in rural areas.

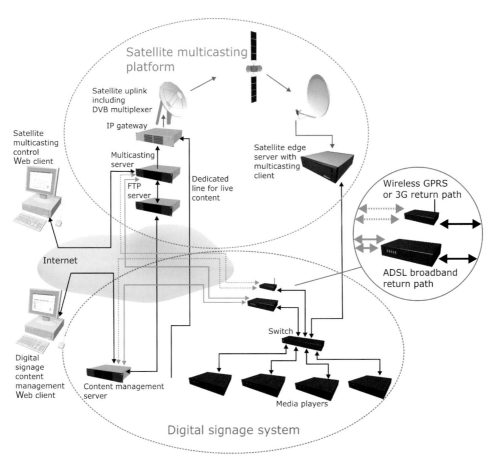

Figure 9.12   A full-featured digital signage broadcast system.

Multicasting for content delivery combined with an optimized unicasting return path is the digital signage network without compromises.

By now, you should have a picture of a complete digital signage system with all supporting equipment, such as a rendering server and a CRM system. You should also know where to find the suitable content to convert and update. However, what does it take to operate a digital signage system in an efficient way? What are the things to take into account when choosing means for distribution? Digital signage systems also call for new ways to plan the traffic. This can be complicated, since things might happen in real-time, near-real-time, or non-real-time. Chapter 10 covers these areas.

10

OPERATIONAL ASPECTS

When establishing a digital signage network, it is crucial to choose a system-suitable solution for your content management, distribution, and networking.

In this chapter, we will summarize operational aspects of the various alternatives. We will start with an analysis of traffic patterns for the various ways of distribution. Also, we will review some more general operational aspects of digital signage systems, as well as alternative technologies to consider.

CONTENT DISTRIBUTION

Digital signage distribution methods include manual creation and shipping of physical media (CDs and DVDs), broadband networking, and satellite multicasting (Figure 10.1). But, how do you choose the right solution?

Physical Media

Small-scale systems that cover only a handful of locations can be handled manually. It is quite easy to set up a system based on DVD recorders or computers and to distribute the content on CDs or DVDs. The main problem of manual systems is that you rely on your staff at each location to load new content into the media players.

The amount of content to be sent to the shops is limited only by the storage medium. DVDs can store up to 4.7 GB—that's a few hours of

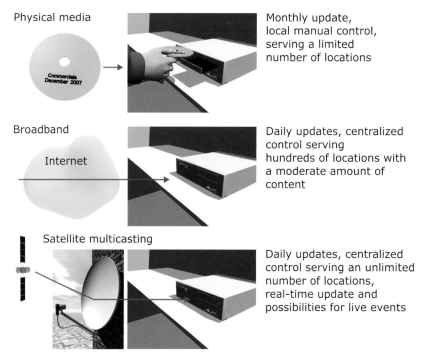

Physical media — Monthly update, local manual control, serving a limited number of locations

Broadband / Internet — Daily updates, centralized control serving hundreds of locations with a moderate amount of content

Satellite multicasting — Daily updates, centralized control serving an unlimited number of locations, real-time update and possibilities for live events

Figure 10.1   Digital signage distribution options: physical media, broadband networking, and satellite multicast networking.

video, most likely sufficient for a small-scale system. The challenges relate to manual duplication, shipping, and installation, making this kind of distribution quite slow. To ship new content more than once a month is probably not practical. Of course, Blu-ray and HD-DVD discs will make it possible to handle more capacity such as for high-definition (HD) commercial spots. But still, most digital signage operators will probably prefer to move to broadband or satellite distribution rather than develop the physical media further. The biggest issue with these kinds of systems, based on distribution of physical media, is the complete lack of control of what appears on the screens. Changes take a lot of time, and it is very hard to synchronize advertising campaigns.

Even manually operated systems like this need a simple, manually operated content management server. Simple systems like this will still generate central maintenance costs.

Broadband Networking

As the number of signage locations increases, manual content distribution is no longer sufficient; a unicasting broadband networking solution will be much better. There are two options, manual and automatic, for broadband networking.

In a manual content distribution setup, the local personnel use a computer to fetch the content manually from a central server. The downloaded content is then saved in a flash memory and transferred to the media player. This is essentially the same as distributing content on physical media, but it eliminates the need for physical mail. This is not a tremendously practical solution for a complex signage network. In shops with many media players, it will take too much time to update the media players one by one. Manually fetching content from a common server via the Internet might be practical for a system where you provide new content no more than once a week.

A better option is to configure the media players or an edge server to fetch content automatically from a central content management server using the Internet. Because it operates independent of human input, content could be updated quite often, even once a day or more. The ability to update content at any time makes the capability of the broadband distribution chain the only limiting factor of the system.

There are two things that determine the capability of the system: the content management server's streaming capabilities and the backbone connection between the content management server and the Internet. Of course, the local Internet connection in the stores also affects the performance of the system, but this is not of significance today since most broadband connections reach bitrates of several megabits per second (Mbps).

Let's make a simple calculation. We would like to transfer a 150 MB video file. Assuming a system has a streaming server with the capacity to stream 50 Mbps to the Internet and a backbone connection with at least the same capacity, we get the following situation. Each broadband connection is assumed to have an average maximum speed of 2 Mbps. This allows for 25 sites to be served simultaneously. Since we are using the Internet for distribution, we must communicate in unicast mode—the file, 150 MB, has to be sent to each location individually. As a result, we can calculate

Table 10.1 Time required to transfer a 150 MB file to various numbers of locations using a 50 Mbps distribution server and backbone connection

Number of locations	Time required (minutes)
25	10
50	20
75	30
100	40
500	200 (3.33 hours)
1,000	400 (6.66 hours)

the following: 25 (locations) $\times$ 150 (file size in MB) $\times$ 8 (bits per byte) = 30,000 Mb have to be transferred. At a rate of 50 Mbps, this would take 600 seconds (10 minutes).

Table 10.1 shows the time required to download a 150 MB video file (5 minutes of MPEG-2 video at 4 Mbps) to various numbers of locations.

Careful planning is required to serve a large number of locations with large content files using broadband Internet connections. An additional problem is that it might not be acceptable to use the shop broadband connections during business hours, to keep that line of communication open for sales transactions. If a retail chain is open from 9 A.M. to 7 P.M., there are a maximum of 14 hours that can be used for file transfer alone (Figure 10.2). Of course, time zones must be taken into account when planning for distribution.

The calculations of transmission time assume perfect conditions, where no retransmissions are required and the Internet connections are reliable. In real life, there would be additional overhead, which might be hard to calculate.

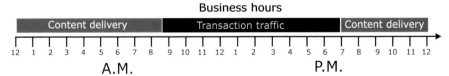

Figure 10.2 Broadband distribution of content requires careful planning, especially if files can be transferred only during nonbusiness hours.

The costs involved in a broadband digital signage network are not just the broadband connections in the shops. Many shops have broadband access already. But the content management server becomes more expensive as its streaming capabilities are increased. The cost for the Internet backbone connection also increases.

There are obvious limitations to how much content can be updated using broadband distribution when it comes to serving many locations. It may take several hours to replace a video clip, and this might be an issue if there is a need for an update that was not been planned in advance.

Despite these caveats, taking the leap to automatically fetching the content from the content management server provides much more efficient control of the digital signage network than manual handling of the media players.

Satellite Multicasting

When the number of locations exceeds the capacity of a broadband network, the next most efficient method is satellite multicasting. If there are 100 or more shops and the content to be distributed is quite large, multicasting might be the answer.

Terrestrial broadband requires an increasing backbone connection speed and increased server capability as the number of locations served increases, but the multicasting server only has to send each message once and is not even aware of how many receiving computers exist. Therefore, the cost for distribution is independent of the number of receiving sites. Also, the time required for distribution of a certain amount of data is independent of the number of sites served. Since the content management server has to provide content only to the FTP server at the satellite uplink, the load on the content management server is insignificant and is independent of the number of sites served, at least from a content delivery point of view.

As a consequence, one content management server in a satellite multicasting system might serve several digital signage systems instead of just one. Sending files to the uplink FTP server is very much the same task as sending files to one single media player or a single store (if several message channels are involved). From a content management server point of view, the satellite multicasting solution is very favorable.

Since the load on the server for content delivery is lighter, more bandwidth can be used for return path traffic handling.

In satellite multicasting systems, the same distribution channel is used by all stores served and therefore the bitrate may be much lower than in a broadband-based system. We will now take a closer look at the implications of this.

With the other assumptions the same as for the broadband distribution system—a 150 MB video file is now distributed in a multicasting system at 0.5 Mbps—we can calculate the distribution time as 150 (file size in MB) × 8 (bits per byte)/0.5 (transfer speed in Mb) = 2,400 seconds (40 minutes). This is equal to the time required to distribute the same file to 100 locations using broadband (assuming perfect transmission with no retransmissions needed). The advantage to satellite multicasting, however, is that in the same amount of time, an unlimited number of locations can be served. Using a less expensive 0.25 Mbps satellite link would double the time required to 80 minutes but also cut the costs of the satellite segment by 50 percent. Still, we have a fixed amount of time but can reach an unlimited number of sites.

Satellite is regarded by some people as an expensive distribution method. However, it is a very cost-effective method of serving a large number of locations with a suitable bitrate.

Assuming a transponder cost of $150,000 (U.S.) per year per Mbps would result in distribution costs of $37,500 for a 256 kbps channel. In a retail chain with 500 shops, the annual cost of distribution per shop would stay at $75 ($6.25 per shop per month). When comparing costs of broadband and satellite, the more advanced content management servers and high-speed Internet backbone connections for broadband have to be taken into account. Sending content to only an FTP server, as is the case for satellite, would require less than 0.5 Mbps streaming capability and a slim backbone connection.

It is interesting to try to find the point at which it is profitable to implement a more advanced distribution method. However, the choice is not just economical. Moving from distribution of manual media to broadband networking is very much a matter of being in control of the system. Also, the decision to move from broadband unicasting to satellite multicasting must consider whether there is a need for near-real-time applications or live event broadcasting. The ability to make quick corrections to faulty content also affects the choice between broadband and satellite. But it is the number of locations and media players to be served that is of the utmost significance when making these decisions.

Figure 10.3 shows the relation between distribution cost and number of sites served, and you can see the points at which the methods intersect, becoming more or less efficient than the others. It is impossible to put definite figures to points A and B, but industry experience suggests that point A is between 10 and 50 locations and point B is around 100 locations.

Figure 10.4 shows the time required to distribute 150 MB of content over a broadband network and a satellite connection. The cost for distribution of satellite IP and the time required to distribute a file is independent of the number of receiving sites because the same satellite capacity is available to all receiving sites.

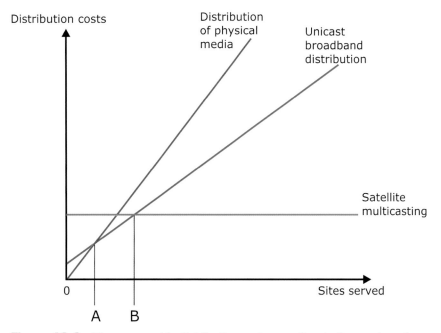

Figure 10.3 The comparable distribution costs according to the number of sites and medium (physical media, unicast broadband, and satellite multicasting).

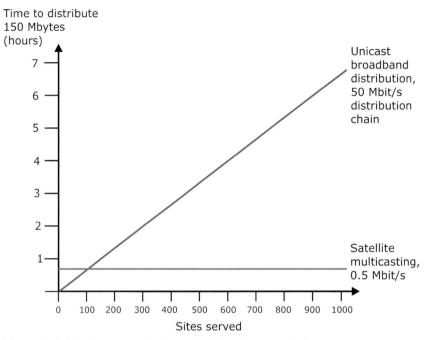

Figure 10.4   The comparable speed of distribution of 150 Mbytes via unicast broadband and satellite multicasting as the number of sites increases.

Simultaneous Transfer of Multiple Files and Queuing   Using several multicasting channels is one way to avoid queues, but queues are almost inevitable since there is a stochastic nature to when files are sent to the multicasting server. Another problem is large video files that take time to pass through the channel. Combining larger files with smaller ones is especially likely to cause problems. *File interleaving* is one way to solve this problem. Interleaving means that all files in the multicasting distribution process equally share the distribution capacity. As a result, smaller files will outrun (finish quicker than) larger ones.

This is very handy because smaller files are often used for near-real-time updating of content such as news tickers, betting odds, and stock market information, and they must be delivered and displayed as quickly as possible. Larger video clips are often transferred according to a schedule and it does not matter much if they are delayed slightly.

Figure 10.5 illustrates the various file transfer options. At the top, you see the small 1 MB file (the *green* line) is ahead of the large file (the *red* block). It transfers quickly and doesn't disrupt the large file.

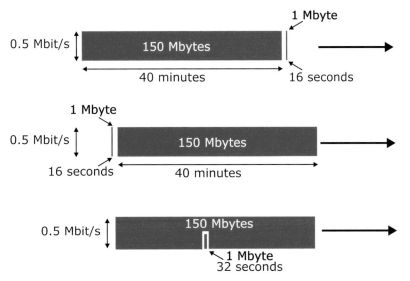

Figure 10.5 Transfer of more than one file. If the small (1 MB) file is transferred first (*top*), it goes quickly. If the large (150 MB) file is transferred first (*middle*), it delays the small file by 40 minutes. Interleaving the files for transfer (*bottom*) means that tiny files can be delivered during the transfer of larger files.

In the middle, you can see that transferring the large file first means the smaller file is delayed by 40 minutes—not ideal. With file interleaving (the bottom illustration), the system shares the bandwidth with both files, so the small file is delivered quite quickly (twice the time, 32 seconds, is required), and the large file continues its lengthy download with a barely noticeable delay. It is quite important, however, not to try to transfer too many files at the same time when using file interleaving. This will cause the traffic to slow down, and it puts a lot of pressure on the multicasting server as well as the multicasting clients. This might affect the system's stability. Separate queues for different kinds of traffic (near-real-time and non-real-time) may be a better choice in such situations

Efficient IP Multicasting In a streaming application, it is evident how to use the distribution channel's capacity. As an example, it is unlikely anyone would even think about pushing a faster signal through a 4 Mbps TV distribution channel. However, in file transfer systems, that thought occurs all the time, and there is the risk of overloading the channel. If an upload channel is faster than the multicasting channel, you might end up with too much content waiting in the upload folder and in the multicasting server to get through the system.

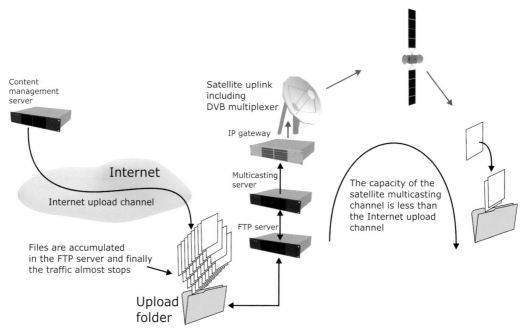

Figure 10.6 The use of a multicasting channel for file transfer requires wise planning of traffic so that files do not pile up and get stuck in the FTP server.

A 256 kbps channel has a maximum capacity of $256 \times 3{,}600/8 = 115.2$ MB per hour. It is necessary to carefully plan FTP uploads to avoid too much content getting stuck in the distribution chain. You could say that the FTP server acts as a kind of a funnel that may get filled up with files if you do not wait for the files to disappear in the other end (Figure 10.6). If we assume a capacity of 0.5 Mbps in the multicasting channel, the maximum capacity that can be transferred is 3.75 MB per minute, which is 225 MB per hour or 5.4 GB per 24 hours.

It is important that the content management server does not deliver more data than the capacity of the multicasting channel; otherwise, the file transfer process cannot be interleaved for maximum efficiency. The average bitrate of the stream of files from the content management server is just as important as the correct setting of the bitrate that is provided from a video encoder for DVB or IP streaming.

One way to avoid these problems is to not use a higher upload speed than the multicasting channel bitrate.

GPRS and UMTS Content Delivery

Some applications need small antennas and must work even in mobile situations, such as LED text displays on busses and at bus stops. At these locations, there might be no access to ADSL and it might not be practical to install a satellite dish. For these applications, General Packet Radio Services (GPRS, the GSM data channel) and 3G (Universal Mobile Telecommunications System, UMTS) data channels may be the most appropriate carriers for content. Bitrates vary but are in the range of 80 to 200 kbps (Figure 10.7).

These alternatives are point-to-point unicast connections, and separate communications sessions have to be set up between the content management server and each terminal. A terminal consists of a radio modem, a media player, and some kind of display device. The cost for distribution will rise in relation to the number of terminals served, just as is the case for digital signage broadband networking.

To achieve multicasting to mobile units, various broadcast solutions must be used. In some countries, there are separate data channels

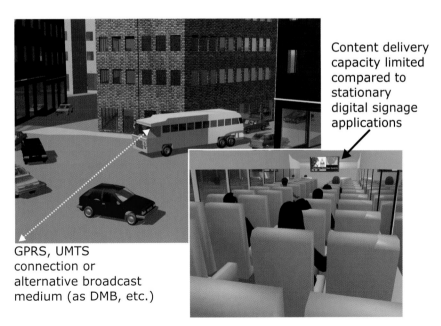

Content delivery capacity limited compared to stationary digital signage applications

GPRS, UMTS connection or alternative broadcast medium (as DMB, etc.)

Figure 10.7 Low-bitrate digital signage applications may use GPRS or UMTS for content delivery.

that piggyback on FM radio transmissions. Of course, new radio broadcast media, such as DAB (Digital Audio Broadcasting) and DMB (Digital Media Broadcasting), may be used for digital signage content delivery as well. As with satellite distribution, these systems have a fixed cost for distribution capacity, regardless of the number of receiving terminals.

GPRS and UMTS are useful solutions to create a return path from media players and edge servers in digital signage broadcasting systems where content delivery is done by satellite.

Hybrid Unicast and Multicast Distribution Systems

There are occasions when it is not possible to install a satellite dish. As an alternative, that particular site can be served by broadband for content delivery while the other sites use satellite. As discussed previously, the load on the content management server, like the demands on the content management server and the backbone Internet connection, will increase with the number of sites served by broadband. However, by keeping the number of sites that pick up content by broadband to a small percentage of the population, high-quality digital signage content delivery can be achieved everywhere (Figure 10.8). This is yet one more example proving the benefit of using the right media or combination of media to get optimum results.

Remember that serving the FTP and multicasting severs at the uplink does not require much more capacity for content delivery from the content management server than is required to serve one single shop using broadband unicasting. Appendix A contains more information on how to make basic traffic analysis calculations when choosing unicast and multicast solutions.

Which Delivery Method Is Best?

Most digital signage systems of today use broadband networking. As discussed, broadband is point-to-point communication, and satellite multicasting is point-to-multipoint. One of the most important things to analyze when selecting the distribution method for a digital signage network is what traffic is point-to-point and what is point-to-multipoint.

Broadband networking means an almost symmetrical channel, where almost the same amount of information is transferred in the forward and return paths. However, the need for content delivery

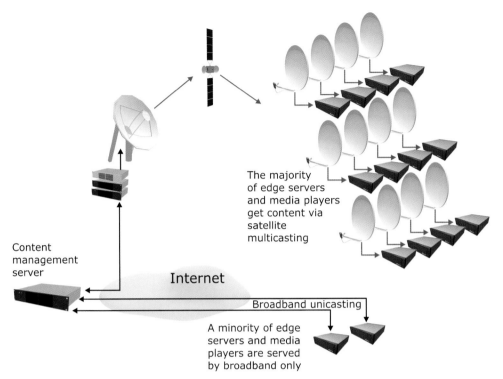

The majority of edge servers and media players get content via satellite multicasting

Content management server

Internet

Broadband unicasting

A minority of edge servers and media players are served by broadband only

Figure 10.8 Digital signage networks can use both broadband and satellite distribution methods.

is much larger in the forward direction than in the return path in the opposite direction. Content delivery is most often a point-to-multipoint task, but media distribution puts a heavy load on the broadband connection of the signage location. For this reason, as mentioned, broadband content delivery is often prohibited during business hours if there is not a separate broadband connection for content delivery.

In these systems, night transfer of files is quite common. If you have large amounts of data and a large number of sites to distribute to, you may not be able to update all the locations in just one night. A solution may be to use a dedicated broadband connection for media. However, that is not always possible and satellite multicasting may be a more efficient way to solve the problem. Using satellite multicasting for content delivery combined with broadband return path traffic is a solution with no compromises (Figure 10.9).

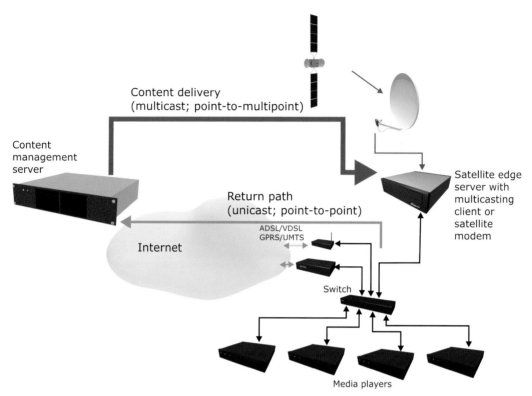

Figure 10.9   Analyzing the kind of traffic and choosing distribution methods accordingly might lead to a digital signage distribution system that uses satellite multicasting for content delivery and unicast broadband for return communication.

THE RETURN PATH

A significant difference between terrestrial broadband and satellite is that with satellite IP broadcasting, you can choose whether or not to have a return path. In a broadband digital signage system, the return path is essentially at no extra cost. But in a satellite multicasting system, it may cost extra to have a return path. Some would say that it is impossible to run a digital signage system without a return path for playlogs, heartbeat signaling, and alarms.

On the other hand, if you think of a digital signage system as a pure broadcasting system, the system could be operated without return traffic, which would save some expense. In a system with several

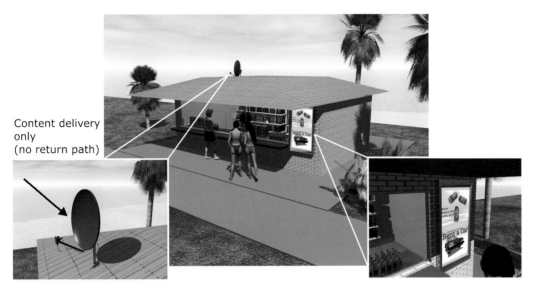

Content delivery
only
(no return path)

Figure 10.10 Staff can take the place of a return path—they can request technical assistance as needed.

thousand screens, the resemblance with TV broadcasting networks is evident. Such systems will certainly appear in the years to come.

Figure 10.10 shows a situation where a return path would not be necessary. Because the kiosk is staffed, that person could alert the technical support team that the digital signage is not operating correctly. If the digital signage application was not under constant live monitoring, such as the billboard in Figure 10.11, a return path would be invaluable for signaling when there is a problem with the system.

A return path can be designed for narrowband operation. As a result, it may be acceptable to use the existing broadband connection even during business hours (Figure 10.12). An economical return path also allows mobile return path solutions such as GPRS and UMTS (3G) modems. If these alternatives are used, the system will be completely wireless.

Even if the demands on content delivery should increase, the return path traffic is not expected to increase to the same extent.

The return path is a typical point-to-point task.

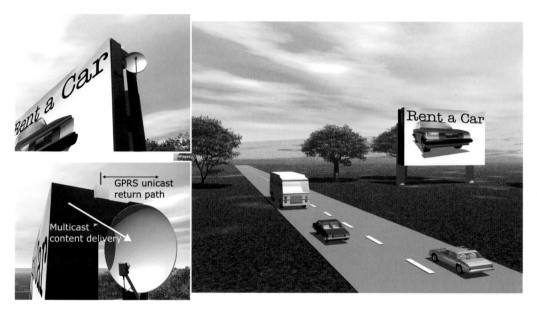

Figure 10.11 Digital signage systems that are not staffed need a return path so the system itself can notify the administrators of a problem.

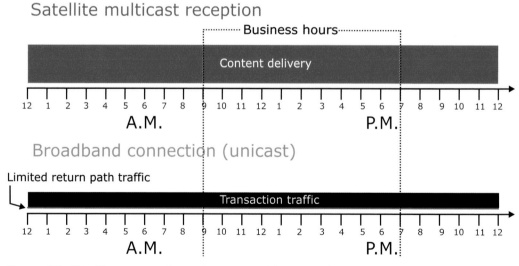

Figure 10.12 The return path may be optimized for narrowband operation and could be used even during business hours.

CONTENT STORAGE

Digital signage systems are far more complicated than traditional broadcasting systems because content is stored not only in the content management server but also in the edge servers and in the media players.

Cleanup Procedures

Anyone with a digital set-top box with a hard drive knows that the drive will eventually get full if old files are not removed. The same is true with content management for digital signage systems—old content must be removed or replaced to make room for new content. There are several ways to handle this.

Downloading a file that contains a list of current files is one solution. The media player or the edge server reads the file and then erases all the files not included in the list.

Another solution is to assign an "expiration date" to each file. Once that date has passed, files are automatically erased.

Another very simple solution is to reuse old filenames for the updated filenames. This means that old files are overwritten by new ones and there will be an automatic clean-up of old data (Figure 10.13). This concept is particularly valuable for near-real-time applications, where files are updated frequently.

REPLACING HARDWARE

Replacing faulty hard drives or flash memories can be tricky because the correct content must be transferred to the new drive as part of the installation process.

In a broadband digital signage network, the replacement unit will start downloading proper content from the content management server as soon as it is attached to the broadband connection.

In multicasting systems, it is more complicated, and if the scheduled content update is infrequent, there might be problems getting all the content on the replacement drive. There are several ways to solve this problem, depending on how often the system is updated.

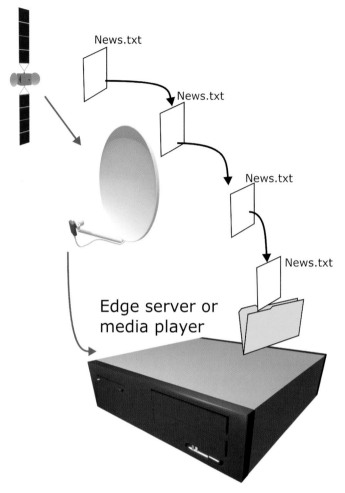

Figure 10.13 Overwriting old files by reusing filenames is a simple way to control the storage space on the hard drive.

Of course, a redundant edge server in the store would do the job, but another way might be to see that a collection of backup players are always connected to the system. This way, one of these spares—which has current content because it was already part of the network—can be sent out as the replacement drive.

Another alternative is to equip the service personnel with a laptop that contains all the current content. As the service personnel install the replacement drive, they can upload the content to the replacement unit (Figure 10.14).

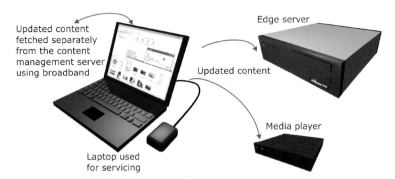

Updated content
fetched separately
from the content
management server
using broadband

Edge server

Updated content

Media player

Laptop used
for servicing

Figure 10.14 Laptops can be used to transfer data manually to load content on replacement units.

It may also be feasible in a hybrid broadband/multicast system to let the replacement unit fetch content on a broadband connection for its initial content installation. Finally, there is the alternative of using the multicasting channel to send all content once more even though it is needed in just one location.

UPDATING SOFTWARE

As with any computer or digital TV set-top box, software needs to be updated. In this context, the software is referred to as firmware (Figure 10.15). Most digital signage systems allow for this. The media

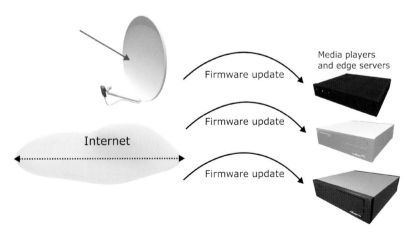

Media players
and edge servers

Firmware update

Firmware update

Internet

Firmware update

Figure 10.15 The firmware of most media players can be updated remotely by broadband or via satellite.

Poster People Will Become Service Personnel

Some people will argue that jobs will be eliminated because it will no longer be necessary to distribute and hang printed posters and signs. However, a digital signage system will actually create many jobs. On the content creation side, the dynamic media will require much more content to be produced, which will increase the load on advertising agencies and production houses.

At the other end, lots of people will be required to service the equipment. The work of replacing the posters will disappear, but media players and screens will still require some attention.

player can retrieve new software from the content management server or the edge server. Then, using a command file recognized by the player, the software installation is initiated. The ability to update the media player's software is important because this enables new features—such as the introduction of new file formats—to be supported without replacing the hardware.

PRESERVING DISPLAY DEVICES

Like any other digital device, LCD and plasma screens have limited lifetimes. One way to decrease the maintenance costs is to turn off the screens when the stores are closed. In many digital signage systems, this is done automatically from the content management system. Some media players can even read status data from the screens to produce alarms and confirm that a screen is in operation. In some cases, it is desirable to have the screens in operation even when the store is closed. If the screens are visible through store windows, they can continue to advertise a store's products, increasing their value and functionality. But leaving the systems turned on 24/7 will lead to a need for a sooner replacement.

In the long run digital signage networks will probably become very extensive, creating a much more dynamic market for outdoor as well as indoor advertising.

In addition, future digital signage systems for home use will have large similarities to conventional broadcast networks (discussed in Chapter 12).

11

CREATING DIGITAL SIGNAGE ENVIRONMENTS

The benefit of digital signage applications for point-of-purchase and other public areas is not only that it can spread a message in lots of locations. It can also create a certain environment or atmosphere in the same way at many places at the same time. The ability to centrally control what is being shown at many locations gives new possibilities to publicizing a certain profile, which is important when branding products.

In this chapter, we will take a closer look at some environments using digital signage systems. These installations are all over the world, including my home country, Sweden.

Large indoor LED screens, such as the aquarium scene in Figure 11.1, are very impressive but also expensive and therefore rare. Most large LED screens are outdoors, such as showing performers at concert venues to those with seats far from the stage.

RETAIL CHAINS

Using digital signage may be a way of extending a product's branding—the "personality" of a product that consumers will recognize and come to expect. The ability of digital signage to spread the same message everywhere is of utmost importance in successful branding.

Unlike printed signs, digital signage opens the opportunity to do things simultaneously. When you are making an advertising campaign, you need the correct timing for your TV commercials in

Figure 11.1   Large LED screens create a fantastic atmosphere, even though the picture is built from tiny LEDs.

Figure 11.2   Flat-panel displays provide an addition to the shop environment instead of putting a load on it. The displays do not require more space than printed signs do, but they add dynamics and flexibility.

Figure 11.3 Using HD video clips in portrait orientation is a very powerful way to display clothes. This orientation of the screen is natural and very efficient for displaying people in standing or walking positions, as shown on these screens from Panasonic.

relation to the outdoor advertising and advertising in the shops. Digital signage helps to get this timing right because you always know what is shown, where, and when. Advertising is not only adapted to the season but also to the day of the week and the hour of the day, which might have an effect on sales (for example, promoting breakfast in the morning and dinner in the evening).

GROCERY STORES

Grocery stores have to find new ways to sell their products. One informative and creative way to use digital signage in a grocery store is to have the store chef offer dinner suggestions, including instructions, recipes, and where to find the items in the store. This method of providing information tends to be more appealing and attention-grabbing than pure advertising (Figure 11.4).

In larger grocery stores, the displays are often spread across a vast area. Often there are groups of larger displays. Each group of displays is covering a certain department of the store (Figure 11.5).

The major issue is that the environment in such stores is quite noisy, meaning the customers are exposed to a lot of impressions. Using helpful information rather than advertising is one way to get attention.

Figure 11.4   Digital signage can show commercials at the point of purchase as in this case from RTV digital signage.

Figure 11.5   This Swedish supermarket uses RTV digital signage to enhance the produce department.

Shelf-Based Digital Signage

In contrast to the large displays that you find in some shops are the small, shelf-oriented displays. These displays are located close to the products they promote and will sometimes catch the customer's

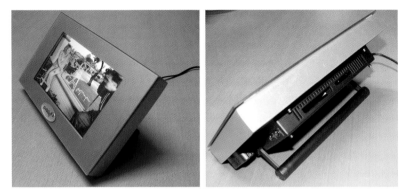

Figure 11.6 A shelf display from Publiq.

attention in a better (more product-related) way than the larger screens. Figure 11.6 shows a 7-inch display with integrated media player that can be mounted or placed near specific products. Devices like this often have flash card readers but also can be fed through local area networks.

CINEMA APPLICATIONS

Digital signage is suitable for any kind of media industry. Cinemas are no exception. Just as for other point-of-purchase applications, there might be digital signage screens in the foyer replacing the traditional cinema posters. The digital poster content might be changed according to what movies are shown at a particular hour of the day. Replacing the traditional film with electronic media has been a dream for a long time.

Cinemas are very dependent on being able to do things simultaneously and according to schedules and playlists. For this reason, cinemas are probably one of the most challenging environments for digital signage.

Preshow advertising is the least demanding application within the cinemas. This requires moderately priced projection systems and DVD-quality signals.

There are two quality levels used to show movies in cinemas using digital techniques (as described in Chapter 9): *E-cinema* (electronic cinema) and *D-cinema* (digital cinema). E-cinema uses high-brightness HD projection systems; the higher-quality D-cinema is an HD reproduction at studio-quality bitrates and compression.

Other important applications are customer terminals and kiosks that let visitors view movie trailers at their request, to facilitate movie selection.

The possibilities to introduce electronic games that are one way or the other connected to the visitors' cell phones are endless. Of course, it

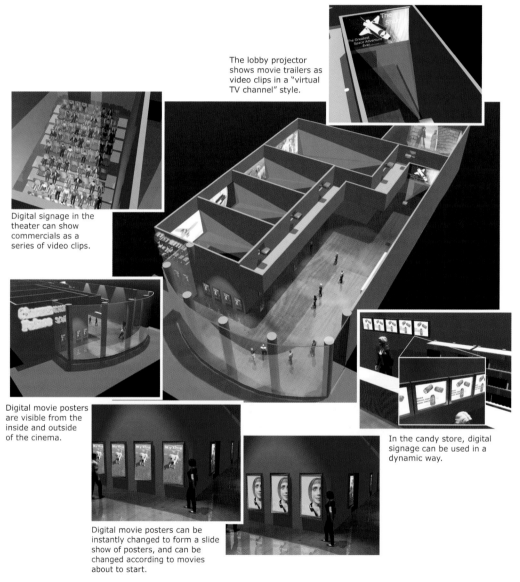

The lobby projector shows movie trailers as video clips in a "virtual TV channel" style.

Digital signage in the theater can show commercials as a series of video clips.

Digital movie posters are visible from the inside and outside of the cinema.

In the candy store, digital signage can be used in a dynamic way.

Digital movie posters can be instantly changed to form a slide show of posters, and can be changed according to movies about to start.

Figure 11.7   Cinema digital signage applications are quite varied. In the long run, D- and E-cinema will replace all remaining analog projection systems.

may be eventually possible to download trailers to cell phones using Bluetooth. These trailers have to be supplied in formats and file sizes that are suitable for the capabilities of today's cell phones.

Finally, cinema auditoriums could also be used to show television events such as boxing matches and other wide-interest sporting events.

This means that in a purely digital cinema environment, all formats, resolutions, and quality levels of video clips have to be handled (Figure 11.7). Cinemas are no doubt one of the most challenging environments for digital signage, and there is much room for experimentation and development.

In large environments like cinema lobbies and trade show displays, it might be desirable to combine several 42-inch or 50-inch screens into one large display, to show either one very large picture divided into segments or to create an artistic collection of image sizes and shapes. Note in Figure 11.8 that a variety of aspect ratios is achieved by combining the screens in different ways. Such combined screens may become very impressive, though you would not want to watch an entire movie this way.

Figure 11.9 shows what can be done with indoor LED displays. By combining several sections of LEDs, any aspect ratio can be achieved, creating a new canvas type for digital art. This kind of application is suitable for cinemas as well as hotel lobbies and reception areas in larger companies.

Figure 11.8 Combining several screens into larger ones (from Panasonic). Varying the number of screens and their orientations can yield both wide and very narrow configurations.

Figure 11.9   Interesting artistic effects can be achieved by combining segments of LED displays.

BANKS AND POST OFFICES

In retail locations where customers may have to form a line to wait for the next available staff person to assist them, digital signage can offer new and improved methods of communicating with customers. A queue ticket display and clock immediately catches attentions since it provides information that is of immediate use to the customer (Figure 11.10). Digital signage also promotes products or services to customers waiting in line—the practical information about the queue draws attention to the advertising message.

KIOSKS

Kiosks are a kind of advanced customer terminal that provide two-way communications. Customers can withdraw money from their bank accounts, purchase products, or request additional information about an exhibit or product. Depending on their purpose, kiosks might include credit card readers or even more sophisticated devices like web cameras and microphones.

Kiosks are customized to their particular application, and they can also take on many different designs, as shown in Figure 11.11.

Figure 11.10 This digital signage application from Publiq shows the next queue ticket in line (981) and where to go (counter 4) combined with a commercial for home improvement loans.

Figure 11.11 Kiosks (like this selection from Publiq) are often customized according to use and location. They are used for gaming, in banks, as unemployment offices, and so on.

Customer Terminals

Customer terminals can be regarded as simplified kiosk terminals. They often consist of a touch-sensitive screen connected to a media player or, as in Figure 11.12, with a built-in media player. This is a highly advanced, near-real-time satellite multicasting service. The screen content is on a background image on top of which is overlaid text files with the odds data. The overlay files are updated as soon as there is a change in the database where the odds are stored.

This terminal also has a continuously updated news ticker, and the user can select which game is shown and select the desired page within a game. The media player is a flash memory device where the user can select a playlist and move around within a playlist by touching the correct regions (buttons) on the screen.

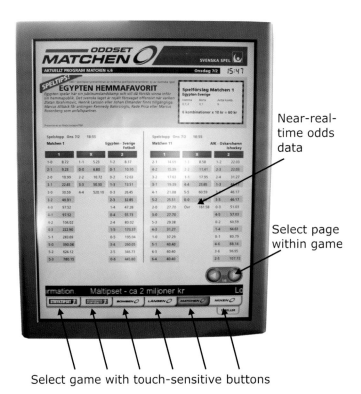

Near-real-time odds data

Select page within game

Select game with touch-sensitive buttons

Figure 11.12   A near-real-time odds customer terminal application from MultiQ (text in Swedish).

Figure 11.13 This large IR touch screen from Panasonic works like an art museum; the user chooses from hundreds of paintings to be displayed in large format.

When the screen has been untouched for a while, the media player returns to its default playlist promoting its various features to entice the next customer to interact with it.

Customer terminals like this may be used in digital signage broadcasting systems to provide local interactivity. Figures 11.13 and 11.14 show some additional uses for customer terminals.

If several download alternatives are available, a touch screen enables the user to press a specific button on the screen to make a selection.

Finding Surfaces for Digital Signage

A classic problem in advertising is finding space for the signs. A way to solve lack of space is Intellimat, a carpet display device that you can step on (Figure 11.15). Floor space may be used this way. Another alternative that maximizes its footprint is a spinning, cylindrical LED display. These displays create a dynamic and exotic impression in cinemas and at tourist attractions (Figure 11.16).

Figure 11.14a Electrosonic digital sign with Bluetooth download capability makes it possible for users to download coupons and other information directly to a cell phone.

Figure 11.14b Another way to use the customer's cell phone is to let him or her send an SMS to interact with the content on the screen. This is used by many TV stations, as in this example from NEVER.NO. It can also be used for digital signage applications. Games voting and customer contact are possible applications.

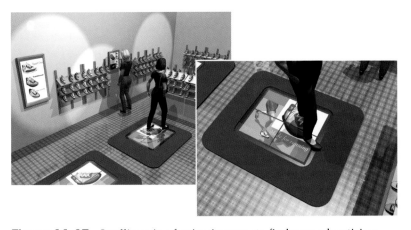

Figure 11.15 Intellimat is a fascinating way to find new advertising space—on the floor.

Figure 11.16 CNN headquarters in Atlanta uses a number of cylindrical digital signs.

OUTDOOR DIGITAL SIGNAGE ENVIRONMENTS

Of course, it is desirable to be able to put signs outside the stores to get the customers to go inside (Figure 10.17). In malls, the signs may be located outside the shop even though they are still indoors. In this usage, conventional plasma or LCD displays that do not withstand outdoor climate may be used.

No doubt, the most spectacular digital signage applications are the large outdoor LED screens. Until recently, they were used primarily at events like concerts and in sports arenas. But in the last few years, outdoor LED displays are seen in more and more places. Las Vegas has created some of the most spectacular outdoor LED displays.

Outdoor digital signage requires very expensive installations, but outdoor applications are increasing everywhere. In addition to event-like displays, displays in street environments are getting more popular (Figures 11.18 and 11.19), and in the long run, these will replace the large-scale printed posters and wall advertising.

In metropolitan areas, it may be hard to find new places to locate commercial signs because so much space has already been claimed. In the years to come, many of the locations used for printed signs will be converted into digital signage.

Figure 11.17 Digital signage can be placed outside a store to promote the products sold within. The digital signs on each side of this bookstore's window change to display books or magazines.

Figure 11.18 LED screens are very bright and provide adequate contrast around the clock. Las Vegas streets are lit with very large screens.

Figure 11.19 Another Las Vegas outdoor LED screen advertises a show and changes to promote a contest related to the show.

A current limiting factor in the creation of outdoor displays is that the choice of outdoor display devices is limited to LED displays because they are powerful and withstand cold as well as hot weather. LCDs get damaged if exposed to extreme temperatures. The major drawback of LEDs is that the individual LED is quite large, which means the screens have to be very large in order to provide acceptable resolution. The larger a screen is, the farther away viewers need to be for optimal viewing (Figures 11.20 and 11.21).

However, there is one indoor location that so far is quite unexploited for outdoor digital advertising—store windows, where digital signage can be directed toward people outside in the street. Because it is protected from the elements, LCDs can be used.

In contrast to the extremely large LED screens that are used for outdoor advertising in metropolitan areas and for billboards placed along roads, there are small LED text display systems used at bus stops and even on busses and other public transportation. Still, the reason for using LEDs is that they tolerate a wide temperature range and are bright enough to provide a sufficient contrast ratio night and day.

Figure 11.20   Some of the more extreme, large-scale LED digital signs in Las Vegas.

Figure 11.21   Night-time view of one of the spectacular Las Vegas outdoor screens.

Outdoor Screens in Three Dimensions

The latest addition to outdoor LED screens is to build screens in three dimensions, following the walls of a building or curving screens, as in Figures 11.22 and 11.23.

Figure 11.22   At the Miracle Mile Shops in Las Vegas, the LED screens wrap around the building, creating a very exotic effect.

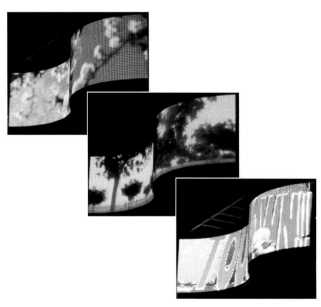

Figure 11.23   This curved LED display from Billboard Video, Inc. is another example of digital signage in three dimensions.

Figure 11.24   The LED screen displaying the TV coverage may provide the same detailed view of what's happening to the audience on location as to the TV viewer.

Sports Arenas

The activities in sports arenas are often associated with television—they are broadcast for worldwide viewing. In many cases, the TV viewer has a better view than the visitors at the arenas because cameras provide a close and unobstructed view.

One way to improve the view for onsite spectators is to use large outdoor LCD screens, as shown in Figure 11.24. Often, the TV signal that is sent to the TV viewers at home can be used in the sports arena itself.

No doubt, digital signage makes its contribution to indoor as well as outdoor environments. Dynamic and flexible content will become part of the building when used outdoors and part of the décor when used indoors.

12

THE FUTURE OF DIGITAL SIGNAGE SYSTEMS

The future will most certainly provide larger, better, thinner, and cheaper display devices. This greatly increases the number of possible applications for all kinds of digital signage. The future may also provide completely new kinds of display devices that we cannot imagine today.

As with all technology developments, another thing to be expected is that the cost of hardware will decrease, and the cost of storing immense amounts of data will be very low. This will allow for very advanced digital signage systems with large movie or music libraries that can be combined with all other kinds of content.

As discussed previously, advanced digital signage technologies are based on file transfer and live streaming IP. Using these basic elements, it is possible to create all kinds of new and exciting media. But what will eventually happen will depend on what new display devices are introduced.

This book has focused on public retail and entertainment applications for digital signage. For the next few years, we will find most applications for digital signage in stores and other public areas, such as museums and transportation hubs. This is an interesting reversal of history, as the first electronic signage applications in shops were based on the old VHS technology and TV sets that were first used in homes and then migrated to retail uses. However, the public retail environment is where digital signage is likely to develop and gain acceptance, before evolving into home applications. The possibilities to provide all kinds of information, entertainment, and dynamic digital art in the home go beyond the borders of your fantasy.

FOUR DEVELOPMENT PHASES OF DIGITAL SIGNAGE

Digital signage will likely go through four development phases as it gains widespread use and acceptance.

Phase 1: Manual Duplication and Distribution

The first phase is manually handled displays located at a limited number of locations for advertising products in stores and providing additional information in other public spaces. The content is distributed using physical media, such as DVDs. Content production is also manual, as are the copying process and mailing of DVDs.

Phase 2: Terrestrial Broadband Unicasting

In the second phase, the manual distribution of content is replaced by a broadband unicast-based distribution network. This means some content is added manually while other content is retrieved from sources already available through the Internet. At the time of writing this book, most digital signage systems are in this phase.

Phase 3: Network Multicasting

In the third phase of developing the digital signage media, the amount of content to be distributed has increased and so has the number of sites in the network. There is also a need for near-real-time and real-time distribution of content. Systems like this need multicasting, using either satellite or local area networks that allow for multicasting.

Phase 4: In-Home Digital Signage

The fourth phase is when digital signage becomes a consumer medium. This requires mass-market multicasting channels. There are different ways to meet this challenge. On a national or international level, satellite broadcasting may be the first alternative. Also, using multicasting-enabled local area networks will result in the next generation of cable TV networks. Another way of handling local or regional multicasting is, of course, through terrestrial transmitters.

As an interesting consequence, this digital signage network looks very much like the present-day infrastructure for distribution of digital television (Figure 12.1).

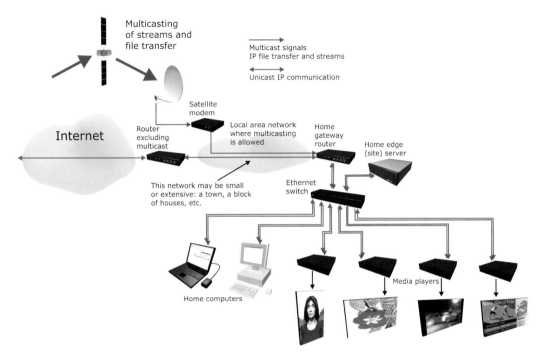

Figure 12.1 Digital signage home site servers or media players combine multicasting for content delivery and the common Internet broadband connection in applications where a return path to the content provider is required.

Multicast distribution of digital signage to the home may be done using satellites and local area networks (Figure 12.2).

DISTRIBUTION MEDIA OPTIONS

Satellite is very efficient for multicasting IP across vast areas, such as a country or a continent. This is very appropriate for public digital signage applications. Retail chains, hotels, railway stations, and airports are frequently spread over a vast area, and satellite will be the most appropriate means for broadcasting to these distant sites.

However, for future in-home IP broadcasting applications, with lots of receiving sites everywhere, even terrestrial transmitters and cable TV networks may be suitable distribution media. DVB then may be

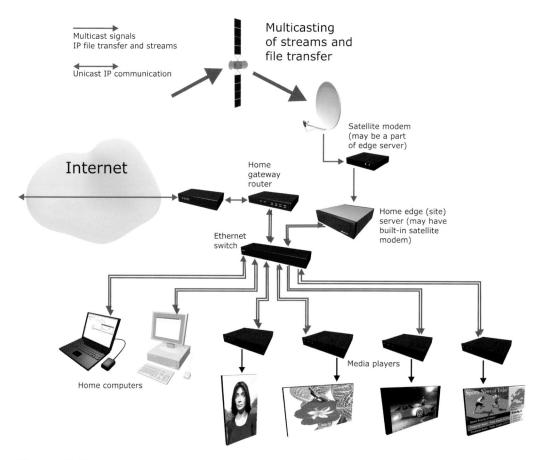

Figure 12.2   If no local area network carrying the multicast signals is available, a direct-to-home satellite dish may be used.

used to carry IP in these distribution systems as well. On top of this, of course, all kinds of multicasting networks are of interest.

Terrestrial Multicasting Using Landlines

One option is multicasting on a national or international level using terrestrial broadband based on optical fibers combined with local area networks. However, there will always be a need for the telecom operators to control how the capacity on these networks is used. A completely free use of multicast capacity on the Internet is not to be expected. However, telecom operators may choose to interconnect local area networks in different geographical areas using optical fibers. This is very similar to the way digital cable TV has evolved, where local cable networks in different cities may be interconnected by optical fibers. These interconnecting links need a specified quality of service with guaranteed bitrates. IPTV providers also work very much this way already and use a common headend for all their local networks.

Terrestrial Transmitters

Local or regional distribution of the multicast signals also can be handled by terrestrial broadcasting transmission systems. In spite of all the satellites and fibers in the world today, the terrestrial broadcast systems have survived the new technologies. This is largely because of the possibilities to use existing rooftop antennas and because the signals can be received using mobile equipment. This is not the case for cable and satellite.

Europe and many other places use the DVB-T standard for terrestrial TV and the DVB-C for cable. In North America, the Advanced Television Systems Committee (ATSC) standard is used. Only time will tell to what extent these systems can be used to carry IP intended for digital signage applications as well.

New terrestrial broadcast media, such as DVB-H and DMB, are based on IP distribution and the basic principles of file transfer and streaming. Therefore, they use principles similar to those described for digital signage in this book.

A conclusion might be that the digital signage medium, when distributed to the end consumer, will use a combination of the distribution channels that are in use today. Some people use cable and others use direct-to-home satellite distribution or off-the-air reception from terrestrial transmitters.

IP Broadcasting

Efficient means of distribution will be required to distribute the large files and live streams for digital signage to a larger number of sites. The Internet of today is not suitable for large-scale multicasting purposes. However, in a world where most people have access to broadband Internet in their homes, the Internet is perhaps the best choice as a return path to the content provider in applications where a return path is needed.

In Chapter 7, IP broadcasting was discussed. By combining the versatility of IP packets (today mostly used for telecom) with broadcast technology (today used for distribution of digital television signals), a new and powerful medium—digital signage broadcasting—is created. The use of IP packets and broadcasting means distributing any kind of information anywhere, simultaneously, and to an unlimited number of receivers. This has never been possible before. Combining the best characteristics of two partially competing technologies provides perhaps the most flexible medium ever known.

CONSUMER APPLICATIONS

A digital signage system may eventually replace the conventional TV set because it can provide live IPTV as well as background visual effects such as digital art and information. In the future, our homes will probably have many more display systems than today. With at least one flat-panel display system in each room, the possibilities for digital art will grow, and flat-panel displays will become a part of the furnishing in every room. This would mean that the display systems will be used in many more ways than just for television and home theater applications (Figure 12.3).

Background TV and Information Display System

In addition to watching original broadcast programming, many people use their TV sets as a source of background information. For this kind of application, digital signage may be a better choice than conventional television because a live broadcast channel can be combined with news or stock tickers, weather maps, or sports results that are continuously updated.

For such a background source of information, digital signage regions and layers created from a selection of files—possibly combined with one or more live streams—may be a better choice than conventional television. We will now look more closely at the reasons.

Customizing Content

Since the final content on a screen in a digital signage system may be selected individually for each screen (the final selection is done by the playlists used in the media player), the result may be adapted to each specific environment of a home. Theoretically, the user may

Figure 12.3   Larger, thinner, cheaper, and better display devices are the future of digital signage and may be a part of the future digital home.

choose what to show in each region or specific layers of the individual screen, as well as to add tickers according to taste and interest.

For those looking for a faster way to configure the various displays in their homes, future systems will likely offer ready-made themes that can be selected at each media player. This spares the users the need to go through the tedious and complicated process of building a playlist from scratch for each screen element.

Once a theme is selected, modifications can be made to customize it for specific interests or purposes (Figure 12.4). Themes might include kitchen, living room, or bedroom. Other kinds of themes may be used at different times of the day, such as the morning/breakfast theme, the midday theme, or the evening theme. Themes could also be adapted to specific viewer groups by age or interest, such as teenagers, sports, or nature.

Themes may require a subscription fee, but providers may leave some of the regions open to advertising in order to subsidize their costs so consumers can receive the rest of the content free. This

Figure 12.4   Viewers can customize the content to be shown on different parts of the screen.

"free-to-air" digital signage concept is an example of simultaneously displaying commercial information and entertainment. Commercial TV stations can only show commercials during breaks in the programming, which is not the case for digital signage.

Digital Art and Information

With large screens at home, digital art can create a specific atmosphere or be used as a part of the room's furnishings. Digital art will really begin to take off as soon as the right displays have been developed and are reasonably priced for home consumers. Good examples are the desktop background pictures in computers and in cell phone displays. Perhaps people will change the art on their walls every day or by the season. An interesting possibility is to add sound to the digital art to be able to intensify the experience (Figure 12.5).

The Digital Newspaper

Another dream of thin display devices is the digital newspaper. A digital newspaper device may contain an integrated media player that is loaded with content overnight (instead of printing and distributing the newspapers).

Chapter 3 describes the basic elements of the content shown on a digital sign. A digital sign requires either files or digital streams to create the content of the individual sign. The same basic principles

Figure 12.5 Digital art will become much more important as the number of display systems at home increases. A piece of digital art like this may be presented along with sounds of sea, wind, and waves.

apply to a digital newspaper based on future digital paper presentation. Figure 12.6 shows a digital paper application where the airport magazine is automatically downloaded to an integrated media player as you enter the airport.

As described in Chapter 2, the development of new electronic paper display devices will probably be the core of this medium, which may be regarded as a branch of digital signage. Electronic paper technologies might also be used for signs as large as sports arena screens and as small as price tags.

Wallpaper Television

The introduction of digital paper also means the possibilities to make extremely thin displays that cover larger areas of the walls. If OLED or other technologies succeed in providing low-cost display devices, the "wallpaper" television set or digital signage screen that is glued to the wall may very well become a reality within the next few decades. Being able to cover an entire wall with a display system will result in a completely new impression of media, as shown

Objects on digital paper (text, pictures, and video clips) are files being presented as regions and layers by an integrated miniature media player.

Figure 12.6   The future digital newspaper really consists of the same content that the newspapers use today for the printed product but distributes them digitally.

Figure 12.7   The futuristic "wallpaper" television set or wallpaper digital signage display would require a high-definition digital signage system to provide interesting content.

in Figure 12.7. The display device will really become a part of the room. But in order to fill the "walls" with interesting and dynamic content, a powerful digital signage system is required behind the scenes.

THE NEED FOR STANDARDIZATION

In order to get digital signage systems to work in your home, you must be able to buy media players from different manufacturers that could work with one another and with standardized content management servers. Today there is next to no standardization, but organizations such as POPAI (Point of Purchase Advertising International) are working to establish a common standard (see Chapter 3).

Eventually, there probably will be some kind of standard for home use of digital signage systems. What is most important to achieve is a playlist standard to get all media players to interpret playlists the same way. Also, there is a need for handling of groups of playlists and how these playlists should affect different regions, layers, and tickers on the screens.

Standardization is an achievable goal, since all digital signage systems are based on standardized file and stream formats. What is missing is just the standardization for the administration of the files and streams. You could say that this is very similar to the problems that were solved when establishing the Digital Video Broadcasting (DVB) standard. The MPEG-2 and audio Musicam standards existed and what was needed was a standard that could handle the administration of the different components of the signal.

If no standard is set, there might be a few digital signage systems that survive; in the long run, manufacturers of media players will work together with different brands of content management servers. Darwin's law of evolution also applies to the development of electronic hardware and software—it is truly the survival of the fittest.

Important Standardization Issues

A number of issues have to be settled to be able to create a standardized digital signage system.

Like the standards for digital TV, such as the DVB standard, it is practical to use a generic digital signage standard that focuses on how the media players interpret an incoming signal or message. This allows for future improvements on the back-end side, that is, in the content management and rendering servers. This is much the same as the possibilities for older digital TV set-top boxes to take advantage of

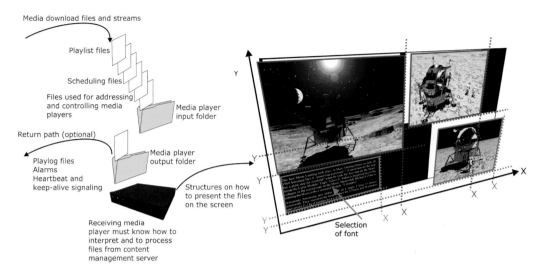

Figure 12.8   A number of parameters have yet to be standardized for digital signage systems.

improved encoding and other advances on the transmission side in digital TV distribution systems.

Parameters to Be Standardized   Parameters to be standardized to allow any brand of media player to be used in any digital signage system include (Figure 12.8):

- Structures for how layers, regions, and tickers are to be presented on the screen based on incoming playlists
- Playlists
- Scheduling files
- Ways to address and control the media players, such as telling them what message they are to provide (message channel)

If a return path is to be supported, file formats covering the following features have to be standardized:

- Playlogs
- Alarms, heartbeat signaling, and other housekeeping information signaling

Distribution File Formats   Chapter 9 describes why it is better to break down larger publishing files into separate files for audio, video, images, and text. Doing so is a way of achieving flexibility when it comes to insertion of local content, getting fast updating of near-real-time data, and making the distribution chain as economical as possible. Therefore, the standard should contain a set of basic file formats for forming screen content.

For those who produce Adobe PDF or Microsoft PowerPoint files, it would be an advantage if future versions of Adobe Acrobat and PowerPoint had export filters where the publication is split into a set of the distribution files along with a standardized playlist. Having such features would mean a big leap ahead in adapting to the digital signage medium.

No doubt the question about what file formats to be supported by a digital signage system is among the most critical and difficult issues. The question of which file formats to be handled on the content management back-end side and which on the media player client side could probably be debated forever.

Finally, there are electrical interfaces that may be mandatory or optional. A problem is that the standard must be open for introduction of new file formats since the use of IP is much more versatile than conventional broadcasting systems.

Probably, there are many more parameters to be set and future standardizations commissions will have much work to do before media players reach a standardization status similar to TV digital set-top boxes. Also, the terminology for digital signage has not yet been finally set. In the Glossary, I have tried to summarize the known terminology of today, but there are many alternative terms to choose from.

THE DIGITAL SIGNAGE CONTENT PROVIDER OF TOMORROW

After looking at the figures in this chapter, it should have become quite evident that the content provider of tomorrow will be some combination of TV and radio channel production facility, newspaper editorial staff, and Webmaster's office. All kinds of content have to be handled by this new kind of media-providing company. Also, advertising agencies will probably have to work somewhat differently than they do today to take into account simultaneously several aspects of media and adapt the content to this new way of content management and distribution. Combining IP and broadcasting creates a very versatile medium able to handle any kind of information, anywhere, and to anyone.

It is interesting to see that most companies in the media market have already started to move in this direction and already work in a more integrated way. Radio and TV stations are well established on the Web. Virtually all newspapers around the world are well established on the Web, and many of them have formed partnerships in the radio or television business.

General, large-scale, content management systems for TV stations and others are aiming at being able to support various publication channels, such as radio, television, the Web, and printed media. Digital signage is probably next on the list (Figure 12.9).

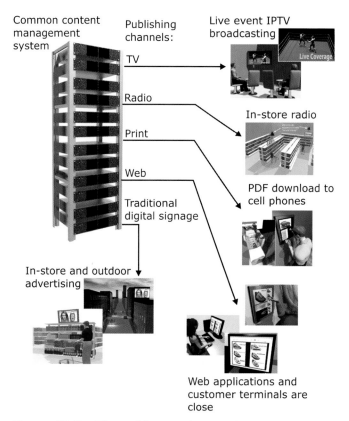

Figure 12.9   The goal for most large-scale content management systems is to provide support for any possible publication channel. Digital signage may become the "all-in-one" publication channel of the future.

Content Customization

It is obvious that digital signage operators must be able to provide a variety of non-real-time as well as real-time or near-real-time content. Consumers will use the content in different ways than they do today. They will want whatever they want whenever they want and in a much more customized way than today. Therefore, content providers will have to provide a selection of files, streams, and playlists (themes) to appeal to consumers. And the final appearance of each playlist will probably be decided by the consumer.

Today, TV stations and program providers supply us with ready-made broadcasts, and web sites are also completed selections of content. The user can search for specific things, but the design and functionality of a site is predetermined. Digital signage means consumers will require something to be served but in the way they want it. So playlists that can be adjusted according to taste (creating your own themes) may be one of the key features of the future.

Consumers may want more services than just information and entertainment with commercials mixed in. Such services may include digital art for customization of the home environment. Today, the closest model for digital art customization is cell phone companies that provide additional background themes, animations, and ringtones so customers can create a unique and individualized phone.

File and Information Transfer

One of the most important properties of digital signage systems is that they are based on distribution of IP packets. Compared to other broadcasting media, IP has the advantage of being able to transfer any kind of information, and this opens up completely new media that are more than just content on a screen. Inventing a new medium is more or less only a question of developing new presentation devices and new file formats. The ability to handle all kinds of information means that it will become possible to maintain the existing infrastructure in local area networks even though completely new services are introduced.

Three-Dimensional Objects and Holographic Data

Figure 12.10 shows what could be possible with the proper holographic technologies. A new car model can be introduced using a 3D holographic display system. The car itself is reproduced from a 3D file.

Figure 12.10 Three-dimensional digital signage systems most certainly will be based on IP technology since existing infrastructure can be used for distribution.

The presenter is also created from a 3D animation file. The 3D text above the car is from a text file, as is the text on the rotating 3D ticker below the car.

The dynamics of such a potential system are impressive. The 3D model of the car could be exchanged for another car model in a fraction of a second, and the presenter's script would change to promote the features of that car model.

The concept is the same as for today's digital signage systems. Each element displayed originates from a separate file. If a display device like this is introduced, the existing IP distribution infrastructure could be reused. If this technology is combined with live distribution, live performing artists could be included instead of a prerecorded animated announcer. The possibilities for using live events for promoting products at many locations simultaneously will eventually find new dimensions.

Who knows what the future will bring when it comes to 3D and holographic technologies? And who knows, sometime in the future these systems also might be used to transfer stimuli for all our senses, even smell and taste. IP can carry any kind of information!

Appendix A

TRAFFIC CAPACITY CALCULATIONS

Digital signage systems involve real-time as well as near-real-time and non-real-time applications. As a result, calculating the capacity required in such a system means taking several things into account.

CALCULATING THE MINIMUM BITRATE

The maximum transfer time allowed for content is the variable that determines the minimum bitrate. Normally, it is not possible to buy a variable bitrate, so the minimum bitrate has to be selected prior to installation.

First, figure out the amount of content to be updated in each media player each day. How many files need to be updated and what are their sizes? Summing up the files to be updated each day gives a hint of an average bitrate that could do the job in 24 hours.

In this example, each store has 10 media players. All players are updated with, and always contain, the same content. But, they do not necessarily play the same content at a given time.

Here are some files that might be updated to the media players during a normal 24 hours:

- 4 video clips, 40 MB each (approximately 1.8 minutes of 3 Mbps video)
- 52 JPEG pictures, 1.5 MB each
- XML data that is continuously updated at an average rate of 50 kbps

Each day we have to transfer $(4 \times 40) + (52 \times 1.5) = 238$ MB (excluding the XML data, which is added in later). To calculate the average bitrate, multiply the MB size by 8 (to convert to Mb) and divide by $(60 \times 60 \times 24)$ (60 seconds in 60 minutes in 24 hours = the number of seconds in 24 hours). The total size of data to be transferred is 238 MB and the average bitrate required will be $(238 \times 8)/(60 \times 60 \times 24) = 0.022$ Mbps. Divide by 1,000, and the result is 22 kbps.

Adding the 50 kbps XML data file stream, which runs constantly, makes the total 72 kbps. This is a very low bitrate, and it will take 24 hours to get all information through.

There might be additional requirements, such as the ability to correct a 1.5 MB JPEG picture that contains errors. If there is a request to replace one of the JPEG pictures in 5 minutes, the required bitrate can be calculated as follows: multiply the MB file size by 8 (to convert to Mb) and then divide by 5×60 (the number of seconds in 5 minutes to get the bitrate in bps). A bitrate of $(1.5 \times 8)/(5 \times 60) = 0.04$ Mbps $= 40$ kbps will be required, and a total of 90 kbps will be necessary to include the XML data stream as well.

If the requirement is to transfer one of the video clips in less than 30 minutes, the requirement will be (using the same formula): $(40 \times 8)/(30 \times 60) = 178$ kbps plus the 50 kbps of XML data, adding up to 228 kbps.

UNICAST VERSUS MULTICAST SYSTEM SERVER LOAD

The major question in digital signage is probably whether to choose an Internet-based unicast system, or a solution that allows for multicasting as a private terrestrial IP network, or a satellite solution.

Unicasting Calculations

If the amount of content is limited and/or the number of sites to be covered is low, an Internet unicast solution might do. The possibilities for real-time streaming in unicast systems are not very good when there are multiple sites.

The basic problem of unicast systems is that a separate transfer of data has to be set up with each player. This means that the content management server has to be able to deliver the bitstream required

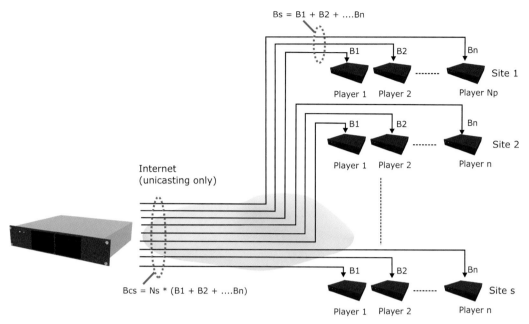

Figure A.1 In unicast distribution, a separate bitstream has to be set up to each media player; this requires a huge bitstream from the content management server.

to each media player. The load on the content management server system will depend on the number of players (Figure A.1). In the earlier example, we decided that in order to fulfill all requirements, the bitrate had to be at least 228 kbps. In our example with 10 players in each store, a system with 100 shops would include 1,000 media players. If there are 1,000 players that should receive the same content, the server must provide 1,000 × 228 kbps = 228 Mbps.

If the number of media players to be covered or the amount of traffic to be transferred doubles, the required bitrate would increase to 456 Mbps. Two thousand media players may sound like a lot, but if there are 10 media players in each store, it only takes 200 stores to reach that 2,000 capacity.

Here are some variables used in calculating the total bitrate needed:

- Bcs = Required minimum streaming bitrate from the content management server and in the Internet backbone connection.
- Ns = Number of sites to be served.
- Np = Number of media players to be served in each store.

- Bs = Bitrate required from the broadband connection in the store.
- Bn = Bitrate of information to be distributed to media player n.

Content is assumed to be individual to each media player at one site:

$$Bcs = Ns \times (B1 + B2 + \ldots Bn)$$

If the amount of content to be distributed to each media player is assumed to be the same (B), the total bitrate required from the server and the Internet backbone connection is $BC = Ns \times Np \times B$.

In our example, that means $Bcs = 200 \times 10 \times 228\,\text{kbps} = 456\,\text{Mbps}$.

So far, extreme Internet bitrates may be hard to find, but large servers do exist, and the technology is always developing. And if we need to increase the number of media players from 10 to 20 in each shop, the required bitrate from the content management server will approach 1 Gbps. To build a system with this performance, we would probably have to use several decentralized servers located in different cities to handle the load on the connections to main routers on the Internet. The same problem occurs if the traffic doubles to each player due to new demands from the advertisers. Thus, using unicasting across the Internet is very sensitive to traffic increase, and traffic planning might be difficult.

Note that the load on the Internet broadband connection in each store is the sum of the bitrates to the media players:

$$Bs = B1 + B2 + \ldots Bn$$

The solution is to use multicasting networks, which are much less sensitive to such changes.

The problem of unicast systems is that the load on the content management server increases with the number of sites and media players to be covered. One way to partially solve this is to use an edge server. With edge servers, a file does not have to be transferred more than once to each site. When all media players use the same content files (e.g., customer terminals all used for the same kind of information, the same commercial video clips used for preshow advertising in different auditoriums in cinemas), edge servers are particularly efficient.

Multicast Calculations

Adding site servers in broadband distribution systems may ease the load on the content management server. An even more efficient way of handling higher distribution requirements is to use multicasting or even the combination of multicasting and edge servers. Figure A.2 shows the very efficient combination of a satellite multicasting system and satellite edge servers.

Multicasting solves the problem of the load on the content management server, which increases as the number of sites increases. All files and streams are distributed just once. The content management server delivers files only to the FTP server at the uplink station and nowhere else. Therefore, the load on the content management server is independent of the number of sites served.

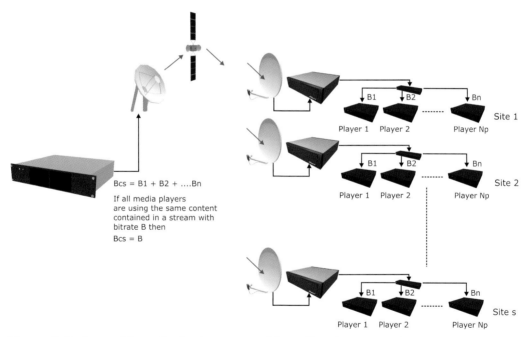

$Bcs = B1 + B2 + ...Bn$

If all media players are using the same content contained in a stream with bitrate B then

$Bcs = B$

Figure A.2 In a multicast distribution system with satellite edge servers, the content management server is completely unaffected by the number of receiving sites. The same thing applies to a system where the edge servers are replaced by satellite modems and media players that have integrated multicast clients.

If content is unique to each media player at one site, then

$$Bcs = (B1 + B2 + \ldots Bn).$$

If traffic increases, the bitrate in the single bitstream has to be increased accordingly, but the required capacity is independent of the number of sites served. As a result, the bitrate required from the content management server and the multicasting platform normally will be within reach of standard equipment. A satellite transponder may house up to 40 Mbps or more, and this capacity can be available at each reception site.

In the example, a simple content management server and a satellite channel providing a bitrate of 228 kbps will do the same job as the 456 Mbps content management server in the unicast network. And as a matter of fact, it would do the same job for any number of sites.

On the other hand, if all media players in the shop needed to be updated with different content, assuming the same requirements (10 media players in each of 200 stores), the satellite channel would have to be 10 times as wide, 2.28 Mbps. The unicasting server could have stayed at 456 Mbps, since unicasting has the advantage of being able to supply unique information to each media player. Figures A.3 and A.4 illustrate the case discussed above.

The unicast and multicast systems are designed to have the same performance at 2,000 media players. When the number of media players increases above 2,000, the unicast system requires more time to update the media players with the 40 MB video clip file at the same time as the 50 kbps XML file is transferred to the players. In 30 minutes, the 40 MB video file and 11.25 MB of XML data are transferred to all media players (Figure A3).

You can also see that we actually use only a small portion of the capacity of the system. A 228 kbps channel will provide $0.228 \times 24 \times 60 \times 60/8 = 2.462$ GB in 24 hours. So clever traffic handling can save a lot of capacity.

It is very difficult to compare unicasting and multicasting because it is essentially comparing apples and oranges. Unicasting is a point-to-point method of distribution and multicasting is optimized for point-to-multipoint distribution. In digital signage systems, there is

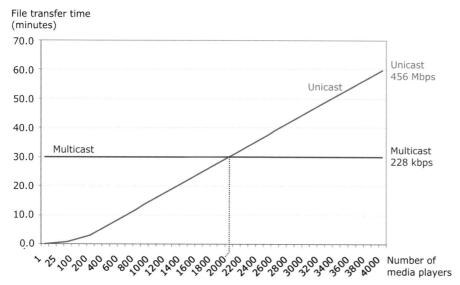

Figure A.3   In multicast systems, the file transfer time is independent of the number of media players served. Here, a total transfer time of 51.25 MB (40 + 11.25) is shown.

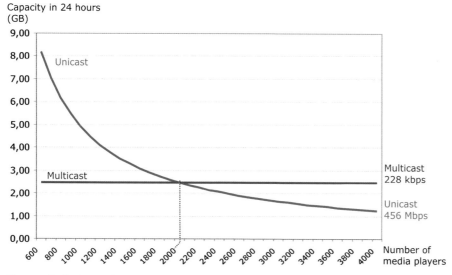

Figure A.4   In multicast systems, the capacity that can be transferred to the media players during 24 hours is constant; in unicast systems, the capacity is affected by the number of media players.

often a mix of these two needs. In general, the greater the number of sites and media players that use the same content, the better multicasting is likely to be. In systems where a small number of sites get more individual content than common content, unicasting might be the best choice.

Unicast and Multicast Break-even Formulas

At what number of media players to be served is the time for transfer the same?

Is it possible to use some simple formulas to decide the break-even point between unicast and multicast distribution. It is known that unicast is advantageous when there is a small number of locations to be served and that multicast is better for serving a large number of locations with the same content.

The calculations are based on the assumption that the same content is to be distributed to all sites, that there is only one player at each location, and that no edge servers are involved.

Transfer Time Break-even

Ac = Amount of content to be transferred (bytes)—multiply by 8
        to get number of bits
N = Number of sites to be served
T = Time for transfer of content
Bu = Bitrate provided by the unicast server (bits per second)
Bm = Bitrate provided in the multicasting channel (bits per second)

- Unicasting: $T = Ac \times 8 \times N/Bu$
- Multicasting: $T = Ac \times 8/Bm$
- Transfer times for unicast and multicast systems are equal when:
  $Ac \times 8 \times N/Bu = A \times 8/Bm$

From this, we can deduce that the required transfer times for content are equal when the number of sites, N, is:

$$N = Bu/Bm$$

As a consequence, the break-even for capacity per 24h can also be calculated using the preceding formula.

Example

$Bu = 50$ Mb/s (broadband unicast bitrate)
$Bm = 0.5$ Mb/s (satellite multicast bitrate)

- Transfer times are equal when the number of sites to be served is: $N = 50/0.5 = 100$
- Break-even is at $N = 2000$ in Figures A.3 and A.4; this can be calculated using the same formula.

Distribution Cost Break-even

$Cu = $ Cost per bandwidth (bits per second) in the unicast backbone connection
$Cm = $ Cost per bandwidth (bits per second) in the multicast channel
$Ctu = $ Cost for distribution using unicast
$Ctm = $ Cost for unicast using multicast

- Unicasting: $Ctu = Ac \times 8 \times Cu \times N$
- Multicasting: $Ctm = Ac \times 8 \times Cm$
- Distribution cost is equal when: $Ac \times 8 \times Cu \times N = Ac \times 8 \times Cm$

From this we can deduce that distribution costs are equal when the number of sites, N, is:

$$N = Cm/Cu$$

Example[*]

$Cu = 850$ USD per Mb/s and year (broadband unicast dedicated capacity)
$Cm = 150{,}000$ USD per Mb/s and year (satellite multicast)

- Distribution costs (just comparing broadband backbone capacity and satellite multicast capacity) are equal when the number of sites to be served is: $N = 150{,}000/850 = 176$

Costs for servers and content gathering must be added when establishing a real budget for the distribution part of a digital signage system.

---

*Cost may vary considerably due to amount of capacity leased and choice of broadband or satellite operator, respectively

Remember that server costs are much higher when using unicast than for multicasting if a large number of sites are to be served. Also, costs for separate broadband connections in shops must be added if required. Reception equipment costs should be added if satellite multicasting is used. However, the preceding formulas can still give a quick indication of where the break-even point is when chosing between unicast and multicast distribution for digital signage systems.

Again, multicasting is superior if it is important to be able to update content simultaneously and when it comes to live streaming of radio or television to many locations. There are very few cases where unicasting beats multicasting, except for the return path for playlogs and alarms. This is typical point-to-point communication. Therefore, a hybrid system using satellite multicasting for content delivery and broadband for the return path is very hard to beat.

Appendix B

MORE ABOUT IP ADDRESSING

Without digging too deep into IP (Internet Protocol) addressing, we will cover the basics, as they relate to digital signage systems. As introduced in Chapter 5, an IP address consists of four three-figure groups separated by a dot, such as 162.117.114.201. The Internet is based on a number of networks and hosts (computers) within each network. This means that the IP address of a certain computer is identified by the number of the network to which it belongs and the identity of the computer itself within that specific network.

For this reason the IP addresses are divided into classes. Classes A, B, and C are used for unicasting, and class D is used for multicasting.

To separate the A, B, and C classes, different subnet masks are used. The subnet mask is a way to filter which part of the IP address is used for identifying the network and which parts are used for identifying a certain host within that network.

Class A identifies a small number of very large networks. The first group identifies the network and the other three the computers within that network. The subnet mask is 255.0.0.0.

Class B identifies a much larger number of networks since the first two groups are used to identify the network and the two last groups identify the hosts (up to 65,534). The subnet mask is 255.255.0.0.

Class C is used to identify small networks with up to 254 hosts. The first three groups identify a large number of networks and the last group identifies the hosts. The subnet mask is 255.255.255.0.

Two of the addresses defined by the fourth group (000 and 255) cannot be used for identifying computers. 000 is the address reserved for the network itself and 255 is reserved for broadcasting messages within the network.

There are public IP addresses that are visible on the Internet. However, private IP addresses may be used behind the router gateway. To the outside world, only one public IP address is visible, but in reality, several computers (hosts) may share this IP address.

The IP addresses used behind the gateway router are private IP addresses. These addresses do not exist in the public Internet but only in closed local area networks such as a network used for digital signage in a store. In class C addresses, the address range from 192.168.0.0 to 192.168.255.255 is reserved as private IP addresses, and in class B, the address range from 172.16.0.0 to 172.31.255.255 is reserved as private addresses. These addresses are never used in the "public" Internet.

In the private network behind the gateway in Figure B.1 the network address is 192.168.000.000 and the broadcast address is 192.168.000.255. All other addresses in the range 192.168.000.001 to 192.168.000.254 may be used to address computers or media players.

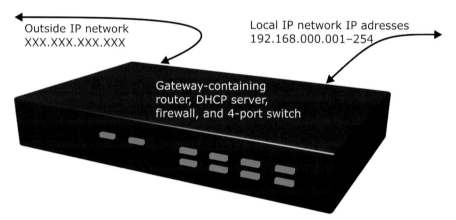

Figure B.1   The gateway-containing router, DHCP server, firewall, and a four-port switch. The single IP address to the left "XXX.XXX.XXX.XXX" is provided by the Internet service provider; the router provides the private addresses within the network 192.168.000.XXX.

On top of all other tasks, the gateway contains a firewall to limit the possibilities for intrusions from outside. On top of the IP address, IP traffic uses port numbers to differentiate traffic that originates from different applications. By controlling which port numbers are open, unwanted access behind the firewall is avoided because the intruder has to have access to at least one port number to get through.

THE MAC ADDRESS

A computer may be assigned a different IP address every time it boots up. The IP address is either set manually by the user or automatically by a DHCP server that resides in the same network as the computer. However, there is one thing that, in most cases, never changes: the MAC address (Media Access Control). The MAC address is individual to each computer's network card.

The switch keeps track of the computers by using the MAC addresses. The switch learns at what port a MAC address is located and then filters the Ethernet packets accordingly. So, the switch itself does not use the IP addresses.

The switch operates at the Ethernet link layer (called layer 2) and the router operates at the upper network layer (layer 3).

THE OSI MODEL USED TO DESCRIBE IP TRAFFIC

What may make IP communications seem complicated is that it is often described as divided into seven layers, three of which are shown in. This is referred to as the OSI, Open Systems Interconnection, model.

The bottom layer, layer 1, is the physical layer that connects the computers and network devices, such as the cabling and other physical connections.

The second layer is the link layer. In this case, it includes the signaling according to the Ethernet protocol. Ethernet is a packet-oriented protocol, meaning that all data is inserted into packets. Using packets makes it possible for several data streams to share one channel. The

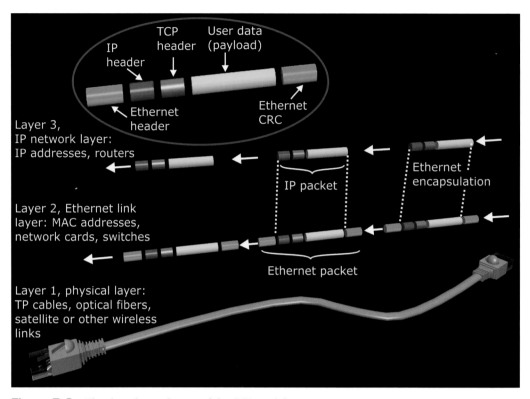

Figure B.2 The three lower layers of the OSI model.

switches and the computer network cards (with their MAC addresses) operate on the ethernet level.

The third layer is the network layer, which can be controlled by various protocols. In this book, we use only the Internet Protocol. The IP packets are encapsulated in the Ethernet packets. Routers handle IP addresses and work in layer 3. There are seven layers in the OSI model, with the applications on top.

Glossary

Asset: A number of content files, along with metadata covering that content.

Azimuth angle (of a satellite): The bearing angle, counted clockwise from the direction to the north, toward a satellite.

Block: Often refers to a set of files that is defined by a playlist.

Channel: Just as in television, the content sent to the screen. In a store or other location with digital signage, there might be several screens with different channels or messages (message channels).

Content: Any kind of information used in digital signage systems. Content include all kinds of video, audio, and text files, as well as all other kinds of information that may be of use in the shops.

Content distribution server: Another name for content management server, often used in digital signage systems based on broadband networking.

Content management server: The heart of the digital signage system. The server is responsible for storing and managing the content in the system. It may include authoring and content creation as well as content gathering tools. It is also responsible for administering the distribution of content to the edge servers and the media players, as well as controlling the final playout on the screens.

Customer relations management (CRM): A system closely connected to the content management server that handles the orders from customers and the billing of the system. The CRM system also keeps track of what content is needed to provide the services to the advertisers.

Customer terminal: In this book, something between a conventional digital sign and a kiosk. The customer terminal might be a touch screen device with a built-in media player. The customer can decide what is going to be shown by choosing the playlist and by moving to various locations inside a playlist.

CVBS (Composite Video Blanking and Sync) (PAL or NTSC) interface: The common analog video interface for the combined black-and-white and color TV signals.

Day parting: Dividing a day into smaller time segments, displaying different messages and using different playlists. (See *scheduling*.)

Demultiplexer (demux): A device that splits a common digital stream that contains several streams related to audio, video, or other data into its original components.

Digital cinema (D-cinema): The highest quality of digital cinema concepts. This technology replaces the analog film in all respects and requires signals of studio quality.

Digital signage: A medium to produce dynamic electronic information, entertainment, and advertising in shops and public places (possibly also in homes). Depending on the distribution method, digital signage may provide non-real-time as well as near-real-time and real-time information. Digital signage systems may also include interactive customer terminals where the user may decide what content is to be shown on the screens. Digital signage content may be based on separate content files that are combined in an individual way on each screen.

Digital signage broadcasting: A new revolutionary medium that is created by combining digital signage techniques with the broadcast media. Digital signage broadcasting has the potential to replace most existing electronic and printed media.

Digital signage network: Any kind of digital signage application where there are several media players at several locations. The network may be administrated using manual distribution of media, broadband networking, satellite broadcasting, or any combination of these distribution methods.

Digital Video Interface (DVI): The digital interface used mostly with computer graphics cards and computer screens but also in older flat-panel TV sets and monitors.

Display device: Any kind of device for displaying content. From the early technology of cathode-ray tubes, the number of display devices has increased to include plasmas, LCD screens, various computer-type TFT screens, OLEDs, projection systems, and electronic ink techniques.

Distribution server: Another word for content distribution or content management server. This term is used in digital signage broadband networking, where the content management server handles broadband distribution to each media player as well as to store and manages content.

Downlink signal: The signal that is received from a satellite.

Edge server: A local server that retrieves content from the content management server and serves as a central storage of content in a shop or other location where there is a larger number of media players. Also known as site server and media server.

Electronic cinema (E-cinema): A more modest level of *D-cinema*. E-cinema is used for preshow advertising and other cinema applications where moderate quality is accepted.

Elevation angle (of a satellite): The angle describing a satellite's angular height above the horizon.

Encapsulation: Embedding an IP stream into a higher-level distribution protocol as the DVB transport stream protocol.

Event information (metadata): Information sent along with TV programs that describes the content, such as the duration of a program, actors, and date released. Also may include upcoming content.

F connector: Standardized connector used in satellite receivers and other devices all over the world for RF (radio frequency) input and output signals through coaxial cables.

File interleaving: Sending several files simultaneously through a multicasting channel.

Graphical interface (video interface): The electrical connection between the media player and the display device. Common interfaces are VGA, DVI, and HDMI, in addition to analog composite and component video interfaces.

Groups of pictures (GOP): A GOP is a number (often 12) of consecutive pictures in a video signal to be compressed. After compression, only the first picture of each GOP and the differences between the remaining pictures are included in the compressed signal.

HDTV: High-definition television.

Heartbeat signaling: Signals are sent back from a media player or edge server to the content management server to indicate that the device operates properly.

High-Bandwidth Digital Content Protection (HDCP): Copy protection system for HDTV.

High-Definition Multimedia Interface (HDMI): Digital audio and video interface for HDTV signals.

IEC connector: Standardized connector used in TV sets and video devices (especially in Europe) for the RF (radio frequency) input and output signals through coaxial cables. (IEC stands for International Electrotechnical Commission, a professional organization that defines international standards.)

Interlaced scanning: An old technique of avoiding flickering pictures in CRTs by drawing every other line on a TV screen during a vertical scan and then drawing the lines in between during the next scan.

Internet Protocol (IP): First developed for military purposes in the United States to define the communications within a very robust and dependable packet-oriented network for computers. The name Internet originates from the fact that one of the primary goals was to build a network that could connect different military computer networks.

Internet Protocol television (IPTV): Television that uses IP packets to carry digital audio and video signals.

IP address: In the Internet Protocol, the unique numerical address that identifies a computer in a network.

Keep-alive signaling: See *heartbeat signaling*.

Kiosk: An advanced customer terminal that allows two-way communication with a customer. Kiosk systems often include smart card readers to enable ordering and purchasing products and services.

Layer: A digital sign consists of virtual graphical layers superimposed on one another to form the complete screen content. Each layer is described by one or more content files. *Layer* is also used to describe communication layers such as those in the OSI model (see Appendix B).

LED: Light-emitting diode.

Letter boxing: Adding black bars to the top and bottom of a screen with a regular 4:3 (1.33:1) aspect ratio to be able display widescreen 16:9 (1.78:1) programs.

Media player: Device that decodes and plays media files to be displayed by various kinds of display devices. Media players also may have permanent storage capability, such as a hard drive or a flash memory. Some media players can be used to decode IPTV streams. Media players can be computers equipped with media player software or more dedicated hardware media players that resemble set-top boxes.

Media server: See *edge server*.

Modulation: The process of using a radio wave to carry information by changing the amplitude, frequency, or phase of that carrier according to the information.

Multicasting: Simultaneous distribution of IP packets to a group of computers or media players without setting up a separate communications session with each player. Multicasting does not require confirming return traffic from the computers or media players.

Multichannel media player: A media player with several graphics cards that support more than one screen.

Multiplexer (mux): A device that combines several bitstreams that contain digital audio, video, or data signals into one bitstream.

Near-real-time: Refers to content that might have a slight delay in the distribution chain, compared to live or real-time distribution.

Non-real-time: Refers to content that may be stored for a long time to be called when requested either by a playlist or a customer using a customer terminal.

Orbital slot: The geostationary satellites are located at orbital positions—slots—that are stationary in relation to the surface of Earth. The orbital slot is identified by the longitude of the location on Earth's equator that is directly below the satellite.

Organic light-emitting diodes (OLEDs): Light-emitting diodes built up from layers of organic materials. Light is emitted by electrons recombining with a lack of electrons (electron holes).

Peer-to-peer network (P2P): Several computers distribute content to one another. P2P is used in file-sharing systems and might also be used for digital signage applications to relieve the load on the content management server, which distributes content to only some of the media players, which then share content with the remaining players.

Playlist: A list with instructions as to what files are to be displayed and for how long. The playlist is usually contained in its own file. Content specified by a playlist is called "block."

Playlog: A file containing information on what content has been shown on a specific screen. It is a kind of receipt of delivery of the content on the screens. It may include other technical status data. A return path is required to collect the playlogs if this is to be done automatically.

Point of purchase: The physical location where the customer makes the purchase, such as in stores, restaurants, and hotels.

Progressive scanning: All lines in a scanned picture are covered in one single scan, as opposed to interlaced scanning, where the scanning process is divided into two scans, each covering every other line.

Quadrature-phase shift keying (QPSK): The most common way of modulating digital signals in satellite links. The radio wave can use one of four phases to symbolize the 00, 01, 10, and 11 combinations of two binary digits.

Real-time: Refers to information that is transferred instantly without being stored in the distribution chain.

Region: Part of the screen that can display content. It may also be called a *zone*.

Return path: An IP connection from the media players or the edge servers to the content management server. In broadband distribution systems, the return path is obvious. In multicasting systems, the return path is a separate connection implemented using a broadband connection such as ADSL or a mobile connection such as GPRS or 3G (UMTS).

RJ-45 connector: The most common connector used with twisted-pair cables in Ethernet networks.

RSS: May be short for Rich Site Summary, RDF Site Summary, or Really Simple Syndication. All mean feeds used to distribute continuously updated information on the Internet. RSS feeds can be used to update news tickers, stock market news, weather information, etc. in digital signage systems.

SCART connector: European standardized connector for analog composite and component video signals. The connector also carries analog stereo audio. (SCART stands for *Syndicat des Constructeurs d'Appareils Radiorécepteurs et Téléviseurs*.)

Scheduling: Deciding when content is to be presented, whether in a day, a week, or longer. The schedule may be contained in a scheduling file.

SDTV: Standard-definition television.

Site server: See *edge server*.

Sony/Philips Digital Interface Format (S/PDIF): Digital audio interface for multichannel audio. It exists both as an electrical and an optical interface.

Stream: The transfer of IP packets. Live IPTV streaming is perhaps the most important streaming application of today, but many other kinds of data are transmitted in IP streams.

Thin film transistor (TFT): The technology used in more advanced LCD screens to control the liquid crystals that are used to block light passing through each pixel.

Ticker: Area on the screen with text that scrolls horizontally or vertically. Tickers often contain a repeated advertising message or updated news, stock, or weather information.

Unicasting: Two-way point-to-point communications used on the Internet and in other IP networks.

Uplink signal: The signal that is sent from an uplink station toward a satellite.

YPbPr component connection: Analog video interface that may also carry high-definition signals. The interface includes three connectors—*Y* for luminance, *Pb* for the difference between the Y and the blue signal, and *Pr* for the difference between the Y and the red signal. From these three signals, the red, green, and blue signals may be calculated. In digital video for component video signals, the related term YCbCr is used instead. However the terms YPbPr and YCbCr are often used together.

Zone: See *region*.

INDEX

ABOUT THE AUTHOR

Lars-Ingemar Lundström has worked with television distribution platforms and other media projects for more than 25 years. Besides his professional career, he is a well-established freelance writer in Sweden with hundreds of articles to his credit.

Lundström has been a pioneer in several new areas, including the introduction of satellite, cable, and digital TV. Throughout the years, he has collected his knowledge in several books that describe the various advances in media technology.

In 2006, Focal Press published his book, *Understanding Digital Television*, which explains complex technical solutions in an easy-to-comprehend manner including hundreds of illustrations created using the latest 3D graphics methods.

For the last few years, Lundström has been managing digital signage and IP broadcasting development projects for Teracom, a broadcast service company owned by the Swedish government. Combining these technologies creates the powerful new medium—Digital Signage Broadcasting—that he describes and explains in this book.

More information about the author and his books is available at *www.digitalsignagebroadcasting.com*.